Gridiron Journeys:

How I Fell In Love With College Football

By

Mike McMackin

FIRST EDITION 2024

Copyright © 2024 Michael McMackin

Gridiron Journeys: How I Fell In Love With College Football / Mike McMackin.

ISBN 979-8-218-47834-6

All rights reserved.

No part of this publication may be reproduced, distributed, or transmitted in any form or by any means, including photocopying, recording, or other electronic or mechanical methods, without the prior written permission of the author, except in the case of brief quotations embodied in critical reviews and certain other noncommercial uses permitted by copyright law. For permission requests, email to mcmackinwrites@gmail.com with "Attention: Permissions Coordinator," in the subject line

Email: mcmackinwrites@gmail.com

Cover design by: Vanessa Lowry

Back photo by: Patrick Flynn

Table of Contents

INTRODUCTION 1
   Troy at Appalachian State; September 17, 1004, 6:42p.m.

CHAPTER 1: A HALL OF FAME CAREER IS BORN 7
   Appalachian State at Wake Forest; September 3, 1983

CHAPTER 2: MY FIRST TASTE OF THE BIG TIME 33
   Georgia at Clemson; September 19, 1987

CHAPTER 3: IRON BOWL ON THE PLAINS 49
   Alabama at Auburn; December 2, 1989

CHAPTER 4: GOOD GUYS WEAR CRIMSON 85
   Miami vs. Alabama; January 1, 1993

CHAPTER 5: LESSON LEARNED 129
   Georgia Tech at Clemson; September 11, 2004

CHAPTER 6: "WE ARE!" "PENN STATE!" 155
   Michigan State at Penn State; November 18, 2006

CHAPTER 7: UPSET FOR THE AGES 191
   Appalachian State at Michigan; September 1, 2007

CHAPTER 8: WOFFORD'S NIGHTMARE 281
   Wofford at Appalachian State; October 31, 2008

CHAPTER 9: AN END OF AN ERA 325
   Appalachian State at Montana; December 12, 2009

CHAPTER 10: A PAIR OF POWER 5 WINS 369

    Appalachian State at North Carolina; September 21, 2019

    Appalachian State at South Carolina; November 9, 2019

CHAPTER 11: SEPTEMBER TO REMEMBER 461

    North Carolina at Appalachian State; September 3, 2022

    Appalachian State at Texas A&M; September 10, 2022

    Troy at Appalachian State; September 17, 2022

EPILOGUE 627

ACKNOWLEDGEMENTS 651

ABOUT THE AUTHOR 659

To Mom and Dad

Who gave me a love for books and sports

"Always do more than what is expected."

Jerry Moore, Appalachian State Football Coach, 1989-2012.

2014 College Football Hall of Fame Inductee

Paul –
Enjoy the game!

SAME ENJOY THE
X-MAS! PAUL.

Introduction

Troy at Appalachian State

September 17, 2022

6:42 p.m.

It was the greatest day in Appalachian State University history. So far in September of 2022, the Mountaineers had been the talk of college football. On opening weekend App State had hosted the University of North Carolina (UNC) for the first time and a record crowd of more than 40,000 people watched the teams play a shootout. The Apps lost 63-61, despite scoring 40 points in the fourth quarter. The next week, they went on the road and beat number six Texas A&M. Because of those two exciting wins, ESPN's *College GameDay* had decided to come to Boone to do their show today. More than 2.2 million people watched the three-hour show from 9 a.m. until noon. In the final 11 a.m. to noon hour viewership was more than 2.8 million. It was one of the highest rated early-season *College GameDay* shows ever, and there weren't really a lot of big games that day. There were several thousand students who had camped out the night before so they could be in prime spots close to the stage and get on TV. Dozens had made signs. All this exposure was priceless for a school like Appalachian, nestled in the northwest corner of North Carolina. Most of the media attention was focused on the "Big Four" schools in the Atlantic Coast Conference, or the schools in the state's major cities. Many App fans felt *College GameDay* was long overdue in making the trip to Boone.

Since 2000 Appalachian State's football team:

- Was the first Division I football team since the 1930s to win three straight national championships from 2005-07;

- Was the first Football Championship Subdivision (FCS, 63 scholarship players) team to beat a ranked Football Bowl Subdivision (FBS, 85 scholarship players) team with the upset of Michigan in 2007;

- Was the first FCS team to receive votes in the Associated Press (AP) poll. As a result of the Michigan win, the AP changed their rules to allow FCS teams to be included in the poll;

- Was the first school in college football history to earn a bowl bid and win the game in the first six years of eligibility;

- Since it made the move to FBS in 2014, Appalachian had an 80-20 record. Only Alabama (104-10), Clemson (99-13), Ohio State (93-11), Oklahoma (86-19), and Georgia (86-21) had better records; and

- Was the first FBS school in North Carolina to win 13 games in a season.

So finally, Rece Davis, Kirk Herbstreit, Lee Corso, and the rest of *College GameDay* folks were on Sanford Mall in the middle of the App State campus. In addition to all the people watching live, there had been millions of views on social media about the set-up and lead-in for Saturday's show.

App State got to show the world the passion of its fans, the beautiful campus, and what it means to be a Mountaineer. Country music star Luke Combs, App State's most popular alum, had flown in after doing a concert in Green Bay, Wisconsin, the night before to join the *College GameDay* stage and be the celebrity game picker. The sacrificial lamb that day for the game was Troy University, a team Appalachian had beaten at Troy the year before, 45-7. The Trojans, however, were not being good guests. There were two seconds remaining in the game. Troy led 28-26. App State had the ball at their own 47-yard line, and it was fourth down. It was too far to try a field goal. There was a sense of despair among the 34,406 fans packed into Kidd Brewer Stadium, also known as "The Rock."

Luke Combs had gained a lot of his popularity from a song with lyrics saying, "Beer Never Broke My Heart." However, football had broken the hearts of App fans many times over the past several years. Despite the program's overall success, when Appalachian had gone against the so-called Power 5 teams, they would play a close game, but usually came up short, like two weeks before, against UNC. They had lost games in overtime at Tennessee and Penn State. There were some who felt App State had choked when playing teams that had more resources in their athletic department. When App State was finally ranked in the AP poll in 2018, they lost their first game as a ranked team, to arch-rival Georgia Southern. They promptly dropped out of the poll. And after millions were watching that morning, hearing about how great App State is, they were seconds from losing at home to a team they had beaten four times in a row.

As Appalachian players leave the locker room to take the field, they touch a sign that is shaped like the state of North Carolina, with a star in the northwest corner, marking Boone. It says on it: "Today I Give My All For Appalachian State." The players had been giving their all for almost three games and with all the attention it seemed to have taken its toll. Could they give their all for another two seconds? Would even that be enough?

Was this going to be another heart-breaking failure to handle the spotlight situation? The Mountaineers had pulled out many close wins over the years, especially at The Rock, but could they do it again?

This game is just one of the many memorable moments I have experienced as a college football fan. There have been many joyous occasions, but there has been plenty of heartbreak too. Growing up in North Carolina, I liked college basketball better than college football. But once I got to Appalachian as a student and as I got started in my career working in television, I realized what a great sport college football is and what an emotional roller coaster it can take you on.

Chapter 1: A Hall of Fame Career is Born

Appalachian State at Wake Forest September 3, 1983

When I got accepted to Appalachian State University in the fall of 1980, I wasn't sure that was where I wanted to go to college. I had been to Boone many times. Our family camped a lot at the campgrounds near Boone and spent a lot of time driving on the Blue Ridge Parkway. I had always had more of an affinity for the mountains over the beach. There were so many beautiful overlooks on the Parkway and the Dan'l Boone Inn was a great place to eat. However, as I got older, most of our family vacations were at the beach instead of the mountains. During fall break of my senior year in high school, my mom and I went up there and took a campus tour. Since it had been a while since I had been in the Boone area, being back around the mountains helped me decide Appalachian was the best place for me to go. Besides, I enjoyed the cold and was looking forward to the snowy winters!

I had only been on campus a few days when I heard the student radio station, WASU, was looking for DJs, newscasters, sportscasters, and other positions. At the time, I was going to be a business major, but they said it didn't matter what your major was, you could still work at the station. I went and applied and got a shift doing a five-minute sportscast once a week. I was terrible and very nervous but enjoyed it and the managers at the station gave me advice on how to improve. I thought perhaps the media could be a way for me to get involved with sports.

Although I was a big sports fan, I wasn't very familiar with Appalachian's athletic teams. I started paying a little more attention after I had been accepted there and I knew the basketball team had made the National Collegiate Athletics Association (NCAA) tournament in 1979. One of the starters on that team had gone to my high school. I was disappointed the basketball head coach, Bobby Cremins, had left to take the job at Georgia Tech the summer before I got there. Cremins wasn't the only Hall of Fame coach to leave Boone that summer. When I arrived in August of 1981, men's soccer was one of the biggest sports at App. Hank Steinbrecher, who was the head of U.S. Soccer during the 90s, had been the coach but left for Boston University before the 1981 season. In 1980, App State had beaten Clemson and made the NCAA tournament. Since App had beaten them the year before, Clemson came to Boone to play us and that was a huge deal. I went and had a great time despite Clemson winning the game 2-1.

However, the day before, the football team won the first Appalachian game I had ever seen in person, 48-9 over Lenoir-Rhyne College. They also won the next game against James Madison University and were 3-0 for the first time in four years after a 31-14 win over University of Tennessee-Chattanooga (UTC). That was the first time the Mountaineers had beaten UTC. I thought this was awesome and wondered if a bowl game could be in our future? Sadly, no. The team didn't win again that year.

In 1982 the NCAA had decided that conferences that didn't have high enough attendance would be dropped down to Division I-AA (the NCAA changed the name of 1-AA to FCS prior to the 2006 season), and the Southern Conference, of which Appalachian was a member, was one of the conferences affected. I-AA only applied to football. Appalachian was still a Division I school, and the basketball team could make March Madness and all the other sports could compete for the Division I NCAA Championship. A lot of people weren't happy with that decision. It didn't bother me. In the college football world in 1982, App State was a minnow in the ocean. In I-AA we had a chance to be a big fish in the small pond. For one thing, they had their own rankings. The way the program was then, App State was never going to be ranked in the AP poll. They just didn't have the facilities or budget to compete against the bigger schools. The other thing was that I-AA had a playoff and that was something we could do. But in 1982 Appalachian was a long way from winning a conference championship. The record was 4-7 and head coach Mike Working was fired.

"It was kind of strange. Mike Working went off his rocker a little bit," said Ed Boyd, a guard from 1981 to 1985. "He had lost the team. We were an exciting offense, but he had differences with seniors."

Boyd and I were classmates at South Mecklenburg High School in Charlotte. He got his first start against Virginia Tech in game eight his freshman year and remained in the starting lineup for the next four years. Danny Squires, the tackle he played beside as a freshman, was also a South Meck grad. When Boyd and I were reminiscing about those days, I told him I said Southern California may have had the Student Body Right (a running play), but App that year had the South Meck Left. Boyd was first team All-Southern Conference in 1983 and '84 and named All-American in 1984. He was inducted into the Appalachian Sports Hall of Fame in the fall of 2022.

When Coach Working was fired, I was still working at WASU, and no one at the radio station knew much about the new coach that had been hired. His name was Mack Brown. He was 32 years old and was from Cookeville, Tennessee. He had played quarterback at Florida State. He arrived at Appalachian after being the offensive coordinator and quarterbacks coach at Louisiana State University (LSU) for one year. Alan Risher was the quarterback at LSU in 1982 and although he only played for Brown that year, he had a great year, breaking several of LSU legend Bert Jones' school records. The Tigers made it to the Orange Bowl that year and lost to Nebraska.

I had gotten to know Brian Hoagland at WASU. Brian also worked at *The Appalachian*, the student newspaper. He was the sports editor for two years.

"I didn't know much about Mack when he came," said Hoagland.

Boyd said Brown came in and made some needed changes.

"Mack got rid of a few people who probably shouldn't have been on scholarship and cleaned up some other things. It was definitely good for the program."

Brown felt like one of the things that needed to change was to re-establish the team's confidence.

"The biggest thing was to let them have positive moments in practice," said Brown. "Going on the road to face an ACC [Atlantic Coast Conference] team in the opener was big. We would emphasize win the kicking game and turnover battle."

The biggest problem with being I-AA, I felt, was that scores would be listed differently, and we wouldn't be publicized as much, but Appalachian wasn't getting much attention anyway. That was something Brown felt like he could change. Tim Wooten was the sports director at WASU in 1983 and liked the energy Brown brought to the job.

"Such a dynamic personality and he was so kind, nothing egotistical about him," said Wooten. "He had incredible leadership skills and was someone I always looked up to."

Boyd could quickly sense the difference, "As far as Mack, he brought class to the locker room. A top-notch guy."

Jeff Owen had graduated in the spring of 1983 but was keeping an eye on the football program and liked what he saw.

"Mack brought a whole different level of coaches," he said. "We had been hiring some older, retread guys, but Mack showed you could be successful bringing in new, fresh-faced guys."

"I remember how accessible he was," recalled Wooten. "You could reach out to him, and he was always accommodating, never in a rush and would give you his full attention."

Hoagland echoed that sentiment.

"He was a cool coach to work with. He was so different than Mike Working, who could be abrasive. He would take care of the college newspaper. Not intimidating, super nice, super cordial but he stood up for his team. After each game we did a report card and graded each position. We gave the linebackers a C or D in one game, he called me on it. He called me in and let me know why he disagreed with me and explained why he felt that way. But that didn't change our relationship. He was professional."

The 1983 season would kick off against Wake Forest University at Groves Stadium in Winston-Salem, my hometown. I saw my first ever college football game there in 1970 as a 7-year-old. Wake defeated North Carolina State that day on their way to an ACC championship. I still remember the quarterback, Larry Russell and the star running back, Larry Hopkins. The Wake Forest-Appalachian State game had become a pretty good rivalry drawing some of Wake's biggest crowds of the year. The two schools first met in 1975 with the Mountaineers winning 19-17 but Wake Forest had won the last four games. I had been to the two previous games. App State had a 14-0 lead in 1981, but the Demon Deacons scored a late touchdown and got the two-point conversion to eke out a 15-14 win. I was disappointed with the result, but it was my first exposure to Wake's tradition of "Rolling the Quad" after a football game win, which started when campus moved from its namesake town near Raleigh to Winston-Salem in 1956. On the old campus, there was a bell that students could ring to celebrate something. On the new campus, after the game was over the scoreboard flashed, "Roll the Quad!" Though there was a bell in Wait Chapel, the students couldn't ring it. The new campus tradition meant covering the branches of the trees along the Quad in toilet paper.

"That was our money game, what we called the annual sacrifice to fund the athletic department," said Boyd. "We always got pumped up for the bigger teams. We had a chip on our shoulder. Most of these guys had been recruited by these schools, but we didn't get an offer. And we wanted to show them we could play. We had nothing to lose. We'd go at 'em!"

One thing we had learned about our new football coach was that he was full of energy and worked very hard at getting the student body excited about the team. Attendance hadn't been very good the past two years, averaging less than 13,000 a game. I had always enjoyed the games and was a very vocal supporter. I felt then, and still do, that the crowd can influence the game and the players. Coach Brown felt that way. During his pre-game interviews with Wooten, Brown would implore students to come to the game and make a lot of noise. Wooten invited me to sit in on one of those interviews one week and it was impressive to see Brown's energy and passion. That energy paid off on the recruiting trail too.

Boyd was impressed with what Brown was doing.

"You could see it the next two years in the guys he brought in. We probably wouldn't have gotten some of the guys who joined the team had he not been there."

Brown had his eyes on a running back named John Settle from Rockingham County High School north of Greensboro. Hoagland remembered being impressed with Settle signed to be a Mountaineer.

"That was a big-time recruit for App. He was a top 50 in-state recruit. He was going to go to Duke, but they wanted him to play D. You could tell why Mack was such a great recruiter and still is."

"Settle was an amazing story," said Brown. "It was the first recruiting weekend. There was about 28 inches of snow on the ground, and we were wondering if we should cancel the weekend. Someone said, 'We'll get four-wheelers to get them around' and we had 13 kids. They were freezing. We didn't have a recruiting video to show them, so we got one from the university. We told the kids we don't usually have this much snow. Then we showed them the video and it was all about snow skiing and winter stuff. Twelve kids came into the office on Sunday and said, 'Coach, I can't do this. It's too cold.' Settle had been recruited by ACC teams. He came in and said, 'Coach I had always dreamed of playing in the snow' and he committed and became one of the greatest players in program history."

A lot of App students went to the games at Wake. In 1983 there wasn't a four-lane highway all the way from Boone to Winston-Salem like there is now, but it still took less than two hours to drive. Our fraternity had hired a bus to take us to the game and about 40 of us were headed down U.S. Highway 421 to see what our new coach could do. Hoagland had a little different experience.

"I went to that game as fan. Most games I had been there as the sports editor. I had an illness and had outpatient surgery that morning. I didn't like Wake and wanted to beat them. They were the biggest rival when I was there."

The offensive-minded coach got a big help from his defense. Trailing 7-0 in the second quarter, linebacker Joel Carter intercepted a pass and returned it 48 yards for a touchdown. Later, Billy Van Aman kicked a 54-yard field goal and the Apps led at the half.

Boyd remembered those big plays by the defensive giving the team a lift.

"We [the offense] were playing off each other that game. We were all friends and we picked each other up. Mack brought it all together. We became a big family. Before we had been pitted against each other."

Brown wasn't surprised the team was playing so well.

"I think it was just the confidence we had built in the off season," he said. "They accepted the challenge of beating an ACC team."

App extended that lead when Carter picked off the Deacons' first pass of the second half and returned it 30 yards for a touchdown. In addition to his two pick-sixes, Carter had 18 total tackles and recovered a fumble. Another fumble recovery gave the offense great field position early in the fourth quarter. As Boyd says, this was the time in the game when things hadn't always gone App State's way in the games against the "bigger" schools.

"We could hang pretty tough, but in the second half the lack of depth would come into play. The biggest thing I remember that night it was hot and humid. We were cramping. We didn't have any depth and had to suck it up."

One position the Mountaineers did have some depth was at running back. Settle, making his college debut, had the most carries of the running backs with 16 for 48 yards. Junior Cliff Reid had 15 carries for 68 yards and senior Alvin Parker had 45 yards on 11 carries. Reid was the running back after the latest turnover and he scored on a 12-yard run, sparked by a great play by Boyd.

"For me personally I had a double pancake," he remembered. "In this case we were doing zone blocking and me and the center were responsible for the nose guard and the linebacker. The center took the nose guard, and I pulled around got the LB, pushed him back to the safety I knocked them both down and I was in end zone and here's Reid standing over top of me. The block made the highlight film for the Yosef Club [App State's athletic booster club] and I graded out pretty well for the whole game too."

"We were hanging in there," said Brown. "That was fun when people don't think you could do that. We had that chip and an edge for the game. They [the players] saw they had a chance, and instead of getting scared, they put pressure on Wake."

Wake Forest scored a touchdown with 1:12 remaining. The two-point conversion cut the lead to 27-25. But Appalachian recovered the onside kick, ran out the clock, and a hall of fame coaching career was born.

"One of the greatest wins in my history," said Brown. "The win reinforced what the staff had been selling in the preseason."

"By the end of the game we were just exhausted," said Boyd. "It was a good exhausted, but we were exhausted. The bus ride back to Boone was fun. When we got back to campus, the students had ripped down the goal posts and threw them in the Duck Pond."

I don't remember a whole lot about the game. I remembered the two interceptions by Carter, and I remember the late touchdown. I remember celebrating after the game. Our bus stopped by the Wake campus before we went back to Boone.

"It was a blast," said Hoagland. "To beat them and to be there to witness it was special. I went out with some high school buddies who were Wake fans and they weren't happy. I remember taking a lot of satisfaction with that win. It was sweet."

I thought Appalachian may be able to make the playoffs after that game. Wake Forest wasn't that good that year, but they were an ACC team and that was a big win for App. The Mountaineers got off to a 4-1 start and were ranked as high as number 10 in the nation, but injuries and a lack of depth from the previous regime hurt the team but they finished the year with a 6-5 record.

"We had a lot of injuries as the season went on," said Boyd. "It was the first winning season in a while and that felt good!"

I went to most of the home games that season, and we played at Furman University the weekend of fall break and went to the game with my dad. Furman won 49-0 on the way to the conference championship. Furman was coached by Dick

Sheridan, who would later coach at N.C. State and battle with Brown in the ACC.

Over the course of the season, the backfield was one place where Appalachian did have some depth. Hoagland felt that Alvin Parker, a senior who had played well for Working, should be getting more carries instead of Settle, the true freshman. He wrote a column about that and again heard from Coach Brown. Brown told Hoagland that Settle was working harder than Parker and that's why he was playing more.

"Settle was special," said Brown. "We had some good players at that position. He had a thick lower body, and they couldn't tackle him. We put him in and let him grow."

Settle was doing things to win over his older teammates, like the junior Boyd.

"One of the toughest guys I've ever seen in my life," said Boyd. "We were playing N.C. State and two guys hit him and his facemask was just hanging by one of the hooks. He got up and ran off the field. He just got his face mask fixed and came back in."

For the season Settle was the Southern Conference Freshman of the Year. He led the team in rushing yards, pass receptions, and kickoff returns. He would finish his career as the Mountaineers' all-time leading rusher. Despite not being drafted, he would also become one of the most decorated Mountaineers in the National Football League (NFL). He signed a free agent contract with the Atlanta Falcons and in 1988 became the first undrafted free agent in NFL history to rush for 1,000 yards. He was named to the NFC Pro Bowl team after the season and scored a touchdown in the game.

The 1983 season was a big one in the Brown family. His older brother Watson, who I got to know when he coached at University of Alabama-Birmingham, kicked off his major college coaching career the following week. Watson was the coach at Cincinnati, and they went to number 20 Penn State and came away with a 14-7 win.

1983 turned out to be the only year Mack Brown coached the Mountaineers. After that season Barry Switzer hired him to be the offensive coordinator at Oklahoma.

"When I went to App, I planned on staying forever because I loved it there," said Brown. "When I was hired my salary was $38,500. That next spring Barry Switzer offered me $125,000 at Oklahoma and at that point in my life, I couldn't turn it down. It felt awful leaving."

After a year in Norman, he got his second head coaching job at Tulane University then coached at North Carolina and Texas. His most notable win came in 2005 when Texas beat Southern Cal 41-38 in the Rose Bowl to win the National Championship behind Vince Young's great game. After leaving Texas after the 2013 season, he worked at ESPN until North Carolina hired him again in 2019. Brown wasn't happy that Appalachian was on North Carolina's schedule that year. The schools had only played once before in football and the Tar Heels won that one 56-6 in 1940. Appalachian beat UNC in 2019 for their first win over a Power 5 school since the win over Michigan in 2007. Brown got some revenge in 2022 when he brought his Tar Heels to Boone. I'll have more on those games later. Brown has maintained his ties to Appalachian.

"I still have a house in Linville [a community with several country clubs about 20 miles from Boone]," said Brown. "I helped the school with some fundraising when I was doing television. I'm so proud of the program."

Although he only spent that one year in Boone, I think he is responsible for the success the football program is having now. I'm not taking anything away from anyone else, but when Sparky Woods was promoted from offensive coordinator to head coach, most of the staff stayed with him and were there throughout Woods' five-year tenure.

"I feel a lot of pride getting App State headed in the right direction," said Brown. "I think we started a lot of things moving forward. I'm proud of our staff and I was there for two recruiting cycles. We recruited a lot of out-of-state players. Coaches had to drive state cars on recruiting trips. We got that changed to have dealer cars to drive to meet recruits instead. There was a limit on 33 out-of-state players and John Garner [the athletic director at the time] let us recruit who we needed regardless of where they were. When I got there assistant coaches had to teach classes and we got that changed. Things like that. We were trying to upgrade the training table. I wanted steak for the players before that Wake game. But the cook was sick, so we got hot dogs. We told the players, 'If you give us 100 percent, we'll give you 100 percent.'"

In 1985 the team was 8-3 with close losses to South Carolina and Wake Forest. Only 12 teams made the playoffs that year and the Apps didn't get an invite. Finally in 1986 they earned their first playoff spot and hosted Nichols State. I was there. Settle had a big game but got caught on a long run before he made the end zone. Bjorn Nittmo, who kicked for the New York Giants, missed a 42-yard field goal at the end. In 1987, the Apps earned a high seed in the playoffs. They beat the University of Richmond in round one. In round two they defeated the two-time defending national champions Georgia Southern 19-0. It was the first time the Eagles had been shut out since the program had been revived in 1981. Georgia Southern at that time was an independent and didn't join the Southern Conference until 1992. Marshall, a Southern Conference member that App had defeated in the regular season, came to a snow-covered Kidd Brewer Stadium for the semifinal and beat the Mountaineers.

These runs in the playoffs had created two things that App football hadn't consistently experienced before: fan support and expectations. I knew Woods wouldn't stay at Appalachian forever, but in 1988, I thought we had kept him through the usual post-season hiring season. But South Carolina coach Joe Morrison, who had re-energized the Gamecock fan base, dropped dead playing racquetball in February of 1989. South Carolina hired Woods to take over the program. But because of the efforts of a coach who made it to the College Football Hall of Fame, and a lot of other people behind him, the groundwork was in place for another man to forge a Hall of Fame career of his own in Boone.

For me, the experience I was able to get working at WASU was invaluable. I got the chance to do sportscasts and interview players and coaches of several different sports. I had the chance to do play-by-play for a basketball game. I had professors who really pushed me, as well as some of the student leaders at the station.

David Snepp did the newscast before my sportscast in my sophomore year. Snepp was a senior and had also gone to South Meck. I was so impressed with how smooth he was, and he would come to the control room about 10 minutes before airtime and rip AP stories off the wire and barely look over them and read them on the air with such authority! I had been there for several hours re-writing and rehearsing my scripts, and I was never as good as he was. But he saw something in me. Snepp interned at WBTV in Charlotte, the CBS affiliate, while a student at Appalachian and after he graduated he went to work full-time at the station. He helped me get an internship there. In the fall semester of my senior year, I was able to get a class schedule that allowed me to go to Charlotte to work at the station on Friday, Saturday, and Sunday. I was so glad to get a day during the week because the environment around the station was so different during the week from the weekend and I got a true sense of what a newsroom was like.

I instantly knew TV was what I wanted to do. I had never experienced anything like the newsroom on those Fridays. All the people I knew from TV running around, the telephones ringing constantly, the buzz of the police scanners, and editors hollering about getting the video they needed. It was organized chaos and I loved it. WBTV was a very technologically advanced station in the early 1980s. They used a computer system in the newsroom that few stations were using at that time. I had hoped to get an internship in sports, but they already had an intern. I also learned that in 1984 Charlotte didn't have much of a sports scene. This was before the Hornets and Panthers and there wasn't much except the two NASCAR races, an occasional appearance of UNC or Duke at the Charlotte Coliseum, and high school sports. At least in news I was getting to cover shootings and other spot news. I would go with the photographer and try and get what information I could from the police at the scene. They would let me write the story, but I never got to do a story on the air. I did save a lot of the stories that I did to put together some on-camera things for me to send out to stations. That fall there was a highly contested race for the U.S. Senate between incumbent Jesse Helms and Jim Hunt, who was governor. The weekend before the election I got to go out with the reporter and photographer covering Hunt as he was making a last-minute appeal for votes. Bill Whitaker was the reporter. He worked in the Raleigh Bureau for the station but was in Charlotte that weekend. Whitaker would be hired by CBS News after the election and was a correspondent for *60 Minutes*. I got the photographer, Gregg Pell, to get a shot of me asking a question to Hunt and I used it on my resume tape as well as a class project that the professor loved. I worked the election night too and that was a great experience. Election days are always big days in the newsroom.

After graduating in May of 1985, I kept working at WBTV as a weekend desk assistant. That summer, I went on an interview trip to nine stations in four states in a week that cumulated with interviews at the two stations in Florence, South Carolina. The CBS station, WBTW, hired me to be the anchor and reporter from their Myrtle Beach bureau for the 11:00 news. My path from the mountains had led me to the beach! It wasn't the job I had hoped for in the sports world, but it gave me an on-camera job in TV just a few months after graduating. And I was going to give news my best shot.

Chapter 2: My First Taste of the Big Time
Georgia at Clemson
September 19, 1987

I was enjoying my time living in Myrtle Beach. As a recent graduate, being able to hang out in Myrtle Beach on weekends was a little bit of a dream. I had a good group of friends I had met, including Dwayne Ward, who I'd known from WASU and was working as a DJ at the top rock station. He put me up for a few weeks until I found a place of my own to live.

It was a little weird for me to have my first bit of "fame." Not long after I had been hired, the station had a photo shoot with me and Sherena Gainey, who was the 6 p.m. bureau anchor. Those pictures were put on three billboards around the Grand Strand and were also used in *TV Guide* ads. Occasionally, someone would ask if I was the guy from TV and when I went to Charlotte, people I knew said they saw me on TV or saw the billboard. I spent most of the weekend days playing volleyball on the beach. It was a good time. I enjoyed covering the news there and Gainey had introduced me to all the people I needed to know around town. I was even getting to cover some sports. I would shoot high school football games around Horry County for the high school football highlight show after the late news on Friday night.

In January, they told me wanted someone who looked older in that position, so I moved to Florence to the main station. I moved into an apartment with Bob Juback and Pete Yanity, the station's two sports anchors. WBTW is a CBS affiliate, so on fall Saturdays they had college football games on, and we didn't have a 6:00 newscast. Yanity, the weekend anchor, would usually cover the games in Columbia if the Gamecocks were at home, and Juback would go to Clemson, since it was across the state and longer travel. I tagged along with Bob a few times in the fall of 1986 and fell in love with Clemson's stadium. The skyboxes between the first and second levels were so cool. The press box was first class.

Clemson's stadium is officially known as Clemson Memorial Stadium. But football fans know it as Death Valley. The moniker gained widespread acceptance in the 1950s when Clemson was frequently ranked in the national polls. One of the great features of seeing a game in Death Valley is when the Tigers run down the hill before kickoff. A Clemson grad who had traveled to Death Valley in California had brought a rock from the valley to Frank Howard, Clemson's coach at the time and the man who the field is named in honor of. The rock was mounted at the top of the hill in 1966, but Clemson players didn't start rubbing it before taking the field until the next year. Back in the day, Clemson's players dressed at a fieldhouse away from the stadium and the closest way into the stadium was down the hill in the west end zone. In 1970, locker rooms were built under the stands in the east end zone and coach Hootie Ingram didn't see the point in going all the way to the other side of the stadium to run down the hill. So, the team didn't run down the hill for several years. But in 1972, the seniors wanted to run down the hill for the season finale against South Carolina. After the first game in 1973, the tradition was re-established.

Ten minutes before kickoff, the players board three buses and ride behind the north stands and get off the buses under the scoreboard above the hill in the east end zone. With modern video capabilities, the whole process is shown on the video screen in the stadium. Anticipation builds and the crowd starts cheering as the players and coaches gather on the top of the hill. Then, the cannon fires, the band plays "Tiger Rag" and the players run down the hill on an orange carpet. That was an awe-inspiring sight for me as a 23-year-old. I still get goosebumps every time I experience that. I could just imagine what it was like for a player to run down it.

"Just don't fall down" was what Clemson offensive lineman John Phillips was thinking the first time he ran down the hill as a freshman.

"We were playing Western Carolina," recalled Phillips. "My parents were there, and I was scared to death I was going to fall. 'Please don't fall' was all I was thinking about."

In 1983 the second deck was completed on the north side and capacity was more than 80,000, ranking it as one of the largest on-campus stadiums in the country. Clemson routinely ranked in the top 10 nationally in attendance until the mid-90s when the team averaged barely more than six wins a season.

"You always loved playing at home," said Phillips. "We had an advantage at home and didn't lose much."

On September 17, 1987, I was lucky enough to be one of the 82,500 people there to see the Tigers host the Georgia Bulldogs. Rain and clouds didn't dampen the spirit of any of those fans in red or orange. Clemson was ranked number eight and the Bulldogs number 18. The game was nationally televised on CBS and in 1987 having a game nationally televised was a big deal. Very few games were televised. CBS announcer Brent Musburger captured the atmosphere as he signed on with his trademark, "You are looking live. … It's one of the most spectacular settings in all of college football!"

In 1987 Juback left the station and Yanity was promoted to sports director. For a game as big as this one, he wasn't going to miss it. I was his photographer for the game.

"First game I ever saw in Death Valley," said Yanity. "I thought, so that's what 80,000 or so sounds like."

The two schools are only about 80 miles apart. They first played in 1897 and despite being in different conferences, had played many times and had been playing every year since 1967. Phillips, a senior in 1987, said the Georgia game meant more than all the others. In fact, he said Clemson's two biggest rivals, South Carolina and Georgia, were non-conference games. I asked him which one was bigger.

"Probably Georgia just because they were better," he said.

The Bulldogs had dominated the long series, and the Tigers hadn't won two games in a row against Georgia since 1905-06. Each school had won a national championship in the 80s, Georgia in 1980 and Clemson the following year. Clemson fans love to point out that despite his 2-1 record against the Tigers, Herschel Walker never scored a touchdown against Clemson. After Clemson's national championship, the program had fallen on tough times after the effect of NCAA probation. But with the recruiting limitations in the past, Danny Ford had built the Tigers back up with a strong defense and a powerful running game.

Usually, the games between the rivals were low-scoring, defensive struggles. But Clemson had won the 1986 game in Athens the year before 31-28 with David Treadwell kicking a field goal as time expired. All-ACC running backs Kenny Flowers and Terrance Flagler had graduated, but redshirt freshman Terry Allen was expected to fit right in. One of the pillars of the Tigers' running game was Phillips, now an all-American at guard.

"For me 1986 was a bigger challenge. I had to block Henry Harris. He was a monster. They ran an eight-man front, so we took our angles. We had superior blocking angles, but we had to execute. For a few plays Harris would be out and the guy who I replaced him, number 95, was what we called a fish. Lock him up and he would go. Before the '87 game, we're watching film and I see 95 is starting now, I was thinking this will be easy. But I could tell he had been on a program or something that summer and he had become a monster too."

Number 95 was Bill Goldberg, who later gained fame as the professional wrestler Goldberg.

Coming into the Georgia game Clemson led the nation in defense and was allowing slightly more than a yard per carry. But although Walker was long gone, Georgia still had an impressive stable of running backs. Lars Tate was leading the nation in rushing at more than 187 yards per game coming in. Both programs were led by coaches who would be inducted into the College Football Hall of Fame.

"It was cool seeing Vince Dooley," Yanity said. "I had seen Danny Ford and interviewed him before, but those were two legends."

As the Tigers got off the buses under the scoreboard, the fans could see they were wearing their orange pants, which they only broke out for big games. They were first worn in 1980 against South Carolina and again when they defeated Nebraska to win the Orange Bowl and the 1981 National Championship. Clemson was 11-1 wearing the orange pants. On the broadcast, Brent Musburger said, "One of the great rituals of college football: the arrival of the Clemson Tigers." Georgia was known for their "Silver Britches," but had a sartorial change today too and were wearing red pants for the game. The defenses were dominating the early part of the game.

"Unbelievable play in the trenches," recalled Yanity.

At the end of the first quarter the score was 3-3. Georgia's Nathaniel Lewis provided the game's first big play with a 76-yard punt return to put the Dawgs up 10-3. Clemson fullback Tracy Johnson exploded for a 38-yard run to tie the game at 10. The atmosphere was incredible.

"I had never heard a band play after every play like Georgia did," said Yanity. The teams traded field goals and it was 13-13 at halftime."

Lewis was involved in a couple of important plays in the second half. He was involved in a fake field goal for Georgia that didn't work. But Clemson couldn't take advantage. Later Lewis would fumble a punt inside Georgia's 10-yard line, but Clemson had to settle for Treadwell's third field goal of the game. On defense, Clemson's had shut out the Bulldogs in the half and were hanging on to a 16-13 lead. Georgia finally was able to muster a good drive on the Clemson defense. Starting at their 26-yard line, the Dawgs had some nice runs and a 36-yard pass to tight end Kurt Warner for a big gain. Hampton put the Dawgs back in front with an impressive 8-yard run that he had to break several tackles at the line of scrimmage.

The Death Valley crowd was getting restless, and some were booing. Things were not going well for their Tigers, who had already used all their time outs. There was just under nine minutes left in the game. Clemson's offense was built on ball control, playing with a lead and running out the clock. They weren't built to quickly move down the field.

Runs by Allen and Johnson gave the Tigers a couple of first downs. But a third down completion was short of the first down and the punting team came on the field. Phillips understood the fans' frustration.

"We weren't sure we would get the ball back."

Rusty Seyle came in to punt with 6:56 to go. Despite his earlier touchdown, Lewis was not back to receive the punt after his fumble. Seyle got away a beauty and true freshman John Johnson, a native of LaGrange, Georgia, downed it inside the 1-yard line. That got the crowd back into the game. Yanity and I were standing in the end zone. Phillips had a funny story about how Johnson, who had been committed to Georgia, wound up with the Tigers.

Now, high school seniors fax their signed letter of intent to the university where they are going to enroll. But in the late 80s, you had to get the signature of the player in person. Clemson assistant Tommy West (who was an assistant at App State in 1981 and was an instructor for my PE class) was in LaGrange on Signing Day eve intent to get Johnson's signature.

"Georgia thought they had him and Coach West was in LaGrange and staying at the same hotel as the UGA coach and he said he talked to the coach the night before. He told him 'Sleep well.' Coach West got up first thing and got him signed."

That play by John Johnson brought the Death Valley crowd back to life. On first down James Jackson tried a quarterback sneak and got nothing. On second down, Dooley had Jackson try to run a sweep. Clemson cornerback James Lott grabbed him to slow him down and Gene Beasley came up from his safety spot to tackle Jackson in the end zone to cut Georgia's lead in half. Yanity and I saw the play develop right in front of us.

"I had never seen a defense run like that," he said. "You could really tell in person how fast they were."

The play happened so quickly, the offensive players didn't see what happened, but heard the crowd explode.

"We are having our offensive line meeting with Coach [Larry] Van der Heyden, going over their blitzing and stunts," Phillips recalled. "We really didn't see what happened. It wasn't like we were over there watching it happen."

The free kick was returned to the Clemson 42-yard line. There was 5:31 on the clock. Clemson didn't have any time outs. Despite the two field goals he had already hit, Treadwell had missed from 42 yards earlier in the half. Phillips and the offense had all the confidence in their kicker.

"Get to the 30, we knew he would make it," Phillips said. "Once we got the ball, we thought we could score. We had some momentum. Terry Allen, another Georgia native, was in the backfield, and he was just ripping off runs."

Indeed, he was. And another tailback, Wesley McFadden, picked up a first down on two carries. Then Allen came back in and picked up 12 yards up the middle. It seemed Clemson wouldn't be denied. However, the Georgia defense hunkered down and forced the Tigers into a third and 8 at their 30 with less than three minutes remaining. It was right on the edge of Treadwell's comfort zone. Allen took the pitch, made a beautiful cutback, broke several tackles and made it to the 13 and Clemson had a first down.

A 5-yard penalty on the Tigers slowed them down somewhat. Three runs didn't get the first down but did get the ball to the 4-yard line. With 38 seconds on the running clock Ford sent in Treadwell for the win.

Phillips was on the field goal team, and he never worried that time would run out before they got the kick off. I wasn't so sure and was surprised Ford didn't have Clemson throw an incomplete pass to stop the clock. Back then, spiking the ball to stop the clock wasn't a thing.

"We did that so much in practice, it was just routine," said Phillips. "Coach Ford has us work on that all the time. Two-minute drill and fly out there and over and over and over."

As the clock ticked down, Treadwell came on the field. He calmly positioned his tee where he wanted it on the 11-yard line. (Tees were permitted in college football for field goals and extra points until 1989). He made sure his holder was ready. I was getting anxious watching through the viewfinder of my camera on the endline. The ball was snapped with five seconds on the clock and the 21-yard field goal was good. Treadwell was the hero again. In his Clemson career he never missed a field goal in the last six minutes of a game and kicked six game-winning field goals. The Death Valley crowd was ecstatic.

"The fans were great, and you didn't want to lose and disappoint them," said Phillips.

Fans began coming onto the field. At Clemson, that's not a bad thing. Fans are encouraged to safely come onto the field after games and celebrate with the players. It became official policy in the early 2000s but had been going on since the 50s. Yanity and I did some interviews on the field amid the bedlam, then went to the locker room for more interviews and for Coach Ford's news conference.

"Being on the field and seeing Treadwell make that kick was incredible," said Yanity. "We were standing under the goal post there and the place went crazy. Still probably the best college game I ever saw."

Although that was Yanity's first visit to Death Valley, it wouldn't be his last. In 1990, Yanity was named the sports director of WSPA-TV in Spartanburg, South Carolina, a station that has had close ties with Clemson athletics for decades. He was Clemson's play-by-play announcer for football from 2003 until 2014. As of 2023, he's currently hosting the Clemson football coach's show for the third time.

The win over Georgia looked like the Tigers would be a threat for the national championship. After winning their first six games of the season and getting as high as number seven in the AP poll, Clemson would lose to N.C. State for the second straight year. The regular season ended with a loss to in-state rival South Carolina, but the Tigers were able to beat Penn State

35-10 in the Citrus Bowl on January 1. The final record was 10-2 and a ranking of number 12 in the AP poll.

The Georgia-Clemson rivalry was one of the casualties of the SEC expanding to 12 teams in 1992. SEC teams were playing an additional conference game and Georgia already had a non-conference rivalry game with Georgia Tech. Clemson had the end of the season game with its in-state rival South Carolina. The 2021 game was the eighth time they have played since 1992.

The quality of the football and the electricity in the stadium that day in 1987 really had me hooked. I wanted to keep coming to big-time football games. Little did I know then, that a few months later, I would be in a place where football was about as big as it could get.

Chapter 3: Iron Bowl on the Plains

Alabama at Auburn

December 2, 1989

I was hired by WBRC-TV in Birmingham as the weekend news producer in February of 1988. I seriously considered turning the job down because I wanted to go to the Clemson-Florida State game at Death Valley that fall. That game turned out to be the Puntrooskie game when Bobby Bowden pulled off one of the greatest trick plays in college football history. Deion Sanders had a 71-yard punt return for a touchdown and the 'Noles won, 24-21. It was truly a great game between two top 10 teams. The environment at Clemson was every bit as great as I figured it would be and I was disappointed I missed it. But things worked out okay for me.

Professionally it was a good thing I went to work in Birmingham. WBRC was an excellent station. By the summer of 1989 I had been there more than a year but was still producing the weekend newscasts. I was tired of working weekends and had started sending out some resumes to other stations. One day the news director called me into his office and said it had come to his attention that I had been sending out resumes. At first, I was a little caught off guard, but realized news directors talk to each other all the time and it really shouldn't be a surprise. Anyway, he asked me if I would stay if he made me the sports producer. I didn't even have to think about it and immediately said yes.

Our station did well in the ratings but didn't do well with our male audience. One of the main reasons for that, the station management felt, was that we had inconsistent sports coverage. In 1989 the station brought in two new sports anchors who would change the way residents of Central Alabama would get their sports news forever. Rick Karle was the sports director and would anchor the 6 p.m. and 10 p.m. shows. Mike Raita would do the 5 p.m. show. That show was called *Live at 5* and he would be live, out of the studio as much as possible. The sports producer position was created for me to coordinate everything and produce the live sports shows the station was looking to do. We also had a photographer and Ron Grillo was the weekend anchor who also worked three days during the week. It was a big adjustment for me to get used to the styles of Karle and Raita. We were the first station in town to do a high school football highlight show on Friday nights and it was a big hit. That first year we also did a weekend recap show on Sunday night. It was great working on these shows.

The year before, I was able to get a Saturday off from producing the news and went to the Alabama-Ole Miss game in Tuscaloosa. It was homecoming in T-Town. The Tide were 4-0 and ranked number 12 in the country. Ole Miss was unranked but rallied from a 12-0 deficit to upset Alabama that day, 22-12. Bill Curry was in his second year as the Tide's coach but had never won the Bama fans over. In fact, after that game, a disgruntled fan had thrown a brick through Curry's office window. The Tide finished the season 9-3 with a one-point win over Army in the Sun Bowl.

However, in 1989 Curry had the Tide rolling. They had beaten number six Tennessee in Birmingham, and the following week went to State College and beat number 14 Penn State on a blocked field goal, 17-16. Heading into the Auburn game they were 10-0 and had climbed to number two in the nation. And this team would do something that an Alabama football team had never done: play a game at Auburn.

The Alabama-Auburn football series is as complicated as it is exciting. It was first played in Birmingham in February of 1893. The schools can't even agree on when it was played. Auburn considers it the first game of the 1893 season. Alabama considers it the last game of the four-game 1892 season. There is no doubt about the score. Auburn won 32-22 at Lakeview Field in Birmingham. For a while, I lived across the street from where the game was played. There is now a bank headquarters building on the site. The teams played several games in Montgomery, Birmingham, and Tuscaloosa over the next few years. After the 1907 game, the teams couldn't agree on a per diem for players and after negotiating for much of the year, it was determined that there wouldn't be a game in 1908. The hiatus stretched until after World War II. The peace-time euphoria of the late 1940s finally made it to the "Heart of Dixie." Politicians got involved and the schools would resume the series in 1948 at Birmingham's Legion Field. As a show of the new peace, the presidents of the schools buried a hatchet at Birmingham's Wilson (now Linn) Park before the game. In 1948 Legion Field had 47,000 seats. Denny Stadium (now Bryant-Denny) in Tuscaloosa had 31,000 seats and Auburn Stadium only held 15,000 fans. It made the most economic sense to play the game in Birmingham.

Stadium size had always been a problem for Auburn. From 1923 to 1930 Auburn only played two home games a year because they didn't have a stadium big enough to accommodate big crowds. From 1931 to 1936 they only hosted one game and in 1937 and 1938 they didn't have a home game all season. In 1937 they won the Orange Bowl, so it wasn't because they weren't playing good football.

In the late '20s Ralph "Shug" Jordan was a football player and friends with Jeff Beard, who ran track. They didn't like the fact that Auburn had to play so many football games on the road. They committed themselves to work to make sure Auburn had a stadium big enough to host games.

"It was a dream those men would have for 60 years," said former Auburn AD David Housel.

Jordan is the winningest coach in Auburn history, coaching 25 years and winning 176 games and the 1957 National Championship. Beard was the athletic director who hired Jordan as head coach of the football team in 1951. When Jordan took over, Auburn was consistently hosting three home games a year for the first time. But Florida and Mississippi State were the only SEC teams that would come to Auburn. Even Tulane, who was in the SEC from its founding in 1932 until 1965, played Auburn in Mobile.

Auburn had played Georgia in their first football game in February of 1892 in Atlanta and Auburn had played the Bulldogs more than any other school. In 1919 the two schools started playing in Columbus, Georgia, 36 miles from Auburn) every year. In 1906 Auburn started playing Georgia Tech every year at Grant Field in Atlanta. In 1949 Auburn Stadium was renamed for Cliff Hare, a member of Auburn's first football team. The stadium capacity was increased to 34,500 in 1955. In 1958 Auburn and Georgia would play their last game in Columbus and Auburn would host the Bulldogs for the first time in 1960.

"Georgia was the only one that willingly came in and said let's play football," said Housel.

Georgia Tech started playing in Birmingham in 1960 and would finally start playing in Auburn in 1970 after another stadium expansion that raised capacity to more than 61,000. Auburn hosted Tennessee in Birmingham from 1956 until 1972. Jordan's name was added to the stadium in 1973 and the Volunteers came to Auburn the next year. They would play in Birmingham two more times, before coming for the last time in 1980. In 1980 the upper deck on the west side was finished and Auburn's stadium's capacity was more than 71,000. In 1987 luxury boxes and an upper deck on the east side were finished and Auburn had one of the largest on-campus stadiums in the nation with a capacity of 85,214.

Shug Jordan gave the game its moniker when he was asked after a disappointing Auburn season how he felt about not going to a bowl game.

He responded, "We have our bowl game every year with Alabama."

And with Birmingham's history with iron, the Iron Bowl was born. The Vulcan was the Roman god of fire, metalworking, and the forge. A statue of Vulcan sits atop Red Mountain on the city's southern edge and overlooks Birmingham. Red Mountain got its name because of the prominent seams of red hematite iron ore in the mountain. Mines in Red Mountain provided the iron for Birmingham's steel mills.

So that left one holdout who still wouldn't come to Auburn and that of course was Alabama. Even though Legion Field had added an upper deck on the east side, Jordan-Hare was the largest stadium in the state in 1989. The games produced a lot of thrilling moments. In 1972, Auburn was ranked number nine and was trailing number two Alabama 16-3 in the fourth quarter. Greg Gantt was set to punt for Alabama, but it was blocked by Bill Newton. David Langner picked it up on the run and took it in for a touchdown to cut the deficit to 6. After Alabama's next possession didn't gain much, Gantt was called on to punt again. Newton blocked it, Langner picked it up and ran it in for another touchdown. Gardner Jett kicked the extra point and Auburn had an unlikely win. "Punt, Bama, punt" was shouted by Auburn fans for years. That win didn't generate any momentum in the series and the Tigers lost their next nine in the rivalry.

After Auburn lost in 1980, former Alabama assistant Pat Dye was hired as head coach. Dye, a Georgia grad, had been successful as a head coach at East Carolina University and the University of Wyoming before coming to the Plains. Dye spent eight and a half years on Bear Bryant's Alabama staff.

When Dye was hired, Paul Finebaum hadn't been working as a columnist at the *Birmingham Post-Herald* very long, but he had gotten to know Dye when Finebaum was working in Shreveport, Louisiana.

"I encountered Dye in Shreveport," said Finebaum. "He had called trying to get in the bowl game there. He had been at Wyoming and quit, and I talked to him a lot. He wasn't doing anything, so he had time. I was there when he talked to the team for the first time. You could just tell Auburn was never going to be the same again. The Saban arrival at Alabama was similar."

In Dye's first game against his mentor in 1981, the Tide won and gave Bryant his 315th win as a head coach. That moved him past Alonzo Stagg into first place on the all-time wins list. In 1982 Auburn ended the long losing streak when freshman running back Bo Jackson went "up and over" for the winning touchdown with 2:26 remaining. In '83 Jackson ran for 256 yards and the fourth quarter was played during a driving rainstorm and the threat of severe weather. In 1984, Bo went the wrong way, missed a block, Brent Fullwood was stopped short of the end zone, and Alabama held on to win. In 1985 there were four lead changes in the fourth quarter and Alabama won it on the last play as Van Tiffin kicked a 52-yard field goal. The next year Auburn had the ball deep in Alabama territory trailing late in the game. Auburn had called for a reverse, but wide receiver Lawyer Tillman was on the field, and he was not supposed to be there for that play and was trying to call time out. The refs wouldn't allow it, so Tillman got in his stance, ran the reverse and scored the winning touchdown with 45 seconds remaining. In 1987 Auburn shut out Alabama for the first time since 1957 10-0. In 1988 Auburn won for the third straight year. And in 1989 Auburn would host Alabama for the first time.

David Housel is much more than the former AD at his alma mater. He graduated in 1969 and began working for the athletic department a few years later. He taught journalism at the school for eight years then went back to the athletic department in 1980. When Pat Dye was hired as head coach, he took over as sports information director (SID). He would serve as athletic director from 1994 until he retired in 2005. A year later he was named Director of Athletics Emeritus of Auburn. He's written several books about Auburn football, is the unofficial historian of the university, and loves the place so much.

"When Coach Dye was hired, he didn't want to move it," said Housel of the Alabama game. "He thought it was a recruiting advantage to play the game in Birmingham. But then he saw what the passion to move it was."

"He always made a big deal about it," said Finebaum. "I was a Birmingham columnist and said you can't take that game out of there. There was the pride factor for the city. He told me a story about how the Auburn president was being ushered to seat at Legion Field, and the usher was wearing Bama stuff and the President told Dye, 'We have to do something about this.' He started beating the drum in the early 80s."

Auburn felt the contract with Alabama ended after the 1988 game and they had declared that they would host the game in 1989. Alabama said we would come in 1991, but Auburn held fast.

"Auburn's position was always we would always play that ['89] game at home," said Housel.

Auburn would play the '91 game in Birmingham, but the Tigers would be the "home" team and have the majority of tickets. Then starting in 1993 Jordan-Hare Stadium would host the Alabama game every other year.

Coach Dye passed away in 2020. On an SEC Network documentary on the history of the SEC he relayed a conversation he had with Coach Bryant, his old mentor.

"He said to me, 'You want to move that game, don't you.' I told him, 'Yes.' He said, 'that's not happening as long as I'm coaching.' I told him, 'You aren't coaching forever.'"

"Coach Dye talked about it a lot," remembers Stacy Danley. "He explained what that meant to the Auburn legacy, leveling the playing field, and said we are equal. That was a big deal and Coach Dye made sure we understood that."

Danley, a senior running back in 1989, was one of many Georgia natives on the Auburn team.

"I didn't understand the rivalry between Auburn and Alabama until I got there," he said. "We would go and play them in Birmingham. It was supposed to be a neutral site, but it didn't feel like one. Alabama played there a lot in the regular season, and we would get on a bus and stay in a hotel. It felt like an away game for us."

"I wanted to go and play," said Roger Shultz, Alabama's All-SEC center in 1989. "I was recruited by Auburn. I had friends at Auburn. It was a grass field. I wanted to play on that. We played on Astroturf so much."

With the historic clash lurking at the end of the season, both teams were having good years. Alabama was 10-0 and ranked second in the nation. Auburn lost to Tennessee and Florida State. But with a win over the Tide, Auburn would share the SEC title with Alabama and Tennessee, the third conference title in a row for the Tigers.

"That's the game, beating Alabama," said Danley. "We talk about it in the off season, we talk about it in preseason, we talk about it during the season. You take one game at a time. But regardless of how good you're doing, you know if you lose that Bama game it's not a good season."

Danley said the two losses were a little disappointing for Auburn.

"We came in every year thinking we were going to win the national championship. This was our chance. We had strong leaders and were very focused on what we needed to do. We were tough. That's how we were raised as Auburn men, we were taught to be that way. They raised us right. We had a lot of fun, but we worked hard. We were an experienced team. We were grown men. We had Reggie Slack, Quentin Riggins, Craig Ogletree. We had been there before. Coach Dye was a little under the gun when I got there. They had lost two straight to Alabama, but we got that turned around."

There wasn't an SEC Championship game played then, so this would be the last game until a bowl game. Also, the teams always had an off week before the Iron Bowl.

During the 1989 season each team held a weekly news conference. Alabama had theirs on Monday and Auburn did it on Tuesday. The coach would address the media around 11 a.m. and then the media would eat at the football dorm. The media would request the players they wanted to interview in advance and as they finished with class and their lunch, they would be available for interviews. Raita was always at the news conferences and did his 5 p.m. sportscast live from the respective school. Occasionally, I would get to go. I always enjoyed listening to what the coaches had to say about things, and it was a good way to learn about some of the Xs and Os that the teams were using. It was rare for those conversations to make it on TV, but I felt like you could get some inside background information. It was also nice getting to be around the players. They seemed to be pretty good guys and you could tell some were shy around the media and didn't give great interviews, but others relished the spotlight, and the star players knew they would be interviewed just about every week. Having the off week before the game gave us a chance to do more feature type stories that would air in the pregame show. Sometimes we would do the interviews in a one-on-one setting with a nice backdrop for the person being interviewed. As the season progressed, we would always be thinking about possibilities for stories that would be good for that show.

"When I was a freshman, I was redshirted," said Danley. "Alabama week, I had red jersey. They told me you have to be Bobby Humphrey. I was ready to go and run. D [defense] was tagging me. We were going full speed, scrimmaging. That week off, we were full bore, getting ready. I realized this was different."

John Thomas was a sophomore at Auburn that fall.

"There was buzz. ... It was a big build up," said Thomas. "Everyone was getting hyped as we don't have to go to Birmingham; just roll out of bed."

Michelle Keesee grew up in Auburn and is now works for the university. She was in the ninth grade in the fall of 1989. Her dad was an Auburn grad and knew the importance of this week.

"Monday morning of that week my dad asked me if I could feel it," recalled Keesee. "I asked him what, and he said, 'history is being made here and I don't want you to forget what it feels like.'"

"We had four good days of practice," said Danley. "We were very determined. We knew what we had at stake. We had fans that were there tailgating the week of. Going to class, the fans were there and hollering at us to beat Bama and it was just building up. It was just an interesting two weeks and I'm just glad I had a chance to be a part of it. We were a good team, and they were a good team. Just the fact that we had them on our field, no one wanted to lose. Everybody was on edge a little bit.

We tried to stay low key, go to class and go back to the room. It was a little intense."

"Dye milked it for all it was worth," recalled Finebaum. "That was when the Berlin Wall was coming down and it was compared to that."

"There was so much stuff all week leading up to it," remembered Thomas. "That was the feeling all week there was no way we were going to lose that game."

In Tuscaloosa, the players entered the locker room for practice early in the week to find a cassette tape in their lockers. The tape was a recording of Whitney Houston's song "One Moment in Time." The Alabama players didn't understand what that was for.

"For me the most emotional thing was Friday," said Housel. "I always went and met the opposing team, their coach and their SID and welcomed them to Auburn. When I got to that corner of the stadium where the visitors are and saw Alabama in those crimson warmups, and I realized they were here, and it was going to happen."

After the walk-though for the Alabama players, they were having the team meal in Montgomery, Alabama's, capital, but it wasn't what Roger Shultz expected.

"We had these cards with the itinerary, and we were having a meal at the Governor's House. I thought the Governor was going to be there, but it turned out that was just the name of the hotel where we were staying."

At our station, the game was getting a lot of coverage, and not just in the sports casts. The news department was doing live shots from Auburn as well. We aired our pregame special live from the stadium from 8 to 9 p.m. on Friday, with Karle and Raita hosting it. We liked having the extra week between the games to record some good features about the players and the history of the games. I had put together a story from some of the great games in the series and had really enjoyed meeting some of the players who had made the series what it was. Raita had done a funny story on the drive from Birmingham to Auburn for Alabama fans that had never made that trip. That turned out to be a very crazy day. Not only was it Iron Bowl Eve, but the high school state championship games were also being played that night. I was in the control room back in Birmingham and had to help Karle to get his sports segment in the 10:00 news together. Then at 10:30 we did our *Sideline '89* high school football show to recap the state championship games. There were several schools from our area playing, so I had to make sure the photographers had their highlights edited and Karle had all the information he needed for the highlights and the scores. I rode down early Saturday for the game.

It was finally game day.

"Auburn people that day made a trip they never thought they would, to go to Auburn to see them play Alabama," said Housel.

It's believed that Auburn is one of the first schools to have the tradition of fans lining the sidewalk as players walk from their dorm to the stadium. In the early 60s fans started lining Donahue Street as the players walked from Sewell Hall to Jordan-Hare. The NCAA has since outlawed "athletic dormitories," but the tradition remains intact at Auburn and most colleges let their fans know when to take a break from tailgating and greet the team as they head to the stadium.

In 1989, there were still dorms and most of Auburn's football players lived at Sewell Hall. Danley always enjoyed the chance to interact with the fans and show off a little.

"We used to compete to see who would be the best dressed. Me and my roommate would wait to the last minute to go down and be the last in line so everyone could see us in our clothes. I lived on the back side of Sewell, and we were in our room and heard a roar and we were wondering if we should go out there, but we decided to do our tradition and wait, but it was so loud. Finally, we went out and walked around that corner and I could see the field of orange and blue. Fans were everywhere. Usually, we would have the whole street to walk down but because of the crowd it was single file. I've said this before, to make this walk, I don't care who we played that day. We could have given the Dallas Cowboys a good game that day. There was no way were going to lose."

That was something else that stood out for Karle.

"It was so emotional," he said. "There were grown men crying as those players walked by."

Housel was busy with his duties at the packed press box but took time to look at the Tiger Walk from the back of the stadium.

"It was bigger and wilder that day," he said. "The players understood what it meant. It was pressure, it was excitement, it was anticipation. It was history. For most of the players it was the biggest game they would ever play in. They had the fate of a people riding on them."

Part of his pregame routine was to go down to the coach's office and check in with Dye about the starting lineup.

"Coach Dye looked at me and I looked at him and we both started crying because we knew how much this meant to each other," he said. "He and the players had to control the emotion on the field, and I had to control the emotion in the press box."

Danley thinks Coach Dye did a good job of preparing the players during the week.

"He was in rare form all week," said Danley. "He talked a lot about pride and respect and being disrespected. He made it clear: Alabama didn't respect Auburn. I took that personally and I didn't understand that. We had beaten them three years in a row. He made it clear; they didn't feel like they had to come here. But he said they will respect us from this day forward as their equal. He made sure we understood what it meant for the Auburn family. It wasn't just about us."

"We would get up and start drinking on game day," said Thomas. We would have Bloody Mary's and sit around the house and watch the pregame. We would usually get there about a half hour before kickoff, but that day we were in our seats more than an hour beforehand. The whole stadium was in their seats about an hour before kick-off and they were ready to go."

On the other side of the stadium, as the Tide were getting ready Bill Curry explained why the cassette tapes were in the lockers earlier in the week.

"He had worked that song, 'One Moment in Time' into his pregame speech," said Shultz.

The game was televised by CBS at 2 p.m. local time and at 1:00, the local CBS affiliate, WRBL, had signed on with a pregame show from the corner of one of the end zones. Roger Manis was the sports director, and his co-host was Rece Davis, best known now as the host of ESPN's *College GameDay*. During the prep for the show, Rece had taped an interview with Curry and asked him if he would do a live, pre-game interview with them and Dye on the field. Curry agreed to do it. Later, after he had taped an interview with Dye in Columbus Davis asked him if he would join him and Curry before the game.

"Dye said, 'Bill said he would?'" said Davis. "I told him yes and he said, 'have someone come and get me.' Bill was a man of his word, and he was there. We opened the show with me, Roger, and Bill Curry. We did the interview with Bill, he walked out, and Pat walked in, and we interviewed him. I don't think there is another thing I've done in my career I'm as proud of as pulling that off. Being able to have those guys in that circumstance and that stage was a great accomplishment."

Because their station didn't have a satellite truck to use for the show, they only had one camera that was connected to the fiber optic hookup on the Auburn campus. Most of the show was Manis and Davis pitching to taped stories that they had done in advance.

"We knew how important it was to people in the state of Alabama," said Davis, an Alabama native and graduate from the University of Alabama. "I think because of all that, we were immersed the culture, we captured the magnitude of the moment, and we delivered that to the people and especially to the Auburn people."

When CBS came on the air at 2 p.m. CST, Jim Nantz was doing the play by play. The nation got to see and hear the years of emotion from the Auburn fans being released.

"It was an unbelievable atmosphere," recalled Shultz. "It was so loud. I couldn't communicate with my guard."

"I have not been in many stadiums like that with drama and anticipation," said Davis, who as *College GameDay* host since 2012 is at the site of one of the nation's most important games each week.

In addition to his column in the *Post-Herald*, Finebaum also hosted a radio show in Birmingham before being the first person hired by the SEC Network, before they signed on in the fall of 2014. He graduated from the University of Tennessee in the late 70s and has spent his professional career covering the SEC.

"I've been going to college games for 50 years and I never experienced anything like that," said Finebaum. "Two hours before the game Auburn fans were going crazy. The Bear 315 game [in 1981] was the most electric until this one."

Auburn received the opening kickoff and moved the ball to midfield. Facing a third and 5, Slack hit speedy wide receiver Alexander Wright with a long pass to the 7-yard line and Jordan-Hare went nuts.

"When Slack hit Wright on that bomb, the stadium was the loudest I've ever heard," said Karle. "And most of the Auburn fans were waving orange and blue pompons that had been placed on all the seats."

Thomas's fraternity had seats in the upper part of the student section that gave him a great view of the entire stadium.

"Seeing those orange and blue pompons," he said. "There was a haze of orange and blue across the whole stadium. That was incredible!"

The players on both sides remember that.

"There were all those orange and blue streamers," said Shultz. "And it was a haze."

Danley said, "They had they had these orange and blue shakers, and they were going into the air, and it looked eerie from the field."

Three plays later, Danley's backfield partner James Joseph scored to give Auburn the early lead, 7-0.

Alabama drove deep into Auburn territory, but the drive stalled, and Phillip Doyle kicked a short field goal to get Bama on the board. Later in the first quarter Bama was back in the red zone and was lined up to kick another short field goal. However, Curry had called for a fake, but Auburn was not fooled and the pass into the end zone was incomplete.

Auburn couldn't do much on offense in the first half and Bama took the lead on a touchdown pass from Gary

Hollingsworth to Marco Battle, with a little more than a minute remaining in the half.

"It's interesting for me and a lot of my teammates, you prepare so much during the week, it's a part of your life and the grind, once you take that first lick, I would get the crowd out," said Danley. "The crowd was so loud. I couldn't settle in. I was floating out there. Finally, after about a quarter, I blocked the crowd out. It was hard to settle in."

I asked him if that's why they were losing at halftime.

"I think so. It was weird I didn't realize we were trailing. It never crossed my mind we were losing. We're going to win this game."

In the press box Housel still had confidence in his guys.

"They were ahead," he said. "But I felt like we had the stronger team."

The Tigers retook the lead early in the third quarter when Joseph scored his second touchdown. The Tigers wouldn't surrender that lead. In fact, they scored on four consecutive possessions and the lead was stretched out to 27-10.

Back then, the bowl games would invite the team they wanted. The SEC Champion always played in the Sugar Bowl, regardless of their record. The champions of the Big Ten and Pac-8/10/12 would always play in the Rose Bowl. The winner of the old Southwest Conference would play in the Cotton Bowl and the winner of the Big 8 would play in the Orange Bowl. Even if the champion of the Big Ten and the SEC were undefeated, the two teams wouldn't play in a bowl game. Because of that tradition, it's taken so long to get the BCS, then the four-team playoff, and in 2024, the 12-team playoff in the upper division of college football. If there were ties for the conference championship, the bowls could choose the team they wanted to invite.

"The Sugar bowl was going to take Auburn if they had won," said Housel. "We had been there in '87 and '88. But in the third quarter of the game, they made the decision to take Bama. Auburn went to the Tampa bowl, the Hall of Fame bowl."

The players didn't realize that decision had been made. Hollingsworth hit Battle for another touchdown and the Tide pulled within 10. Bama's defense came up big and gave the ball back to Hollingsworth. Facing a third and goal from the 5 Hollingsworth overthrew Lamonde Russell in the end zone and Doyle hit the short field goal. Auburn recovered the onside kick. Danley, who finished the day with 130 yards rushing, ran for 35 on the drive. When Lyle hit a 34-yard field goal to seal the game, it set off a celebration for the ages.

"It was a great game," said Danley. "I am thankful I was able to play in it."

"Auburn willed themselves to win that day," said Finebaum. "Even though I had been to Auburn games many times before, this had a different feel. You were no longer on Graymont Avenue [the street Legion Field is on]. It was the Auburn fans that made it that way. They were walking on air. They had done something. They had shown the world they were equal to Alabama."

With five minutes remaining in the game, Housel led the reporters in the press box down the elevator to the field, so media members could go to locker rooms for the coach's news conferences and to interview players. The end of the game is a bit of a blur for him.

"I don't remember specifics, just a lot of shouting, hugging, crying," he said. "I don't have specific memories except hugging Coach Dye. I remember that."

As you would imagine, the locker room was crazy.

"Some of toughest coaches we had were running around kissing everyone," said Danley. "I thought Coach [Wayne] Hall was going to kiss me on the mouth! It was just a lot of tears and a lot of cheers as well. A very special moment."

Shultz was gracious in defeat.

"It was the most memorable game for me," he said. "I wish the result was better, but we can deal with it. I felt like we still had the chance to win the national championship if we had beaten Miami."

"There were old-school Bama guys that didn't want to go down there," said Ray Melick, the Alabama beat reporter for the *Post-Herald*. "Truthfully, the Alabama people who complained were glad to have the game at their place too. But that was a defining moment in the rivalry."

Auburn has a post-game tradition of rolling the trees at Toomer's Corner. Toomer's Corner is named after Toomer's

Drugs, a store at the corner of College Street and Magnolia Avenue where the campus meets the town. Stately oak trees lined the corner in 1989 and after each win students and fans would head to the corner and throw toilet paper rolls in the oaks. The Auburn media guide says the tradition is believed to have started because Toomer's Drugs had the only telegraph in town and when the result of the game came across the ticker, the ticker tape was thrown in the trees.

"Everyone rushed over to Toomer's Corner as soon as the game was over," said Thomas. "Everyone stopped by Mom's Store to buy toilet paper. It was wall-to-wall people. It was nuts, just nuts. You couldn't get to the actual corner. I think every person in the stadium went to Toomer's. People who didn't have tickets and watched it at their tailgate were there."

Keesee said that game was the first time she and her friends were allowed to go to Toomer's Corner after a game by themselves.

"We ran from the stadium," she said. "You really couldn't move and there were a lot of 'It's great to be an Auburn Tiger!' chants!"

USA Today named it "The Nation's Best Sports Tradition" in 2018. Sadly, the tradition of rolling Toomer's has been suspended after the trees were poisoned in 2011 and later died. In the 2011 game, Auburn had overcome a 24-0 deficit to win and to go on to win the national championship. Harvey Updyke announced on a call to Finebaum's radio show what he had done.

"He had been on hold for about 45 minutes and gave the name Al from Dadeville," said Finebaum. "He wanted to talk about Toomer's Corner being rolled after Bear [Bryant] died. I had heard some stories about that, but there was no evidence of that ever happening. He was ranting and raving about that. I told him that didn't happen. I lost my cool a little, he wouldn't stop talking. My hand was close to the button [to terminate the call]. He said, 'Here's what I did the week after: I poisoned the trees.' He was upset an Auburn fan had put a [Cam] Newton jersey on the Bryant statue in front of Bryant-Denny Stadium after they beat them. 'Was it against the law?' I asked him. 'I don't care,' he said. Then he said, 'Roll Damn Tide,' and hung up. I literally thought he was a crackpot. We heard from the

Auburn Police Department the next day; they asked us some questions. About a week later he was arrested."

In 2013 Updyke was sentenced to prison but was released on probation after serving 76 days and moved to Louisiana. He died in 2020. Just before the start of the 2023 season, university officials announced the trees were mature enough to be rolled again.

Mom's Party Shop sold a lot of toilet paper when Stacey Danley was at Auburn and has since closed. Danley and his group of seniors finished their career with a record of 39-5-2 that includes the 4-0 record against Alabama. I was only a few years out of college myself, but the dealings I had with these guys, you could tell they were a good group of young men. And Danley hasn't lost that, giving a relative stranger 45 minutes of the day he was moving into to a new home. He's aware of the legacy his class and that team in particular has at Auburn.

"It's an era. It was topped off by that game," he said with pride. "We beat them four in row. When people talk about that game and that era, you can tell what it means to Auburn people, it's special. When I'm together with players or other Auburn people at some point we are going to get to that game."

Alabama's opponent in the Sugar Bowl was against number two Miami. The Hurricanes won 33-25 and wound-up national champions. Six days later Curry resigned his position as Alabama football coach because he felt he would always be a distraction and wouldn't be able to win over the fans. He became the head coach at Kentucky.

"It's the only game and only thing possible that could have made a contingent of Bama people feel good about Bill Curry," said Davis. "If that game had turned out differently, he could have won them over."

His record at Alabama was 26-10, but he never beat Auburn as a head coach at Georgia Tech, Alabama, or Kentucky.

"It felt like something was going to happen," said Finebaum. "At the Sugar Bowl there were a lot of rumors. Even though they were 10-2, Hootie [Ingram, the Alabama AD] was against him, and fans were indifferent. There was a sense of change in the air."

Auburn defeated number 21 Ohio State in the Hall of Fame Bowl in Tampa 31-14 and was ranked sixth in the two major polls.

I attended my first two bowl games after the 1989 season. On December 28, at Legion Field I saw Texas Tech defeat ACC Champion Duke 49-21. Texas Tech running back James Gray ran for more than 200 yards. The next day, Duke coach Steve Spurrier announced he was taking the job as head coach at Florida. I flew to New Orleans that next day to work on our coverage of the Sugar Bowl. That was my first trip to New Orleans and to see a football game played inside. It was quite a trip! Little did I know then that I would be going back to New Orleans in a few years to see an even bigger game between the Tide and the Hurricanes.

Chapter 4: Good Guys Wear Crimson

Alabama vs. Miami
Louisiana Superdome
January 1, 1993

Once upon a time, there was a college football team in Tuscaloosa, Alabama, that hadn't won a national championship in 12 years. They had mostly fallen out of the national conversation. Their history making coach with the great nickname had retired and soon after passed away. They had struggled to find the right coach and were already on their third coach in 10 years and had a 4-6 record the last 10 years against their cross-state archrival.

The year was 1992 – Gene Stallings, an assistant coach under the legendary coach, Bear Bryant, in the 60s, was entering his third season as the head coach at the University of Alabama. In January 1990 Bill Curry resigned as Alabama coach to take the Kentucky job. Despite a 26-10 record in hree years, he never could win over the Alabama fans. He was after all, a Georgia Tech man. There is historical animosity between the two programs. Tech is one of the two schools mentioned in "Yea, Alabama," the school's fight song (Georgia is the other one). In the 1961 game between the two schools there was a controversial hit that left bad blood and may have precipitated the Jackets leaving the SEC. But Stallings had deep roots with Coach Bryant.

Nicknamed "Bebes," Stallings had played for Bear at Texas A&M and was one of the famous "Junction Boys," that survived a brutal summer camp in Junction, Texas, in 1954. Bryant had just come to College Station after leaving Kentucky and felt his team was weak. So, in September, he sent them to Junction for a 10-day camp in a historic drought and heat wave. Less than 40 players "survived" the camp and made the Aggies team. Stallings also served as an assistant for Coach Bryant at Alabama for seven years until 1965 when he left to become the head coach of his alma mater. After being fired at A&M, Stallings was an assistant coach for the Dallas Cowboys. He was the head coach of the NFL's Arizona Cardinals from 1986-89. His only winning season as a head coach in college or the NFL came in 1967 when the Aggies won the Southwest Conference. As a result of the conference championship, Stallings faced his mentor in the 1968 Cotton Bowl and the Aggies beat Alabama. There is a famous picture of Bryant picking up Stallings at midfield after the game. That picture resurfaced after Stallings was hired at Alabama.

"My first impression of him was I was scared to death," said Roger Shultz, an All-SEC center on the 1989 team who would be a senior in 1990. "Bear guy, one of the Junction Boys, he is going to kill us. He walked in the room, sounded like Bear Bryant and looked like John Wayne. Hey, that's not a bad thing, but it was a little scary for a 21-year-old. We knew we would have to work, and we did."

"I was happy to see him hired," said Paul Finebaum, at that time a radio host and columnist for the *Birmingham Post-Herald*. "It was sense of a return to the Bryant era. I saw Paul

[Bryant], Jr., at the news conference when he was introduced, and he said Papa would have been proud. It felt like a renaissance."

Stallings had hired many people who had played or coached for Bryant like Bill "Brother" Oliver, Mal Moore, and Mike DuBose, and fans felt like Alabama would return to the national spotlight they hadn't experienced since Coach Bryant resigned in 1982.

"I'm not sure how good of a coach he was, but he had a great staff," said Ray Melick, the Alabama beat writer for the *Post-Herald* from 1983 to 2005. "[Jeff] Rouzie, [Mike] DuBose. Really an all-star staff of coaches. [Offensive coordinator] Mal Moore was more creative than people gave him credit for. He was the one who had all the creative stuff with [David] Palmer. And he brought in Homer Smith later."

But despite the optimism the Stallings era didn't get off to a good start. The 1989 team was 10-2 under Curry and returned a lot of players. But the first game was a loss to Southern Miss at Legion Field. They had a quarterback named Brett Favre. Then they lost to Florida in Tuscaloosa and in

Athens against Georgia. I was at all three games, and they were all close. At the Georgia game, former Clemson coach and Alabama grad Danny Ford was on the sideline (not in the team area) and after being 0-3 some people were wondering if the wrong Bryant disciple had been hired.

After the Georgia loss, Stallings told the media the team needed to learn to win. Melick was amused that a coach with one winning season in 11 years as a head coach would say his team needed to learn to win.

"I wrote a column, Gene Stallings has one winning season and these guys played in the Sugar Bowl last year," recalled Melick. "Maybe he needs to learn to win. He didn't like that, and we talked about it. But he wouldn't hold a grudge. I've told people he's the only coach I ever covered that I don't think lied to me. It's the highest compliment I could give you. He was always honest and if he couldn't be honest, he wouldn't answer the question."

I was still the sports producer at WBRC-TV in Birmingham, the ABC affiliate. Stallings was very good to us as a station. We would have some unusual interview requests and he would do his best to accommodate us. One time he was not happy with us. The NCAA was requesting legislation to eliminate the "athletic dorms." Most coaches liked the dorms because it was easier to keep up with the players having them in one place. Stallings supported keeping the dorms. He came on the newscast with Sports Anchor Rick Karle to discuss the issue. We had a former Alabama player on as well. The player was in favor of not having the dorms so the players would be more involved with campus life. Stallings felt like he had been ambushed. After the show was over, Alabama's SID Larry White called Karle and told him Coach Stallings wasn't happy about that. He made his point and next time we needed something, he did it.

The team did learn to win. They went to Knoxville and upset number three Tennessee 9-6 (my first trip to Neyland Stadium). But they couldn't maintain the momentum. The next week in Tuscaloosa against unranked Penn State, Gary Hollingsworth threw five interceptions and Bama rushed for only 6 yards in a 9-0 loss. Stallings earned the forgiveness of many Bama fans when he ended the four-game losing streak to

Auburn with a 16-7 win. Stallings became the first coach since Alabama's Red Drew in 1948 to beat Auburn in his first game in the series. It was the seventh straight game the Alabama defense had held their opponents to single digits in points. Stallings' background was defense and with Defensive Coordinator Bill Oliver, they were beginning to play like he wanted.

In 1991 Alabama lost the season opener at Florida but wouldn't lose again. The defense was playing well and had many people returning. Optimism was high among Tide fans for 1992.

"I was at the bowl game, in Miami [in 1991] when they beat Colorado," said Finebaum. "Everyone was saying next year will be spectacular. Everything was aligned."

However, in 1992 change had come to the Southeastern Conference. For the first time since Georgia Tech left the conference in 1964, membership had changed. Arkansas and South Carolina joined. And with a 12-team conference divided into two divisions, the conference was able to take advantage of an obscure NCAA rule that said if a conference had 12 teams and was divided into divisions it could play a championship game between the two division champions. That rule was established because a Division II conference was trying to cut down on travel, but since it wasn't restricted to Division II, the SEC was going to have a championship game.

Most people felt that having to play an extra game against a team good enough to win its division in the SEC could hurt a team trying to win a national championship. There was also a lot of discussion about the make-up of the divisions as well as how the schedule would be done. There was a lot of talk about putting Auburn in the Eastern Division because three of their biggest rivals were Georgia, Florida, and Tennessee. But that would mean if they won the east and Alabama won the west, the two schools would play two weeks in a row: in the traditional, season-ending Iron Bowl, and then again in the SEC championship game. It was decided that would not be a good idea and Auburn ended up in the west with Alabama, LSU, Arkansas, and the two Mississippi schools. Each team had two rivals they would play yearly, and the other game would rotate home and home every two years. That meant Auburn lost the Tennessee game but kept Georgia, the Deep South's oldest rivalry, and Florida. Alabama kept its rivalry game against the Volunteers and got Vanderbilt University as its second rival, which many around the conference rolled their eyes at, but most people were fairly satisfied with their schedules.

One other thing about the 1992 season is it would be Alabama's 100th season of football and there were special events throughout the year. The centennial celebration was kicked off with the A-Day game in April. The Friday night before the A-Day game we hosted a special edition of our *Sports Roundtable* show from the Bryant Museum on the Alabama campus. White, the SID, had set us up with several Alabama football legends who were in town, and Karle interviewed them about their experiences and the traditions at Alabama. One of the guests was Don McNeal, a cornerback on the 1978 National Championship team. In the 1979 Sugar Bowl against number one Penn State the Tide was holding on to a 14-7 lead late in the fourth quarter. The Nittany Lions had the ball on the 8-yard line with a second and goal. Quarterback Chuck Fusina hit Scott

Fitzkee with a pass on the 3 and it looked like Fitzkee could walk into the end zone, but McNeal made an incredible tackle to stop Fitzkee short of the goal line. A third down run was stopped for no gain and the Lions faced a fourth and goal. Penn State's fullback Mike Guman was stopped on fourth down by Barry Krauss in one of the most famous plays in Alabama history. Penn State never scored again, and Bama won the game and the national championship 14-7. Well, while McNeal was talking about that game, Krauss happened to be watching the show at the hotel adjacent to the museum where many former players were staying. Krauss came over to the museum during a break and started messing with McNeal. He was still there when we came out of the commercial break and McNeal told him if he hadn't made that tackle on second down, nobody would even remember who Krauss was. It was great live TV and one of my favorite shows we ever did at WBRC.

Once September and the games rolled around, Vandy would be the Tide's opponent to open the season. Alabama came into that game with a number nine preseason ranking, their highest preseason ranking since 1986. The defense was expected to be strong, but there were questions about the offense and the quarterback, sophomore Jay Barker.

"We knew there was a really good defense," said Melick. "You had Williams and Lassic at RB and Brown and Lee were good receivers. The question was QB. Every year Gene would say, I don't know if I could go another season with Jay Barker as QB."

Barker took over the starting job late in the 1991 season and was undefeated as a starter. However, in four games as a starter he threw fewer than 50 passes for 409 yards and one touchdown. The Tide offense was based on a strong running game and with the defensive expected to be very good, Alabama didn't need much from the quarterback position. There wasn't much experience at quarterback. There were two other quarterbacks in Barker's recruiting class in the winter of 1990. Jason Jack and Steve Christopher were higher rated, and both had won state championships. However, Christopher had left the team and redshirt freshman Brian Burgdorf was listed as the backup. In fact, there had been some speculation that star receiver David Palmer, who was a dynamic quarterback in high school, could spend some time under center. But Barker wouldn't give up the starting job. Burgdorf did play some in each of the first three games, but in the third game at Arkansas, Barker threw three first half touchdowns as the Tide rolled to a 28-0 halftime lead and a 38-11 win.

"Jay wouldn't complete passes in practice," recalled Melick. "But when the lights would come on, he played great."

"It seemed like I wrote the same column every week," said Finebaum. "Is this the worst 4-0, the worst 5-0 team? Same thing every week. But it didn't matter. They kept winning."

The defense flexed its muscle allowing the Hogs 28 yards rushing on 28 carries. In a bit of foreshadowing, Alabama played Tulane in the Superdome and came away with a 37-0 win. Bama rushed for 435 yards and the defense had four interceptions, holding the Green Wave to 58 yards rushing. After the win, Alabama moved up to number four in the AP poll and would head to Knoxville for the annual battle against Tennessee. The Vols were ranked number 18 and the game was nationally televised on ABC. Alabama had won eight straight in the series that had its own nickname, "The Third Saturday in

October," after the day the game was always played. Tradition entailed the winning team would smoke cigars in the locker room to celebrate the win between the two winningest programs in the SEC.

In the 1992 game, the Tide got out to a 17-0 lead behind a strong running game and two Derrick Lassic touchdowns. Tennessee cut the lead to 7 and after Bama fumbled with less than two minutes had a chance to tie or take the lead. But the defense stiffened and kept the Volunteers out of the end zone. Bama got to smoke cigars on the third Saturday in October for the eighth straight year. The defense held Tennessee to only seven first downs for the game. Barker was only five of 11 for 54 yards, but no interceptions.

"Jay Barker was a leader and people respected him," said Melick. "It was the intangible part of his game that made him successful."

There was a win against Ole Miss to run the record to 8-0. After an off-week Alabama moved up to number two in the AP poll for the first time since before the Auburn game in 1989. Now they were headed to the home of another rival, LSU.

Alabama hadn't lost in Baton Rouge since 1969. They wouldn't lose this year either, winning 31-11, allowing the Tigers 22 rushing yards on 35 carries. After the game Alabama's defense lead the nation in scoring defense, total defense, rushing defense, and passing defense.

The next week was the short trip to Starkville, Mississippi. Alabama came away with a 30-21 win. However, in that game the Tide trailed Mississippi State 21-20 going to the fourth quarter. After a field goal gave Alabama the lead, a George Teague interception gave Alabama the ball deep in Bulldogs territory and they would seal the game with a late touchdown run by Chris Anderson. The win gave the Tide a 10-0 record and the SEC's first Western Division title.

There was a week off before the Auburn game was to be played on Thanksgiving and televised by ABC. Things were not going well on the Plains. Before the 1991 season former player Eric Ramsey released tapes he had made alleging among other things, he had been paid by Auburn coaches and boosters. The allegations plagued the program for two years. Auburn was 4-5-1 in 1992.

The ABC national broadcast was airing on our station at 1 p.m. We were going on the air at noon for a one-hour live pregame show from Legion Field. I spent a lot of time with our station engineers, as well as Walter Garrett at Legion Field and Larry White, making sure we had everything we would need to do the production we wanted. We would have several live cameras around the stadium because there would be players warming up on the field. Growing up, my favorite show was *The NFL Today* on CBS. When we got home from church it would be on and I just loved the way they covered all the stories that were going on in the NFL that day. I wanted to cover this game the same way Brent, Irv, and Phyllis would. We had come a long way as a sports department by 1992. Karle and the anchor of the 5 p.m. sportscast, Mike Raita, each had their style and I adapted to them depending on who was hosting the show I was producing. I always liked to have historical aspects and lots of interesting tidbits. They would take care of the entertainment and I'd take care of the information. Karle would be hosting from inside the stadium. Our engineers had helped us set up a feed so that we could have a mobile camera that could roam around the floor of the stadium. Raita was with that camera and was able move around to interview anyone who may be around or to give us good close-up, bumper shots as we were going to and coming back from commercial breaks. We also had a camera on the photo deck that could get us shots of the players we were talking about previewing the game.

Even though it was only Wednesday night, it had been a long week, and I wanted to get a good night's sleep because we would be at the stadium early on Thursday morning. To back up a bit, on a personal note, I had gotten engaged on Halloween. We had gone to Chattanooga to see the new Tennessee Aquarium and Appalachian was playing Tennessee-Chattanooga that night. I proposed after the game. We stayed in Chattanooga and on Sunday went to Atlanta to see the Falcons game (a buddy and I had Falcons' season tickets and I had both of the tickets that day). Anyway, I had planned an evening with my fiancé to have a quick bite to eat and then see a movie to help me relax, so I could get a good night's sleep. We were in the movie, watching *Single White Female*, when I sensed someone walking around the theatre. I looked up and it was my fiancé's mother looking for me. This was in the days before cell phones, and I didn't wear a pager. Karle had her number and called her to look for me and have me get to the station.

The urgency was because Auburn had just announced that head coach Pat Dye would step down after tomorrow's game. They needed me to not only redo the show for Thursday, but to help them get the story done for the 10 p.m. news. By the time I got to the station, it was close to 8 p.m. and we had a lot to do.

The Auburn football coach, especially a legend like Pat Dye, abruptly resigning the night before the Iron Bowl, was a huge story. University President William Muse made the announcement along with AD Mike Lude. SID David Housel said the timing of the announcement had nothing to do with the Alabama game. Karle led the news and most of the sportscast dealt with that news and the effect on the game as well as the future of the Auburn football program. After all that was done, we could focus our attention on the next day's show. It was after 1 a.m. Thursday before I ended up getting home and had to be back at the station to ride to Legion Field around 7.

"It was surreal that he was done," said Finebaum, who had a relationship with Dye before he was named the Auburn coach. "I went to see him the week before to ask him about his future. There were a lot of rumors he was done. I ran into him, and we had lunch, then went to his office. I was peppering him with questions, can you help me out? He felt like if he could win the game, he may have a shot to keep the job. He said, 'I'm not quitting,' but I didn't believe him. That night we went off air at 7:00 and it was announced at 7:01."

Thursday morning, we wanted to get video of each team's buses arriving at the stadium and the players getting off and walking to the locker room. That would be our only chance to get some fresh video that morning for the show. We had videographers assigned to get both teams leaving the bus and entering the stadium. Raita had gotten a quick comment from Coach Stallings as he got off the bus about the news not affecting Alabama at all.

"Wednesday night the coaches came in and told the players Coach Dye was resigning," said Shultz, who was a graduate assistant coach on the 1992 team. "The coaches did a good job of getting the players to just continue doing your jobs. Stallings did a great job of that."

Coach Dye didn't say anything to Raita as he walked from the bus to the locker room.

The show got off to a good start, we showed the video of the players arriving and talked about how this may affect the game. The Auburn players would always play hard against Alabama, but they would really want to send their coach out with a win against their archrivals. Quentin Riggins was a linebacker at Auburn, played in the 1989 game against Bama and was now the sideline reporter for games on the Auburn Network. He and Raita knew each other well from Raita being at Auburn for the weekly news conferences when he played. Raita got an interview with Riggins and was talking live about the situation with the team and also what Coach Dye had meant to him as a player and a person. Riggins was undersized as a SEC linebacker but had plenty of heart and made All-SEC twice. (He began serving a term on Auburn's University Board of Trustees in 2017.) While Riggins was talking, we could see Coach Dye walk from the locker room to watch warm-ups. Raita saw that and wrapped up his interview with Riggins and was talking about Coach Dye. The show producer can talk to the on-air talent through an earpiece system called an interruptible foldback or IFB. Typically, we don't speak to broadcasters while they are talking because it can be very distracting. But Raita had forgotten he had a portable camera and could move around because he usually wasn't able to do that. Mark Jones, the sideline reporter for the ABC broadcast, was approaching Dye to tape an interview. I said in Raita's ear, "Get over there!" and he did and stuck his microphone there. You could see Jones signal to him to keep the mic flag out of the shot and Raita did, but we were able to scoop the network because that interview was going out live! The rest of the show went well. Our other sports reporter, Ron Grillo, was out in the tailgate area and interviewed several fans about the Coach Dye situation and how that may affect the game.

I was very pleased with the show and how the planning allowed us to cover the story the way it needed to be covered. We ended up winning an Emmy award for the show. That was the first Emmy WBRC had won and although it was a regional Emmy, we were still competing with the Atlanta market and all their resources so that was a big source of pride for us.

There have been many memorable Alabama-Auburn games, but the 1992 game won't be remembered for the quality of the football. The first half was scoreless and fittingly, the game's first score came from the Alabama defense. Cornerback Antonio Langham intercepted a Stan White pass and returned it 61 yards for the score. After a field goal, Alabama's offense got on the board early in the fourth quarter and that's how the game and Pat Dye's coaching career would end, 17-0. The only time a Pat Dye coached team was shut out. Dye was crying when he and Stallings embraced at midfield after the game.

"There was always a lot of respect between those two men," said Karle.

Alabama was now in the situation that many people had criticized the SEC Championship game for. A team was in line to play for a national championship, but first had to win this extra game against Eastern Division Champion Florida.

"This was the pressure [SEC Commissioner] Roy Kramer put himself under," said Karle. "If Bama had lost, they wouldn't have played in that national championship game after going undefeated in the regular season."

"The Sugar Bowl officials were nervous," said Melick. "If Florida wins, they get Syracuse against Florida and if Bama wins, they will have number one and number two play. It was the first year number one and number two could play in a bowl game."

"Eleven and oh and nothing to show," was how Shultz explained it.

The opponent would be 11th ranked Florida, who was the last team to beat Alabama, 35-0 in Gainesville early last season. The Gators came into the game 8-3, but they were the defending SEC champions. Early in the season they lost to Tennessee and Mississippi State but ended up Eastern Division champion as a result of beating Georgia and Tennessee losing to Alabama and South Carolina. While Alabama dismantled its arch-rival the week before the championship game, Florida lost at number three Florida State 45-24. Had it not been for the Championship game, Alabama would be set to play number one Miami in the Sugar Bowl.

Keith Rhodes was a student at Alabama in 1992 and wasn't sure what to think about the SEC game.

"It definitely made me nervous," he said. "They [Florida] had been playing very well and they didn't have anything to lose. If they had beaten Alabama, would have shattered our perfect season."

Florida had beaten Alabama the past two years. Steve Spurrier, who won the Heisman Trophy as a quarterback for the Gators in 1966, had returned to his alma mater in 1990 and revitalized the program. Amazingly the Gators had never officially won an SEC title in football before 1991. Their 1984 championship was vacated as a result of NCAA probation.

"Spurrier was already changing the way SEC was playing football," said Melick. "Spurrier had a lot of respect for [Bill] Oliver, even back to when they coached against each other in the USFL [University of South Florida] and Oliver was at Bama when Spurrier played. Spurrier and Oliver were 6-6 against each other all time. I did a story on them that week."

"There was a lot of pressure on us because of that situation," said Shultz. "You don't want to get the players tight. Stallings treated everything the same and that helped. 'You prepare for the game, regardless of the team,' he always told us. Under Curry, if we lost a game, practice would be harder. If we won, easy practice."

The game would be played at Legion Field, and it didn't sell out until the Wednesday before the game. It was televised on ABC, but there was a game on the air before the Alabama game, so we weren't able to do a live, pre-game show. It was a cold day at Legion Field, but Florida started out hot, scoring a touchdown on the opening drive.

"The weather was horrible," said Shultz. "It was cold. It was brutal to stand on the sidelines. I can't imagine what it was like in the stands. That was second best thing after starting this game was moving to Atlanta and inside!"

Alabama would score the game's next three touchdowns to hold a 21-7 lead late in the third quarter. But Florida would battle back to tie. And with less than four minutes remaining, the Gators had the ball and a chance to ruin the dreams of a national championship for the Tide. But Oliver's defense had come up big all year and would again. Langham cut in front of a Shane Matthews pass and returned it 27 yards for the winning score.

"Langham picked off the pass," said Karle. "He high stepped right by us right into the end zone and Alabama was on the way to the Sugar Bowl."

"Of course, everyone remembers the Langham play," said Melick. "I always felt bad for Shane Matthews, he had such a good year. Langham told me, 'I was tired of them completing those short passes. I had safety help, and I was going to jump one.'"

It was the third straight game Langham had scored a touchdown.

So, Alabama, who had won the first SEC football championship in 1933 had won the first SEC football championship game in 1992. It was the Tide's 20th SEC championship, by far the most, and it was the first time a team had won nine conference games in a season.

"It was back-to-back exciting weeks at Legion Field," said Karle.

"Everybody was saying an SEC team is never going to win a national championship," recalled Shultz. "It ended up not being bad at all, in fact it's been a good thing. You have a quality win at the end. It's turned out to be a really good thing, but it was not thought of that way at the beginning."

"I think there was a perception you couldn't go through the SEC undefeated," said Finebaum. "It was justice that they got through, especially how that game ended against Florida."

So, the stage was set. Number two Alabama was heading to the Sugar Bowl on New Year's Night in New Orleans to take on number one Miami. This was the first year of the new "Bowl Coalition," which set up a system that the top two teams would meet up regardless of conference bowl allegiances. It worked out well in 1992 because the Hurricanes were members of the Big East Conference and didn't have a bowl tie in. It was the first time number one and number two were facing off in a bowl game since 1987. The Bowl Alliance was hardly a perfect scenario, but it was a start in what finally became the College Football Playoff in 2014 that would expand to 12 teams for the 2024 season.

This was a bit of a rematch between the two schools that had faced off in the Sugar Bowl after the 1989 season and the Hurricanes prevailed 33-25. Miami was riding a 29-game winning streak and was the defending national champion. If they could defend their title, they would be the first team since Alabama in 1978 and '79 to repeat as national champion. In 1992 their biggest wins were over Florida State and at Penn State. They were quarterbacked by Gino Torretta who won the Heisman Trophy after passing for more than 3,000 yards and 19 touchdowns. Oddsmakers had Miami as an eight-point favorite.

After some practices on campus before taking a break for Christmas, Alabama reconvened in New Orleans on the 26th. My Christmas Day was cut short to drive from Charlotte to Birmingham, and then ride to New Orleans with Raita, Karle, and the sports photographers.

"It's a business trip. You're not going for fun," said Shultz. "You weren't sure who was going to be the national champ. You knew if you won, you were national champion."

Rhodes, whose dad worked for the University Library, had been going to Alabama games for years and had attended several of the road games that season. He and a group of friends were headed to New Orleans.

"We had six of us," he said. "We stayed in French Quarter. We were all crammed into a small hotel suite."

There was a big part of the defense missing when the players arrived. Middle linebacker Michael Rogers had suffered a head injury in a car accident before Christmas and wouldn't be able to play. That forced Bill Oliver to come up with a new scheme for Torretta and their high-powered offense. Alabama alternated days practicing between the Superdome and Tulane's practice facility.

"Oliver was worried about spies, so he personally told everyone what he wanted them to do," said Melick.

Each morning before the practices, there were news conferences by each team. We couldn't believe what we were hearing from the Miami players. Everyone knew how cocky they were because of all their antics in the past and the "Catholics vs. Convicts" thing and the wearing of the fatigues when they arrived at the Fiesta Bowl in the 1986 game against Notre Dame. Linebacker Rohan Marley, son of Bob, was a small guy at 5'8" and 200 pounds but had a big mouth. Every day he was talking about all the things Miami was going to do Alabama and wasn't giving the Tide any respect, calling them "a one-dimensional offense."

"He said, 'I may sing one of my father's songs as I run past you,' said Melick. "Lamar Thomas told Lassic, 'You know me, everyone knows me; who are you?' The Miami reporters were saying that it was a foregone conclusion that Miami was going to win."

I had never been exposed to that kind of trash talking before. I wasn't an Alabama fan, and as a media member, we are supposed to stay neutral, but I really wanted them to win. It's always a better story when the team you are covering wins. It's easier to cover teams that win big games, instead of losing them. I was wanting Alabama to really give it to them. And having spent some time around those guys I knew they were pretty good guys and wouldn't publicly say the things the Miami players were saying. Of course, Stallings wouldn't have any of that either.

"I felt there was this incredible arrogance and overconfidence," said Finebaum. "The Miami players had no respect for the Alabama players. I had been around them for a week and you could see that."

"A couple of the Bama players told me, 'We don't do that kind of stuff. We do our talking on the field,'" said Melick.

It wasn't like the Alabama players were robots. Some of them could be pretty expressive. Wide receiver Prince Wimbley, who was from Miami, was one of them. But he knew when that kind of stuff was appropriate.

"Stallings didn't like that stuff," said Melick. "There were a lot of showboating personalities, but they knew not to do that around Stallings."

"We played them in '90. Some of those guys were on that team," said Shultz. "That year, when we saw Miami guys out, we'd go to other side of road. That's what Curry wanted us to do. But Stallings was from Texas, and he said if you're going to fight, you'd better win."

"We had gotten a tip that the Miami players were going to be at Pat O'Brien's," said Melick. "It was outside of Pat O's when the players ran into each other. Marley called [offensive lineman] Roosevelt Patterson a big fat slob."

Shultz remembers the meet-up. "As a [graduate assistant] it's my job to keep guys out of trouble. We had the confrontation on street, we didn't back down. They weren't sure what to think about that. We wouldn't back down. That was our attitude. That was biggest difference this time."

After listening to the Alabama players during interviews, we could tell they were handling all the talk from Miami pretty well. Once we arrived on the 26th, we started doing live shots during all the newscasts. We had a nice live shot location at Jackson Square during the day. We had a 30-minute show each night. After our show on New Year's Eve, we brought in 1993 on the elevator in the Hyatt Hotel where we were staying.

Despite all the talk from the Miami players, Bama fans were confident.

"I thought we had a chance to win, absolutely," said Rhodes. "With our D we could hold our own against their O."

"I thought Alabama would win. And I have the column to prove it," boasted Finebaum. "As I am writing it, I'm thinking, 'Am I being a homer?' Stallings met with the print media before the game. He was asked if you have a shot and he said, 'We are going to win the game.' And that helped me have the confidence to write that column."

The game was in prime time, after the Rose Bowl, so after all the talk, it was finally time to play football. Miami got the opening kickoff and George Teague let everyone know he had come to play by making the tackle on the 20-yard line. Bama's defense forced Miami to a three and out. David Palmer had a nice punt return, thanks to a nice block by Teague. The short drive bogged down close to the goal line, but Michael Proctor got Bama on the board first with a 19-yard field goal.

Miami responded with a big play when Torretta hit speedster Kevin Williams for a big gain. Tommy Johnson ran him down and tackled him. Rece Davis, the current host of ESPN's *College GameDay* show, was covering the game for WRBL-TV in Columbus, Georgia. He was sitting next to a reporter from a Miami TV station.

"There was a Miami reporter who was very condescending and thought this was going to be a beatdown," remembered Davis. "After Johnson ran down Williams, he said to me, 'That guy must be fast,' and I told him, 'He isn't even their fastest DB.' They weren't expecting a game like that. They didn't grasp how good Alabama was."

A few plays later, Miami kicker Dane Prewitt, who went to the same suburban Birmingham high school as Barker, hit a 49-yard field goal to tie the game. Bama answered with what appeared to be a good drive, but Barker was picked off and the ball was returned across midfield. Lamar Thomas was Miami's leading receiver with 10 touchdowns, but after making a big play, he had the ball stripped by Johnson and the Tide recovered.

Bama had gone almost exclusively to the ground game, and it was working. But Alabama faced a third and 10 at the

Miami 48. Barker threw a poor pass, and it was intercepted at the 23, but the Bama defense got the ball back for the offense. Barker was mixing in some shorter passes with the runs and Lassic ran down to the 1. But he was penalized 15 yards for spinning the ball. That penalty meant Alabama had to settle for another Proctor field goal, this time from 23 yards, but Alabama was back in front 6-3.

Oliver's defensive scheme was affecting Torretta. The 'Canes couldn't run the ball at all on the Bama defense. On the next drive, Sam Shade picked off the Heisman winner.

"It was one of the great defensive schemes Bill Oliver ever came up with," said Melick. "I was surprised how well they could cover them. They used an extra DB and just two linebackers for most of the game."

Derrick Lassic had a 28-yard run to the 3-yard line and this time, didn't spin the ball. On third down, Sherman Williams scored the first touchdown of the game with 6:09 remaining in the half. Prewitt kicked a 42-yard field goal as the half ended to make the halftime score 13-6.

In the press box, the Alabama folks were a little surprised at how well the defense was playing but were expecting more from Miami in the second half. The Hurricanes had only rushed for 13 yards in the half. Lassic was already over 100 yards rushing himself. In the stands, Rhodes was feeling good.

"At halftime. It was the game I was expecting it to be," he said. "The third quarter would be the telling factor."

The Miami defense forced Alabama to punt on their first drive. On the first play Johnson picked off Torretta and returned it to the 20-yard line.

"Torretta was used to the receivers running to spots and he threw it," said Shultz. "We had guys in those spots. It was genius."

Barker converted a third and long with a run inside the 5. Three plays later, Lassic scored, and Alabama was up 20-6. On the next drive for Miami, the Tide lined up the entire defense on the line of scrimmage. Torretta had no idea what to do, so he called time out. The Alabama fans were going crazy.

"Miami's whole offense was based on reads and knowing what the D would do," said Melick. "It was a really remarkable defensive performance, and he only had a week to do it."

The time out didn't help. Torretta, who at this point in the game was 12 of 26 for 127 yards, no touchdowns, and two interceptions, threw it to Teague, who returned it 311 yards for a touchdown and the Tide lead was 27-6. Teague started high stepping about the 10-yard line when it was obvious he would score. Was some of that rubbing it back in the face of the Miami guys who had talked so much all week?

"There was a lot of pent-up frustration," said Shultz. "It was obvious they felt disrespected."

Torretta, who had only thrown four interceptions all year, had thrown two passes in the second half and they were both intercepted. The adjustments the media folks expected to be made at halftime had been made by the Bama defensive staff and Miami had no idea what to do.

When Miami got the ball back, a run lost a yard. On second down, from his own 10 Torretta dropped back against an Alabama blitz and aired it out down the sideline. Thomas had a couple of steps on defensive back Willie Gaston. Thomas caught the ball on the 36 in stride. Gaston had fallen. Teague was about four yards behind Thomas who had caught 10 touchdown passes on the season. Thomas looked back once as Teague was gaining on him. At the 7-yard line, Teague caught him and didn't try and tackle him, but took the ball away from him. His momentum carried him into the end zone before he could turn around and run up the field. Thomas fell down. Miami finally tackled Teague at the 12. It was one of the most amazing things I had ever seen.

"I just thought about it [taking the ball] and did it," Teague told Melick.

"I don't think people realized how fast he was," said Shultz. "He could really run."

"I was sitting next to a Miami TV guy in press box," recalled Melick. "He said 'Holy shit. I had never seen that happen to Lamar Thomas.'"

"Seeing it unfold, it was unbelievable," said Rhodes. "We were in the student section in the end zone. Seeing him run him down and was going to tackle him, then stripping the ball. It was shock and jubilation. Everyone was going nuts. One extreme to another because they were going to score, then we took it away."

The play would go down as one of the greatest plays that never "officially" happened. Alabama was offside, so Miami kept the ball, but Teague had stripped them of their swagger. All the talking Miami had done coming into the game seemed hollow now. The Bama players were doing their talking on the field. And they were speaking loudly. The celebrations on the sideline were intense. Teague was screaming as he made his way to the sideline before he realized the play was called back.

Two plays later Miami punted.

Miami's first three plays in the second half consisted of five plays: interception, interception returned for a touchdown, and a three and out and punt.

But Miami hadn't won 29 in row by lying down. Torretta led them on a long drive inside the Alabama 20. On fourth and 2 from the 12, Alabama applied tremendous pressure and

Torretta's pass off his back foot was knocked away in the end zone by Shade.

Alabama couldn't move the ball and punted back to Miami. Kevin Williams returned the punt 73 yards for a touchdown. Alabama got the ball and went back to the power running game. Lassic capped it with a 4-yard run with under seven minutes remaining and it was 34-13 Alabama. That's how the game would end. Gene Stallings' players had proven they knew how to win. Their winning streak was now 22 games. Alabama had their first national championship since Bear Bryant had died and it was the 12th in their history. Lassic was voted the MVP after rushing 28 times for 135 yards and two touchdowns. As a team Bama rushed 60 times for 267 yards. They had a 12-minute advantage in time of possession. Barker only completed four of his 13 passes for 18 yards, but he won his 17th straight start. Torretta was 24-56 for 278 yards, zero touchdowns, and three interceptions. Miami only rushed for 48 yards in the game, and 42 of that came on the game's final drive against Alabama backups.

"I've become good friends with Gino Torretta," said Davis. "He is good natured around Bama fans. He was a great player and a great dude. People didn't start talking about this defense being one of the best in the history until after that game."

I was happy for Coach Stallings. He celebrated with his family. His son, Jon Mark, had Down Syndrome. He was around the team a lot and would always ride on the team bus with his dad to the stadium.

"Jon Mark said, 'Good job, Pop,' to Gene and he realized his life had changed," said Karle.

Rhodes had grown up in an Alabama family but didn't remember the championship teams from the late 70s. Now he could finally experience a national championship as a student.

"We were super excited. We stayed for the trophy and the celebration and players celebrating with the fans, then of course we left the stadium, and we were out in the French Quarter."

There was one person who had voted Alabama number one in the AP poll all season long. That was Corky Simpson with the *Tucson Citizen* in Arizona. After the rout of Miami, all the other AP voters saw fit to vote Alabama number one. The University had a parade for the team several days later and Simpson was the grand marshal of the parade. Melick wrote a book on the season, *Roll, Tide, Roll: Alabama's National Championship Season*.

Alabama fans couldn't hear enough about the team. *Sports Illustrated* printed a special edition commemorating the win. It was one of the first times the magazine had done that, and it sold out quickly. WBRC wanted to take advantage of the excitement and we did a lot of special programming. Being an ABC station, we carried the game, but apparently most Alabama fans didn't think they would win, or at least didn't think to record the game. I had learned long ago to record everything and if the game wasn't worth keeping, you could record over it. Because of all the calls we got from fans wondering if we would replay the game, we got permission from ABC to re-run it. Several of the Alabama seniors including Teague and Lassic were invited to the Senior Bowl in Mobile. Mike Tucker, our sports photographer, and I went down there and interviewed them about the game and specific plays. We edited those interview clips into the game when we showed the replay. We promoted it heavily and aired it a couple of times, so everyone had their copy of the game.

We also did an hour-long recap of the season. We called it, "Alabama's Sensational Centennial." Karle hosted it from the Bryant Museum, and we had a lot of neat features including an interview with Corky Simpson our sister station in Phoenix did for us. It was a nice recap of the season.

"It was one of the most exciting years to cover," said Karle. "With all the SEC changes, what was at stake for Bama and the end of era at Auburn with Coach Dye retiring."

"That started the nice run for the SEC in national championships," said Melick. "We all thought the SEC was the best, but we didn't know. It was the first SEC national championship in a while, and it has proven over the years they have been the best for the last 30 years."

After Alabama won six national championships under Nick Saban, many fans around the country view the Tide now the same way most of the nation viewed the Hurricanes before that Sugar Bowl game: they win all the time, so they don't like them. But for one game, at least, most of the nation was pulling for them, and they were the good guys against the brash, cocky Hurricanes from Miami.

Chapter 5: Lesson Learned
Georgia Tech at Clemson
September 11, 2004

I left WBRC in July 1998 to take a job in Atlanta at WXIA as the senior sports producer. WXIA, or 11 Alive, as it's known, is the NBC affiliate in Atlanta. It wasn't a good situation for me. My role was different in Atlanta than in Birmingham and it didn't play to my strengths. After 15 months, I decided to leave. A Birmingham coworker's husband worked at The Weather Channel, and he helped me get a job there. I started as a freelancer, and really enjoyed working there. It was a big change, obviously, but it was interesting, and the challenge of writing weather stories was invigorating. They liked the job I did and eventually I accepted a full-time position working on the morning team. Not long after that I took over producing the main morning program, *Your Weather Today*, which aired from

7 to 9 a.m. It meant getting to work at 2:30 a.m., but I loved the folks I worked with, and it was a good fit for me.

When I told people I had gone to work at The Weather Channel, I was met with derision from most of the sports folks I worked with. Weather and sports people usually don't get along at local TV stations, because when the weather folks go long in their segment, that time gets taken away from the sportscast. At 11 Alive when the Falcons made their first Super Bowl appearance in 1999, Fred Kalil, the sports anchor, had mentioned off air that the day of the Super Bowl was a blue moon, the weather guy heard it, and mentioned on his weathercast and infuriated Kalil, because he couldn't use that tidbit. Rick Karle, the sports director at WBRC, was happy I got that job because his father-in-law watched The Weather Channel all the time, and I told him I would give his father-in-law a tour when he was in town. When I did that, Karle's father-in-law had the time of his life and Karle was the son-in-law of that year.

Most people who know me know how much I love sports and they asked me how I was dealing with not going to games for work. I would tell them I loved it, because I could tailgate, drink, and watch the game and not have to run from the field or locker room to edit highlights or an interview. While I had to buy a ticket and didn't get media parking passes, it was nice to enjoy games, especially in Atlanta with so many great events to attend. And working in the morning instead of at night allowed me to do things during the week. Of course, I would be working without a lot of sleep the next day, but at least I could do things.

In 2001 I decided to buy season tickets for Georgia Tech football. They weren't very expensive and growing up as an ACC fan, I would get to see teams I liked. I had good seats in the end zone. I didn't tailgate. I would usually take MARTA and would sometimes eat at The Varsity. Sometimes my wife would go, other times, I would take someone else. I wanted to go to a road game at least once a year too. Clemson and Tech played every year, and the Tigers were probably my favorite ACC team, so that was nice. Plus going to Clemson was an easy trip on the years the game was at Death Valley. I had driven over from Birmingham to see Clemson play at Tech in 1990 and someone had gotten me tickets for the 1999 game at Tech's Grant Field. That game was a shootout between two great quarterbacks, Joe Hamilton for the Jackets and Clemson's Woody Dantzler. Hamilton, who was runner-up for the Heisman Trophy in '99, had more than 400 yards of total offense. Dantzler entered the game when starter Brandon Streeter was injured and ran for 120 yards and a touchdown. He also threw for 185 yards and two touchdowns. Tech won 45-42. This was during a stretch when every game from 1996 until 2001 was decided by three points. In nine of the games between '96 and 2006, the margin was five points or fewer. Pete Yanity was my former roommate from Florence, South Carolina, who took over Clemson play by play duties after the death of Jim Phillips in 2003. He thinks it's one of the Southeast's underrated rivalries.

"I'm not sure either team fully embraced it because they had other games with teams in their respective states they were more focused on," said Yanity.

In 2004 the Jackets would be heading up I-85 to face the Tigers. I had tickets for the game and Mark Stackow was going with me. Stackow worked with me at The Weather

Channel. He's a Notre Dame fan but loves college football and would be making his first trip to Death Valley. I had been to Death Valley several times since I left South Carolina. The Carolina Panthers of the NFL played their home games in their inaugural season of 1995 at Clemson while their stadium in Charlotte was being finished. My parents had season tickets and I went up for a couple of the games. I had been to a Georgia-Clemson game with a bunch of Georgia fans from Birmingham in 1990. I had also been there for the Florida State-Clemson game in 1992.

Up to that point, I hadn't really tailgated at a Clemson game. When I was working in Florence, we walked through some of the tailgate lots close to the stadium, and I was very impressed with what they did. My mom had a cousin who was a Clemson fan and went to a lot of the games. When I went to the game in 1992, I stopped by to say hello to him, but I didn't consider that tailgating. I spent a lot of the time before the game that year with Yanity, who was working for the Clemson pregame show. Yanity and I also had lived with Bob Juback who was working for a station in Greenville and was at the game.

Clemson has a reputation for having a great tailgating experience. Murray Griffin is a Tech grad who goes to a lot of games and has been to Clemson several times.

"They have a beautiful stadium," he said. "They have a great atmosphere for tailgating. You take stuff and set up a table. Have a few beverages. Clemson folks have always been nice. Good folks, devoted to their team."

John Phillips, the former Clemson offensive lineman, has season tickets and enjoys tailgating.

"One thing that I am very proud of is our hospitality for visiting teams, being nice to them, and inviting them to our tailgates."

Sharon Loughran is a Virginia Tech grad and went to Death Valley to see her alma mater play. After the game she was walking past a group of Clemson fans that had a post-game spread going on. The Clemson fans invited Sharon and her group to join them.

"They were so nice, and we were talking about the game, and they were sharing everything with us," said

Loughran. "We realized after a few minutes this was Danny Ford's [the former Clemson coach] tailgate."

John Poteat is another Tech grad but has developed a fondness for Clemson over the years.

"I just love the place," he said. "I spent a lot of money putting my daughter through there. I have three grandkids and they always wear orange. We had a good time that day."

Stackow and I were planning on bar hopping rather than tailgating. The Esso Club is a famous Clemson watering hole. It's a former Esso gas station that had been turned into a bar and was very close to campus. Brent Musburger also talked about the Esso Club every time he broadcast a game from Clemson. Notre Dame was playing Michigan at 3:30 that day and a friend who was a Clemson grad suggested a place downtown to watch that game. The Clemson game didn't kick off until 8 p.m. and was televised on ABC.

We got to town around noon and got parked easily then walked over to the Esso Club. They had a big tent set up. This was week two of the season so it was going to be sunny and hot. We were there for a couple of beers, but I remember not being so impressed. Maybe it was because it was still a long time until kickoff. We headed to that place downtown so we could be situated when the Notre Dame game kicked off. The place, that I don't remember the name of, was great. They had the game on the big screen, so Stackow was happy. The food was good, and pitchers of beer were $5. Notre Dame upset Michigan so that made him feel even better. After that game was over, we headed over to the stadium.

In 2004 Tommy Bowden was in his sixth season as the Tigers head coach but hadn't won over many Clemson fans. Bowden was the oldest son of Florida State coach Bobby Bowden and the older brother of Terry Bowden who had been a coach and was working for ABC. I was familiar with both. The two brothers had different personalities and took different paths following in their father's footsteps. When I started working at WBRC in Birmingham, Terry was the head coach at I-AA Samford University. Prior to that he was the head coach at Salem University in West Virginia, his home state. He was very hands on and felt it was better to work his way up as a head coach at smaller schools. He had success at Samford, getting the Bulldogs to the playoffs a couple of times. When Pat Dye stepped down as coach at Auburn, Terry Bowden got the job and won his first 20 games as head coach at Auburn. He took the Tigers to the SEC Championship game in 1997. Then things quickly went downhill for Terry. There were off the field issues during the off-season and after winning only one of the first six games in 1998, he resigned. His record at Auburn was 47-17-1. In 2004 he was a studio analyst for ABC's college football coverage.

Tommy, on the other hand, worked at larger schools as an assistant coach. He was the wide receivers coach for Bill Curry at Alabama and followed him to Kentucky. After a year in the Bluegrass State, he was hired at Auburn by Pat Dye to be offensive coordinator and stayed in that role when his brother took over. In 1997 he went to Tulane to be head coach. In 1998 the Green Wave were 11-0 and ranked number seven. Clemson hired him the next season. I thought he would be perfect for Clemson. The Tigers had struggled with consistency since the Danny Ford era ended in 1989. I thought Bowden with his experience, bloodline, and Southern roots would play well with the Tiger fans. Coming into the 2004 season Bowden had a record of 38-24. He had won nine games twice but had only finished one season ranked in the top 15. They had beaten Wake Forest in overtime in the 2004 season opener and were ranked 18th as they got ready for Tech.

In 2004 Georgia Tech was coached by another coach I was very familiar with, Chan Gailey. I first met Chan when he was hired to coach the Birmingham Fire in the World League of American Football started by the NFL in 1991. Chan was easy to work with and I always liked him. After the WLAF shut down their American operations after the 1992 season, he was available, and Samford hired him to replace Terry Bowden. After a year there, he was hired by the Pittsburgh Steelers to be the offensive coordinator. The day that news broke, we were trying to chase him down and he said he would be at his son's baseball game and if we came by there, he would talk to us. While with the Steelers he helped develop Kordell Stewart's all-around game that earned him the nickname, Slash because he could play quarterback as well as wide receiver. He was hired by Jerry Jones in 1998 as head coach of the Dallas Cowboys. The

Cowboys made the playoffs both years Gailey was the head coach, but he was fired after the 1999 season. Gailey spent 2000 and 2001 as the Dolphins offensive coordinator, and Georgia Tech hired him in 2002 to replace George O'Leary who had left for Notre Dame.

Optimism was high on the "Flats" in 2004. Gailey had pulled off a major recruiting coup by landing wide receiver Calvin Johnson from Sandy Creek High School in Tyrone, Georgia, south of Atlanta. One reason Johnson chose the Jackets was the academic program at Tech. His mother has two doctorates, and all of his siblings have degrees in medical fields. When he got to Tech, he was 6'4"and weighed 210 pounds. Despite his size, he ran a sub 4.4 40 yards and broke the program record for vertical leap at 42 inches during drills before he ever played a game for Tech. The question would be if sophomore quarterback Reggie Ball would be able to get him the ball.

The game started so late because it was the ABC national, prime time game with Brent Musburger and Gary Danielson on the call. Our tickets were in the visitors' area, at the far end of the upper deck on the south side. That stadium is steep, especially the upper deck. The Tigers were in their orange britches for the game, and I always get goose bumps when they come down the hill (See Chapter 3).

The Tigers had the first chance to get on the board midway through the first quarter, but a third down pass in the end zone was incomplete and Clemson missed a 36-yard field goal. The Jackets then drove to the Clemson 37 and Calvin Johnson made a beautiful catch for his first career touchdown. Defensive back Tye Hill was in good position, but Reggie Ball made a great throw and Tech was up 7-0.

Early in the second quarter, Clemson tied it up when Charlie Whitehurst hit Curtis Baham with a 22-yard pass. Neither team really threatened to score the rest of the half and it was 7-7. I had warned Mark that if the game got out of hand, we would probably leave early because it was such a pain to get out of there and it would be late by the time we got back to Atlanta.

Tech took the second half kickoff and drove to the Clemson 1. On second and goal, a run lost a yard. On third down

Ball threw it to Johnson in the end zone, but he couldn't make that catch and Gailey decided to go for it on fourth and 2. The Tiger D was tough and stopped BJ Daniels at the one to take over on downs. The Clemson offense seemed to get some inspiration from defensive stop and drove into Tech territory. A couple of dropped passes stalled the drive and the Tigers had to settle for a 37-yard field goal.

Clemson's defense forced a punt and it seemed they were ready to put the Jackets away. The Tigers offense got the ball in Georgia Tech territory but had a penalty on third down and Whitehurst's fourth down pass fell incomplete.

In the first two drives of the game, Tech gained 114 yards and a touchdown on 16 plays. In the next 10 drives, they had run 57 plays, but had only gained 154 yards and hadn't scored.

With 8:19 left in the game, Clemson faced a third and 1 on their 38. Tech's defense was up close on the line of scrimmage and when running back Reggie Merriweather broke past the line, there was no one in the Tech secondary to stop him and the Tigers had a 10-point lead. It looked like it was going to be enough to get the win.

On the Jackets' first offensive play, Clemson dropped an easy interception. On third down a Ball run was short, the Jackets punt team came on the field, the Death Valley crowd was going crazy, and I told Stackow we were out of there. If Tech had done something on that drive, I would have stayed. There was 7:19 remaining in the game. Georgia Tech had 268 yards and Clemson had 416.

"I felt like I was playing with house money even before the Clemson game," said Stackow. "The Esso Club was great; I saw Notre Dame sneak up on Michigan and Death Valley was a great environment. I thought it was the right call. I knew it was going to take forever to get out of there and it was late and had been a long day."

My dad, Dick, was very impatient when it came to waiting in traffic after a game. He had season tickets to the Charlotte Hornets when they first joined the NBA and there were always big crowds there and he would hurry us along when the game was over to get to the car as soon as possible.

My mom would always be a little put out by that. "Dickydash" was the term we coined for his jaunt to the car. When I set up their first email account, that's what I used as their email address.

I didn't like sitting in traffic either. Depending on who I was with at the game, I would jog to the car. I knew I would have an easier time passing people on foot in the parking lot than once they were in their cars on the street. I had sprinted across the old stadium parking lot in Boone many times and was one of the first people out of the lot I parked in. Mark was a runner, and I knew he could keep up with me.

"I remember you having me sprint across the parking lot!" he recalled. "But we were still in traffic, even leaving when we did."

I'll have to leave it to the people still in the stadium to describe what was happening.

"I don't leave a game unless it's bad," said Griffin.

"Tech fans were starting to leave and the Clemson fans that were up there were really giving them the business," said Poteat. "It was like walking down the walk of shame. I was with my son who was in high school at the time, and I told him we're not walking through this until the end of the game."

Barry Owens is a Tech graduate who had driven all the way from Chapel Hill, North Carolina, to see the game.

"We were there with friends," he said. "We drove down there three and half hours. We weren't going to leave."

Clemson's offense couldn't do anything with the momentum and had a three and out. Ruben Houston had a nice punt return to give the Jackets good field position. Tech had a third and 3 just inside Clemson territory. At that point, the Jackets were two of 14 on third down. Ball hit Johnson to convert and the big freshman went over the 100-yard receiving mark for the game.

On first down, Daniels had a beautiful 15-yard run with a couple of nice spin moves that gave him 100 rushing yards. Ball hit Levon Thomas for a 19-yard touchdown that pulled the Jackets within 3 with 4:36 remaining. But the Tech kickoff went out of bounds and Clemson had great field position.

This was about the time Stackow and I reached the car. We turned on the radio and listened to Yanity and his color commentator Will Merritt. Whitehurst had a nice 12-yard run on first down. On the next play Clemson running back Kyle Browning, who had scored the game winning touchdown in overtime the previous week, busted through the blitzing Tech defense and went untouched for 54 yards. Stackow and I breathed a sigh of relief that Clemson was going to prevail, and we weren't going to miss an all-time comeback.

The Tigers were excited too. In fact, so excited they committed an excessive celebration penalty and kicked off from their 20. Thomas returned the kickoff to midfield. The Jackets had the ball with 3:11 remaining, trailing by 10. After a completion to Thomas, Ball threw a pass right to Clemson's star cornerback, Justin Miller, but he dropped it. Two plays later Ball converted a third down with a run to the Clemson 23. A pass to the end zone for Johnson was incomplete, but the Tigers were called for pass interference. There were two minutes remaining and the Jackets had the ball first and goal from the 8. Ball's next two passes were incomplete, but on third down Johnson made a great catch for the touchdown, falling backwards, and holding on to the ball.

The Clemson fans at Death Valley were getting nervous. Johnson's heroics had given Jacket fans hope.

"I was surprised when he came to Tech," said Griffin. "He was outstanding. He made a lot of acrobatic catches."

On the radio broadcast, as Stackow and I were driving through Seneca, South Carolina, Merritt said, "Pete, I can tell you there's no one who's left Death Valley tonight." Stackow and I knew differently. Were we going to miss a great finish?

There was 1:49 left to play. Tech only had one timeout, but Gailey didn't do a straight onside kick. It was a line drive kickoff that bounced off a Clemson player and went out of bounds. Clemson had the ball; first and 10 on the Tech 33. Whitehurst ran a keeper and had a nice gain, but he slid, and he was marked short of the first down. The clock was briefly stopped for a measurement and after it was confirmed Whitehurst was short, Gailey called his last timeout. Runs on second and third down couldn't pick up the yard and with 23 seconds left; Bowden sent in the punt team. The snap was bad and dribbled back to the punter. He fell on the ball at the 11-yard line and the clock was stopped with 16 seconds left. On the radio broadcast, you could hear there were still some Tech fans in the stadium and the Clemson fans were stunned.

For some reason, the Clemson defense only had one defender on Johnson who was split wide left. That defender was Miller, who was Clemson's best cover cornerback. He intercepted a record eight passes two years before as a true freshman. After the season he would declare for the NFL draft and was taken in the second round. He played six seasons in the NFL and made the Pro Bowl in 2006. He was very capable. But he was only 5'10". Calvin Johnson was at least 6'4". Miller didn't have any safety help. Ball only looked one way, to Johnson. He heaved it high so Miller wouldn't have a chance to knock it away. Johnson with the 42-inch vertical, went up and got it. Touchdown Georgia Tech. The point after touchdown (PAT) made it 28-24 and Tech fans were giddy.

"That last one he went up and got it," said Griffin. "It was spectacular!"

"We knew he was going to be good," said Poteat. "He was great."

"What a crazy finish!" recalled Owens. "He went up and it was obvious he outjumped the defender. When he caught the pass 400 people went crazy, 70,000 went silent."

But the game wasn't over. There was a celebration penalty called on Tech. Clemson returned the kickoff 49 yards to the Tech 31, giving Whitehurst one play to steal the game back. The Jacket offensive players were holding hands on the sideline, urging their defense to make the play. Whitehurst threw to Kelvin Grant, one of the Tigers' bigger receivers, but he was double covered and couldn't make the catch. The Jackets had won despite trailing by 10 points with less than two minutes to play.

The Clemson fans who had been heckling the Tech fans who left early were forced to eat some crow.

"When the game was over Nick [his son] and I were just hollering at them worse they were giving it to us," said Poteat. "I couldn't talk for a week!"

Johnson finished the game with eight catches for 127 yards and three touchdowns. It gave the nation the first look at the player who would be known as Megatron because of his physical gifts.

On the CBS broadcast after the Johnson touchdown Gary Danielson proclaimed, "Never give up on a game!" I learned an important lesson that day. Never. Leave. A. College. Football. Game. Early.

"I remember it being a great day and I had a great time," said Stackow. "We were kind of kicking ourselves for leaving. It was an unremarkable game when we left."

John Phillips, the former Clemson lineman who played in the mid-80s, didn't make it to that game.

"I was playing in a two-day golf tournament and was paired with a couple of Tech guys," he said. "One of the guys was older and he gave up on the game and went to bed early. We had an early tee time Sunday. He didn't realize Tech had won, I had to tell him."

The only time I left a game early again was on my honeymoon with my second wife. We were in San Francisco at a game between the Orioles and Giants. I have been an Orioles fan since 1970. It just so happened the Orioles were playing in

San Francisco when we scheduled our wedding and honeymoon! I had wanted to see the Giants ballpark and my wife was a Giants fan who had lived in the Bay Area for several years before moving back to Atlanta. The Giants had scored two runs in the fourth and four in the fifth inning and were up 7-1 after six and a half innings. We decided to leave. We walked a long way around the stadium, to see McCovey Cove, and get a good sense of the park. It was incredible. Then we walked downtown. We had reservations for supper and wanted to have cocktails at the Top of the Mark before that, and it was my honeymoon, so I didn't feel terrible about leaving early. I still kept an eye on the score of the game on my phone. The Orioles scored two runs in the seventh and eighth and I was thinking wow! Right before we got on a cable car to get to our hotel on Nob Hill, Johnathon Schoop hit a three-run homer in the ninth to give the Orioles the lead. Zach Britton nailed down the save and the Orioles won. I would have felt worse if we hadn't had such a great time that night!

Clemson finished the season with a 6-5 record. They declined a bowl appearance as punishment for an ugly fracas that broke out between Clemson and South Carolina players in the season finale. Bowden resigned as Clemson's coach midway through the 2008 season with a 72-45 record. He was replaced by Dabo Swinney. Swinney was the Tigers' wide receiver coach for Bowden, who was Swinney's position coach when he played at Alabama. Swinney was on the Alabama team that won the National Championship in 1992 (Chapter 4). He would establish Clemson as a national powerhouse and win the national championship in 2016 and 2018, both times defeating his alma mater in the title game.

Tech finished the 2004 season at 7-5 with a win in the Citrus Bowl. Johnson was ACC Rookie of the Year.

It was truly a pleasure to watch him play for three years. His last year with the Jackets, 2006, Tech won the ACC's Coastal Division with a 7-1 conference record, and he was ACC Player of the Year and first team All-American.

I saw the Jackets play eight times in 2006. They opened the season against Notre Dame at home. I went to the game at Chapel Hill when they clinched the division title. That was a 7-0 thriller. The night before I had driven to Rocky Mount, North

Carolina, to visit Ron Grillo, my former colleague in Birmingham. Grillo and I went to the game in Chapel Hill. I drove down to Jacksonville for the ACC Championship game against Wake Forest. It was rainy, cloudy, and miserable. Wake won 9-3. The best thing about that game was that Tech wore Navy jerseys for the first time since 1994.

The lone conference regular season loss was at Death Valley against Clemson in another ABC prime time game. Yanity had invited me to hang out with him as he did his pregame stuff, and I was on the sideline during the game. That was a great Clemson experience. ESPN's *College GameDay* was there, and the entire town was going crazy. Clemson could have beaten about anyone that day. They beat the Jackets 31-7. Calvin Johnson didn't catch a pass. Clemson speedster C. J. Spiller ran past me on the sideline on the way to one of his two 50-yard touchdown runs. My truck broke down on the way home. A couple of Tech fans picked me up and brought me back to Atlanta.

Once I started going to Appalachian games regularly with Mike Ladd, he always wanted to stay, and I realized I didn't want to miss any crazy plays. That helped me develop the patience to stay and not worry about getting home so quickly. I would be very happy I had adopted that attitude a few years later!

Chapter 6: "We Are!" "Penn State!"

Michigan State at Penn State

November 18, 2006

The Weather Channel had turned out to be a great place for me to work. Although I wasn't getting paid to read the sports section or watch ESPN anymore, I was getting paid to look at maps, something I had always enjoyed as much as sports. I realized what a great earth science teacher I had in eighth grade, because working there I realized how much weather I remembered from her class.

I was producing the *Your Weather Today* program that ran from 7-9 a.m. The show was one of the highest rated morning shows on cable at the turn of the Millennium. In fact, on the morning of Monday, September 10, 2001, we had the highest rated news and information show on cable. Cable news changed forever that week, but that's another story.

Working the morning shift was new for me, but I liked it. I had always been a morning person. Part of the challenges of my job, especially when I moved into more of a management position, was to get the left-side brain scientists to interact effectively with the right-side brain TV producers. We had a good team. Heather Tesch and Marshall Seese were the anchors, Dennis Smith covered weather for commuters and travelers, and Dr. John Scala was our storm analyst. He was a former professor who would cover active severe weather and on a quieter day explain complex weather in an easy-to-understand manner. He left the show to get back into teaching.

There were three finalists for the position to replace Scala who I thought would be very difficult to replace. I was involved with the interview process and the first candidate who came in was Dr. Jon Nese. He was with the Franklin Institute in Philadelphia. He was very knowledgeable and looked good on camera, but I felt he was just so serious. I thought one of the reasons for *Your Weather Today*'s success was the camaraderie and interactions between the anchors and I wasn't sure Nese would fit it with that.

When there was dangerous, threating weather we were talking about, we were serious, but that wasn't the case very often, and we tried to keep things light and engaging to fit the mood of a typical morning show. After Nese did his screen test, Neil McGillis, one of the meteorologists I had a good relationship with, told me he had known Nese when McGillis was a student at Penn State. Nese was teaching then and McGillis said he thought the world of Nese, and he would be a great addition to the show.

Nese was much better than the other two candidates and got the job. Working with the rest of the team, they broke him down and he became light and engaging when it was appropriate. Part of our routine was to meet with the storm analyst after the show to look ahead to weather the next day and what we could do in his segments. Dealing with Scala and Nese was a great lesson in weather and together, we came up with some interesting segments. Nese and I had also developed a close personal relationship. We were similar in age and had similar interests. A faculty position with a lot of teaching came open in the Meteorology department at Penn State and he moved his family back to State College. He told me he wanted me to come up for a game, which was something I wanted to do.

The fall of 2006 was the first full football season since my divorce, and I had planned to go to a lot of games. I had my Georgia Tech season tickets, and they were expected to have a good team, plus I had my mini package of Appalachian games, and they were the defending national champions. We didn't know yet just how exciting they would be with their freshman quarterback, Armanti Edwards. My parents had season tickets for the Carolina Panthers, and I wanted to see them a time or two if I could work it out. I planned with Nese to go to Penn State for the Michigan State game, the last weekend of the regular season.

The 2006 season started for Tech at home, hosting Notre Dame. The game would be the ABC prime time telecast and *College GameDay* was on the Flats promoting the game. The Jackets were unranked, and the Irish were number two.

Despite the lack of a ranking, optimism was high for the Jackets, with Calvin Johnson now a junior, quarterback Reggie Ball was a senior, and they had a solid defense and a good running game. Appalachian was opening the season at N.C. State, and I hated to miss that game, but I decided to see the Jackets. Charlie Wiess was coaching the Irish and Brady Quinn was the quarterback. His favorite target was Jeff Samardzija, who went on to pitch in the majors.

    I tailgated before the game with some friends from The Weather Channel. Jim Gange was another producer who was going to use my extra ticket. There were several Notre Dame fans in our group too. Mark Stackow (Chapter 5) and some of his family were there. McGillis and his wife Jen, both Penn State grads, were there. Jen had grown up in a Notre Dame family near Philadelphia and her younger sister, Jaclyn, a Notre Dame grad, was there with her husband who she met in South Bend, and now lived in Atlanta. Jen broke from her family when she was a junior in high school and decided she wanted to go to Penn State to study meteorology. Neil and Jen left after the tailgate to watch the game at home, but the rest of us had tickets. The atmosphere at Bobby Dodd Stadium that night was one of the best I ever experienced there. Tech isn't known for its rowdy crowds. In fact, most of the time, the rowdiness of the crowds is caused by the visiting fans. Clemson always had a big contingent of fans there and some years the crowd at the Tech-Georgia game was about 50-50 between Jackets and Dawgs. Of course, there were a lot of Notre Dame fans there to spice things up. The Irish prevailed 14-10, but it looked like Tech would be a pretty good team.

I got my first look at Appalachian the following week when I went to Boone to see them play James Madison. Appalachian and JMU were the two most recent FCS National Champions and played every year when I was in school. This game was part of a home and home series the schools had scheduled for 2006 and 2008. The Mountaineers, ranked number one in FCS despite losing the opener to N.C. State, won 21-10. In was in this game Edwards established himself as the best option at quarterback going forward for the Mountaineers. However, despite the win over the Dukes, New

Hampshire would replace Appalachian as the number one-ranked FCS team as a result of their 34-17 win at Northwestern.

The next couple of weeks I was focusing on Georgia Tech. I saw them beat Virginia on a Thursday night and the defense made some great plays down the stretch and held off Maryland. The Jackets five-game winning streak had vaulted them to number 13 in the nation as they would be going to Death Valley to face number 12 Clemson in another ABC prime time affair, but this time the Tigers won going away.

That was the only conference loss for the Jackets and after wins over N.C. State and Miami, could win the Coastal Division with a win at North Carolina. Ron Grillo, my former co-worker in Birmingham had moved to Rocky Mount, North Carolina, and I asked him if he would like to go to the game with me. I drove to Rocky Mount and spent Friday night at his house and then we drove to Chapel Hill on Saturday morning. The game was typical for the Jackets that season, they won 7-0, and as you would expect, it wasn't pretty. The win gave them the Jackets the Coastal title and the opportunity to play in the ACC

Championship game for the first time. I bought my tickets for that game.

But first, I was finally making my trip north to see Penn State and get my first taste of Big Ten football. Penn State was a program I had always respected but didn't really pull for. Our next-door neighbors in Charlotte were from Pennsylvania and were big Penn State fans but they had moved back to the Keystone State. Scott Stroupe, a year behind me in school and a roommate of mine for a while in Birmingham, had always liked Penn State. He was the only person I had known growing up who pulled for the Nittany Lions and didn't have ties to the school or Pennsylvania.

"That old TV movie, *Something For Joey*, was what really got me interested in Penn State," said Stroupe. "They had those crappy white uniforms, but I liked the no names on the back, showing more of a team attitude. I loved Joe Paterno. He was my idol, the Dean Smith or John Wooden of college football."

Jen McGillis had an interesting take on the lack of names on the jerseys.

"I would have liked them there to help keep up with the players," she said. "But the concept is we are a team. And made us as a university to be a part of the team. You don't need to have your name on a jersey to be Penn State."

"I had a cousin that went there, and she sent me a brochure from bookstore," said Stroupe. "I was able to order stuff. You couldn't get any of their things here. All I wore was Penn State stuff. I didn't want to be a Carolina fan. Me and my dad watched the Sugar Bowl between Bama and Penn State in '79, which broke my heart. When I moved to Alabama, I saw pictures of that goal line stand everywhere!"

In addition to Nese and the McGillises there were by far more Penn State grads at The Weather Channel than any other school. They have, if not the best, one of the top two or three meteorology departments in the country so The Weather Channel was a popular post-graduate destination. There was certainly a clique there, and it was obvious how proud they were of their alma mater. I realized it a little more when I worked with Nese as we shared stories about our college experiences.

Growing up in Steubenville, Ohio, Nese wasn't a fan of Penn State. When he decided he wanted to study meteorology in college, none of the Ohio schools had a program he wanted to attend. He visited Penn State in October of 1978, the year before he enrolled and that was when he became a fan.

"I regularly went to games as a student," said Nese. "$35 for a season ticket was great."

The Nittany Lions finished the season undefeated and won a major bowl game in 1968, 1969, and 1973 but hadn't yet won a national championship. They had the tough loss in the 1979 Sugar Bowl against Alabama's goal line stand. In 1982, back in New Orleans, Joe Paterno finally won his national championship.

"I feel like win in the '82 Sugar Bowl over Georgia put Penn State on the map," said Nese. "I went with eight guys in a van. We stayed at the New Orleans YMCA for $10 a night. The game was played on New Year's Day. I bought a ticket from Penn State and still have that ticket. A few years later when we went to the Fiesta Bowl [in 1987 when Penn State beat Miami to win the national championship], I was a grad student. I went with the same group, except this time we flew and stayed at a hotel."

In 1993 Penn State joined the Big Ten after being an Independent since 1892. While an Independent, Penn State's biggest rival was the University of Pittsburgh. The two schools first met in 1892 but played every season from 1900 until 1992 except for a few years in the 30s. With Penn State in the Big Ten and Pitt in the Big East then, the rivalry went dormant, but the schools have played eight non-conference games since then.

"I think I'm old enough to appreciate the Pitt rivalry," said Nese. "I'm over the fact we don't play them anymore. Would I rather see Pitt than Massachusetts or Delaware? Yes, but I understand the realization of scheduling. There are a lot of people my age who long for the way it used to be, but I know it's not going back there."

The Pitt-Penn State game is one of the several traditional rivalries around the nation that are not played annually any longer because of conference shuffling. Perhaps the most famous is the Oklahoma-Nebraska rivalry, which ended when the Cornhuskers joined the Big Ten. Growing up,

Oklahoma was one of my favorite college football teams. I loved the wishbone formation, and they ran it so well. Kansas-Missouri has historical roots that date back before Kansas had statehood. Texas-Texas A&M hasn't been played since the Aggies joined the SEC in 2012. With the SEC expanding to first 12 in 1990, then 14 teams in 2012, the Georgia-Clemson game wasn't being played every year any longer. Even some in-conference rivalries were stopped after division play started in the SEC. Auburn and Tennessee played each other early in the season for years, but when they were put in opposite divisions, they didn't play every year. Of course, Tennessee started a new, early season rivalry with Florida when they were both placed in the SEC's Eastern Division.

With Penn State losing its natural rival, the Big Ten tried to set one up with Michigan State, the two most recent additions to the conference. A story in *The Athletic* says that MSU coach George Perles welcomed Paterno to the conference and proposed their respective schools to play the final game of the season together. Perles had high hopes for the rivalry.

"That's always kind of been kind of a made-up rivalry," said Nese. "They created that Land Grant trophy and jokes are made about it. In the new Big Ten [after USC and UCLA join in 2024] there is no dedicated Penn State rival. That's all you need to know."

The Athletic article states that college rivalries need to be organic and not forced. I agree. Appalachian's biggest rival is Georgia Southern. When I was in school, the Eagles weren't in the Southern Conference and had just re-started their football program. The Mountaineers' rival was Western Carolina, a school App shared geography and many other similarities with then. Once Georgia Southern joined the Southern Conference and had tough games with App State and each school realized they would have to beat the other if they were to win the conference championship. A rivalry quickly developed, especially as the Western program fell on hard times after the death of long-time coach Bob Waters.

The fact the Nittany Lions were playing Michigan State didn't really have anything to do with me going up there that weekend. It was just the best weekend for me. Appalachian had an off week the week before the playoffs would begin and Georgia Tech was hosting Duke. I was looking forward to seeing State College as well as experiencing their football atmosphere that I had heard so much about.

I flew to Harrisburg on Thursday and rented a car. The drive to State College runs along the Susquehanna River as you leave the capital, then proceeds through rolling hills and small towns. There was a severe thunderstorm warning in effect as I was driving, but I didn't drive through too much heavy rain. I met Jon at his office on campus. He took me around town a little and we ate supper at Champs, a sports bar in town where Nese played trivia a lot. The next day we walked around campus and Jon took me to the campus post office where I got to meet a Penn State legend, Mike the Mailman.

Mike Herr had worked at the State College post office for eight years when he was moved to the campus post office in 1976. After his first day in the new position, he came home and told his wife, Katie, "I've found a place I really like."

"I knew I liked it from the first day," Herr said. "The faculty, staff, students; everyone was so upbeat."

There are few people anywhere that are more upbeat than Mike the Mailman. When I called him to talk about his career at Penn State and asked him how he was he responded, "I've never had a bad day!" One reason is because of the environment he created at the campus post office.

"It had to be the most non-postal post office in America," Herr said.

There was an older clerk who was Herr's boss when he started on campus, but after he had retired, Herr had taken over and began to loosen the rules on things. A member of one of the lesser-attended sports had asked Herr if they could hang a schedule poster of their sport in the post office. A member of another sport saw the poster and wanted their sport represented and he said, "Of course!" and a tradition was born. Herr also became a fan of those sports.

"I would try and get to at least one game of all 31 of the sports," Herr said. "The athletes would come into the post office and thank me for being there."

In addition to the sports posters, the wall where the line would form was filled with pictures of Penn State students and graduates would send Mike from all over the world to post.

Herr had met Nese when Nese was a student and Herr had introduced Jon to his future wife Gwen when they were both students at Penn State. When Nese came back to State College to teach, they were able to pick up their friendship.

"He's a true ambassador of PSU and State College," said Nese. "I nominated him for an honorary degree. Except for Joe Paterno, no name is more associated with Penn State than Mike the Mailman."

"You wanted to send a package just to get his smile," said Jen McGillis. "To bring that joy every single day. Everyone left there feeling good. He brought a lot of joy to Penn State."

After hanging out with Mike for a while, I spoke at one of Nese's classes about the role of a producer working with meteorologists to make complex weather systems understandable for viewers. Penn State's meteorology department has its own TV studio and Jon is involved with that. He showed me around and after he was finished with his teaching, we went for a walk along College Avenue, the strip of bars, shops, and restaurants. He introduced me to one of the most popular Penn State game week traditions, the game pins.

"Starting in 1972, a local bank tried to start a tradition," said Nese. "They printed buttons, about an inch and a half or so diameter for each home game. They put a witty saying on it, depending on the opponent. The bank didn't put their name on it. If it was a flop, they didn't want to be associated with it. But they ran out, then printed more. For the second printing the bank put their name on it, because it was good advertising. They ran out again and did a third printing from remaining games. The back of those buttons was metal. That first year, there was a mishmash of three printings of some buttons. In 1973, they did them for all the games and the buttons were all metal.

"Dave Engel [grandson of Hall of Fame coach Rip Engel who preceded Paterno] lived in my neighborhood when we moved back, and he had a great collection. That got me interested in trying to complete my collection. Mike helped me a lot. He would give me boxes of buttons. I have hundreds of them. They hang on a ribbon; each season is a ribbon and they hang down in the order of the games."

We went to the bank to pick up our pins for that game. "No Party for Sparty" was the saying on the button.

Jen McGillis remembers the buttons as a big part of game week.

"Mid-week you would go by the bank and get your button," she said. "My roommate wore them all during the season, I would just wear the one for the game."

"I feel like at Penn State, the whole town is built to the college," said Neil McGillis. "On game weeks you can feel it even before the weekend. I could just feel everyone migrating to the stadium."

One of the things I love so much about college football is the traditions each school has. It's neat experiencing them when you go to games at different places. Penn State has a lot more than just the buttons.

"My favorite was going to a Friday pep rally," said Jen McGillis. "One time we were walking to the pep rally and were joined by Joe Paterno. He asked us about the game and how we were enjoying Penn State. I will never forget that. It was pretty epic!"

"Joe Paterno sightings were the thing of lore," said Neil McGillis. "My roommate saw him one time and said, 'good luck in the game coach!' He responded, 'Thanks!'"

Paterno's house was just blocks from the campus and he had lived in that house for years. He was an assistant under Engle for 16 years before taking over after Engel's retirement in 1965. Nese had pointed it out when he was showing me around.

Another tradition Nese likes is the homecoming parade.

"Homecoming is really big here," he said. "There is a parade on College Avenue Friday for three hours. It's really done nicely."

One reason homecoming is such a big thing at Penn State is because of the strength of the alumni association. The university claims their Alumni Association is the largest organization of its kind among colleges and universities. There are 740,000 Penn State alumni worldwide.

"Some people may say Penn State fans are a cult," jokes Nese. "But generally, they are loyal and support the school financially and otherwise."

Jen McGillis felt a part of the family as soon as she decided to attend the University.

"I felt it when I was accepted to go there, I'm a part of it," she said. "At orientation they talk a lot about the alumni and the Penn State family and how spread out it is. Definitely when you get on campus you feel it."

Neil McGillis felt the same way.

"It's such a huge alumni association and with 100,000 in the stadium, that's one way as a student to see and realize what a big thing you are a part of."

When Penn State grads meet one another, one will say, "We are." And the other responds, "Penn State!"

According to the school, the first use of the phrase is often attributed to Steve Shuey, a captain on the 1947 team who went to the Cotton Bowl in Dallas. Because Penn State's team was integrated, the Black players couldn't participate in all the activities the White players could. Shuey responded, "We're Penn State. We play together or we don't play."

In the 70s Penn State had played at Ohio State and the cheerleaders were impressed with the Buckeye's cheer when someone says, "O. H." and the response is "I. O." The Penn State cheerleaders adopted for their use by saying, "We Are!" and the students were supposed to respond, "Penn State!" It took several years for the chant to catch on. At first it was just used by the students, but eventually it caught on around the entire stadium and beyond. Now, if a Penn State grad sees someone wearing Penn State gear they will say, "We Are," and the other person is supposed to respond appropriately.

"When I teach a statistics class (or when I talk about our large alumni base), I'll often reference a probability problem you can build around the idea that there are a lot of Penn State Meteorology alumni," said Nese. "As an example, say you're interviewing at a company that employs twenty meteorologists, of which four are Penn Staters. The company randomly chooses five employees to go to lunch with you. What are the chances that if you say, 'We Are' at lunch, someone says 'Penn State'?"

I was looking forward to experiencing tailgating at Penn State. It was chilly that morning and with a noon kickoff, we didn't have a lot of time to tailgate. We met up with Mike the Mailman and stopped by some of Nese's friends' spots.

"Now having gone to other places I think Penn State does tailgating as well as anyone," said Nese. "I walk around the parking lot and people are very friendly. Offer you a beer and stuff."

"I'm not a drinker, but I like the tailgate," said Herr. "Sometimes I'll ride a bike so I can get to all the tailgates. I love to eat, talk to people, and remember old games. A lot of times, they will tell me a story about something they remember about me. That's touching."

I enjoyed myself and everyone was welcoming to me and happy to see me there. Some people had even heard of App State. I don't feel like I got the full experience, because we just didn't have the time with the early kickoff.

Because it was the final home game of the season, Nese wanted to get to his seats in time to see the seniors be introduced. He and Herr also like watching the band pregame.

"Marching on the field that's a pretty cool way to do pregame," said Nese. "That's a tradition that makes me smile."

"I like the Blue Band and think that is the best part of the game," said Herr.

Beaver Stadium was very impressive. It's the nation's second-largest stadium with a capacity of more than 107,000 in 2006. Some modifications were made in 2011 and capacity was reduced by about 750 to the current listed capacity of 106,572. It was cold and I was thankful I had the warm clothes I wear to Appalachian games in November and December. Our seats were in the end zone, about halfway up. I like end zone seats because it's neat to see the plays develop and holes open up. I had end zone seats at Georgia Tech for several years and learned to watch the two officials on each sideline mark the play. If they signal time out, it usually means the offense picked up a first down.

On senior day, it's not only the senior players that are introduced to the crowd. If the student who wears the Lion costume for the season is a senior, the student will take off the Lion head and introduce themselves to the student section.

Not only is Beaver Stadium the second largest stadium in college football, but it also has the second largest student section with 21,000 seats available to students. Texas A&M's student section, known as the "12th Man," seats 26,000 students. ESPN game analyst and *College GameDay* host Kirk Herbstreit has declared Penn State as the best student section in the nation. Tickets sell out quickly. Distribution is broken up into classes and each class has a day to buy tickets and there is quite a competition to see which class sells out quickest. In the middle of the section, 700 students wear coordinated blue and white shirts to create a block "S." This was revived in 1999. I thought that was very cool. It also reminded me of the card sections you used to see in stadiums on TV. Card sections began to lose favor in the late 70s, but apparently there are still a few colleges that use a card section during their games.

But for all the traditions, what Beaver Stadium has become best known for is their whiteouts. It had started just a couple of years before in 2004 when the student section dressed in white. It really caught on in 2005 when the whiteout game was against number six Ohio State and Penn State pulled off the upset. The entire stadium participated in 2007. In 2006 the whiteout game was against Michigan and the Nittany Lions lost 17-10. It has developed into something that Penn State fans are very proud of.

"It shows the unity of the fan base," said Neil McGillis. "Everyone is pulling for the same thing, and this accentuates that. It gives me chills thinking about it!"

"People talk about it as soon as it ends. Who will be next year's game?" said Nese.

Penn State has also done what is called 'striping,' when each section of the stadium alternates wearing white and blue. That's been done at several other schools and when participation is good, it looks really cool.

Michigan State was 4-7 coming into the 2006 game, and it would turn out to be the last game for head coach John

L. Smith. Their only Big Ten win had come against Northwestern. The Spartans trailed 38-3 in the third quarter but got a field goal with 13 seconds remaining to cap the biggest comeback in college football history in the 39-38 win.

The Nittany Lions were 7 and 4 coming into the game. They lost to Notre Dame, Ohio State, Michigan, and Wisconsin. In the Wisconsin game, two weeks prior to the MSU game, Paterno was injured in a sideline collision. Nursing a broken leg and torn ligaments, he watched the Temple game from home the next week but would be in the press box for the game against the Spartans.

The 7-4 record was a little bit of a disappointment to Penn State fans. After losing seasons in 2003 and 2004, a lot of people were starting to question if Paterno was staying on as coach so he could become the all-time winningest coach in college football. Paterno was battling with Florida State coach Bobby Bowden for the record. In 2005 Penn State finished 11-1. That included a win in the Orange Bowl against Bowden's Florida State team.

"It's not wrong to have all the respect from what he's done and saying time to step down," said Nese. "He had gotten a little more involved in 2005 and things turned around. Breathed new life into the program. He showed the old guy could still do it. Even with the bounce back it was probably time. He was pretty old [79 years old in 2006]."

Heading into the games that weekend, Bowden held the lead at 363 wins to Paterno's 361.

Despite the senior day emotion, the Nittany Lions started off flat. The Spartans turned two Penn State fumbles into 10 points and led 10-0 at the end of the first quarter. The Nittany Lions got on the board early in the second quarter after a 12-play, 57-yard drive. Anthony Morelli hit Andrew Quarless for a 17-yard touchdown pass.

The Nittany Lions lost two more fumbles in the half. Senior running back Tony Hunt lost his second fumble of the half with less than three minutes remaining and the Spartans were able to tack on another field goal.

PSU came out after the half and had to punt on their first possession. Michigan State had a nice drive into the Penn

State red zone, but the Spartans had three incompletions and missed a 35-yard field goal. The two teams traded punts and Penn State found itself at its own 20-yard line. After a run on first down lost a yard, Morelli went to the air. He completed passes of 23, 23, and 29 yards to give the Nittany Lions a first and goal at the 6. Morelli hit Jordan Norwood in the end zone to give Penn State the lead and the student section something to cheer about.

The defense was able to feed on the emotion and forced the Spartans to punt. It was blocked and recovered by Penn State on the Michigan State 19. But the Nittany Lions only gained 1 yard in three plays and the 36-yard field goal was no good. However, the defense was up to the challenge of stopping the Spartans, keeping them out of Penn State territory on the next two drives. The Nittany Lions were able to add a field goal with 4:30 remaining and lead 17-13.

The Spartans drove to the Penn State 39, but on fourth down, Tim Shaw sacked Brian Hoyer and the Nittany Lions took over. Hunt ran for a first down and the offense ran out the clock. Despite the first half fumbles, Hunt ran for 130 yards for the game.

After the game we headed back to Nese's house to watch the Ohio State-Michigan game. Those two old rivals were number one and number two in the country. This game was the first time they faced off as the top two teams in the country. I joked that I hadn't watched seven hours of Big Ten football in my life before today and I watched the two games today. Ohio State prevailed in that game but would lose to Florida in the BCS National Championship game.

Bobby Bowden also won his game that day and each coach would win their bowl game giving Bowden the two-game lead heading into the 2007 season. Bowden ended up with 377 wins and coached his last game in 2009. Paterno coached until November 2011 and won a total of 409 games. He was fired as coach before the end of the 2011 season in the wake of the child abuse allegations against longtime assistant coach Jerry Sandusky. The NCAA took away some of Paterno's wins, but they were re-instated on appeal. He died of lung cancer in January of 2012.

"It broke my heart all that went down," remembered Stroupe. "I wasn't as much of a fan then, but I hated to see that."

"It's a hard thing for PSU alumni to separate what happened with all the good he did," said Neil McGillis.

I've been fortunate to have had the chance to spend some more time with Mike the Mailman and Nese. A book could be done on Mike. He hosts a bar tour after exams are over in the spring. The first one was held in 1989. I was supposed to go up there for the bar tour in 2007 and even had my name on the T-shirt. Nese and I were listed as security. Something came up and I wasn't able to make it.

It's now known as the Cheers First Class Bar Tour. "This year was the 43rd bar tour," said Herr. Last year was the 31st. When It's your tour you can make your own rules! I like to make everything an odd number. It's all about silliness!"

After I left The Weather Channel in the summer of 2009, Jon invited me up for the bar tour in 2010 and we surprised Herr in the post office when I showed up. It was amazing to watch him in action, walking from bar to bar and so many students shouted, "Mike the Mailman!" or wanted pictures with him. He was so gracious to everyone.

Penn State and Alabama scheduled a two-game series in 2010 and 2011. The 2010 game would be in Tuscaloosa. Nese called me one day and asked if he got me a ticket, would I pick up him and The Mailman at the airport, let them stay at my house, and drive them to Tuscaloosa to tailgate and go to the game. I said, "Of course!"

They arrived Friday night and we went to a restaurant and several of the folks who had worked with Nese met us there. I had never tailgated in Tuscaloosa because every time I had been before I was working. I was looking forward to this experience. I had called a friend who was a Bama grad and went to the games about where they would be tailgating. It was neat. Most people claim a spot on the Quad in advance and park elsewhere and haul everything to the Quad to set up. It is similar to the Grove at Ole Miss (a bucket list destination for me) but not quite as elaborate. Everyone was very nice to us (I was wearing a Penn State shirt) and many engaged Herr and Nese in conversation and thanked them for coming to the game. It was obvious the respect they had for the Penn State program.

"When I was at Alabama, I was surprised how friendly everyone was," said Herr. "I didn't realize Bear [Bryant] and Joe had such a strong relationship. That was refreshing and that's how it should be."

Alabama, the defending national champ, was number one in the nation for that game in week two of the season. The Tide rolled 24-3 over the number 18 Lions but we had a nice time. When I see someone wearing Penn State gear, I ask them if they would be impressed if I tell them Mike the Mailman slept on my couch. I get some interesting reactions.

Herr retired as the mailman on campus in 2016. *CBS News Sunday Morning* did a story on him. There were several pictures of me on the wall in the post office when he stepped down. There was a picture of me at Ann Arbor with the scoreboard behind me after the Michigan win, a picture of Herr, Nese and I at the Tuscaloosa game, and a picture of everyone in Mike's bar tour group from 2010.

I saw him again in 2018 when I was in State College for the App State-Penn State game. He's one of the few people I've met who always makes you feel so much better about yourself just spending a few minutes with him. He still has his boundless energy in retirement and plays a lot of tennis. Penn State is lucky to have such a great ambassador for their school.

I'm always troubled when I come across someone who has ambivalent feelings about their alma mater. I know everyone may not have had a great college experience for any number of reasons. I feel like my four years at Appalachian had quite an effect on how my personality developed because of the experiences I had there and that's one reason I have such strong feelings about the place. I love the mountains in the area. I love the Blue Ridge Parkway. I have a lot of friends who share those passions, and we enjoy spending time together. I always enjoy meeting someone who has such passion for their college, regardless of which one it is. It's interesting hearing their stories about why they feel that way. I think that is one reason why I enjoy the Penn State folks so much.

Everyone has their preferences: ocean or Gulf, pork or beef barbecue, Ginger or Mary Anne. I think it's neat to go to a different school and see the things they do and have that makes that school special to them. I had never really been a fan of the midwestern schools, and I didn't think they played as good a brand of football as the teams in the South do. The game I saw probably won't be shown on the Big Ten Network for classic games, but both Penn State and Michigan State have had excellent teams and won plenty of big games. Michigan, Ohio State, Notre Dame, and Penn State all rank among the top eight winningest college football programs. Regardless, I'll usually pick an ACC or SEC game over a Big Ten game when I'm watching games on TV. Part of that is that I'm more familiar with the teams. But I've learned in my travels to different games in different parts of the country, there are great traditions and neat things to experience. You aren't being disloyal to your school if you admire something another school does. Maybe there's a way you can fit what they do to work for your school. Even the "We Are" at Penn State was modified from Ohio State.

As always, Mike the Mailman puts things in perspective.

"At Alabama, that was where I learned the words to 'Sweet Home Alabama,'" he said. "That was refreshing and that's how it should be. To me, I'd like for Penn State to win every game. That's irrelevant, there's always another game. Everyone's a winner."

Chapter 7: Upset for the Ages
Appalachian State at Michigan
September 1, 2007

When Sparky Woods left Appalachian in early 1989 to take the South Carolina job, Jerry Moore was hired as Appalachian's head coach. Moore had been fired as head coach at Texas Tech in 1985 after winning just a little more than 30 percent of his games in five years. He spent the next two seasons out of coaching before joining Ken Hatfield's staff at Arkansas. In seven years as a head coach, his record was 27-48-2. When Moore arrived in Boone, nearly 40 players had left the program for one reason or another. The starting quarterback and center went with Woods to Columbia. Despite that attrition, buoyed by a fabulous recruiting class, Moore went 9-3 in his first year at App in 1989. Two years later he won the first of his 10 Southern Conference championships. Because I was working in Birmingham and was so busy on weekends with our high school football show on Friday and coverage of Auburn and Alabama on Saturday, I didn't get to go to many App games then. They really became one of the nation's best I-AA teams during the 90s under Moore's leadership. Every season from 1990-99, App State spent at least one week in the I-AA poll. There were six trips to the playoffs and three Southern Conference Championships. There were some tremendous games between Appalachian and Marshall, Georgia Southern, and Furman. Fortunately, I got to see a few of those games on TV. App State had a run against Wake Forest in the late 90s where they won three of four games. The best team of the 90s was in 1995 when they finished the regular season 11-0. The dreams of a national championship were shattered in the second round when Stephen F. Austin came to Boone and upset the Mountaineers. There was frustration in not getting to the national championship game.

  I was enjoying my Georgia Tech season tickets. Not only were they playing exciting football, but I'd get to see some other interesting teams and players that came to town. Often, I would invite a friend who was a fan of the team Tech was playing to the game. I had a mini season ticket package for App, so I could get to a few games and would be able to get playoff tickets. My Georgia Tech season tickets enabled me to get road game tickets so that was how I was able to get the tickets for the game at Clemson in 2004 (Chapter 5). In 2006 I switched to club seats. They weren't that much more expensive, but I got a parking pass and two beers at each game. It was so easy getting in and out of Tech on game day. I didn't live very far from campus and didn't really have any interest in tailgating. If Tech had a 3:30 kickoff, which they did a lot, I could be at home and watch the first half of a game that kicked off at noon, drive to Tech, get parked, and be in my seat for kickoff. I could usually get home in time to see most of the first quarter of the 7:45 p.m. game on ESPN.

The main reason I kept the Tech tickets even though Appalachian had started winning national championships was that the Yellow Jackets were going to open the 2007 season in South Bend against the Notre Dame Fighting Irish. I was going to be able to get tickets and see Touchdown Jesus in person.

The Jackets had opened the 2006 season by hosting the Irish in a game ABC was showing at 8 p.m. The game was good, but the Irish won behind Brady Quinn and wide receiver Jeff Samardzija and the benefit of some questionable officiating. That was one of the high points of the Charlie Weiss era at Notre Dame. Mark Stackow was a buddy I worked with at The Weather Channel, who was also an Irish fan, and I asked if he wanted to go with me to the game in South Bend and he said sure. He had been up there for games several times before.

In early 2007 a game had opened up on Michigan's schedule and the team they got to replace them on the schedule was Appalachian State. Appalachian's success had created a problem. No one wanted to play them. A 1-A school didn't want to risk a loss to a 1-AA team and another 1-AA didn't want to get blown out.

"Back then FCS schedules were almost set up year to year," said Mike Flynn, Appalachian's SID at that time. "We had openings for three non-conference games early in 2007. We had a game against Lenoir-Rhyne scheduled but needed the others. We figured we would have a Division II team come in, but still needed two games. Back then Jay Sutton worked scheduling. I saw something in the news that Michigan had an opening and told him. He said, 'I'll call them right now.' Coach Moore was on board, and they were desperate too. They paid us $400,000. Because of that amount of money we got, we were able to give a guarantee that no other FCS school could give. We gave Northern Arizona a big number to get them here."

"Originally, we had a game scheduled with LSU that day," said AD Charlie Cobb. "But they ended up double booking that day, so they moved us back a year and we had the opening in 2007. We were trying to play six home games every year. If we had home games, we could create revenue. We scheduled the Lenoir-Rhyne game not knowing what would happen."

Thanks to those events, on September 1, 2007, the Mountaineers would play in Michigan Stadium, AKA, the Big House. I couldn't believe App State was playing Michigan, the Victors Valiant, the all-time winningest program in college football history, in the historic Big House, home to the biggest crowds in the sport. This was going to be the first time Michigan would play an FCS school (prior to the 2006 season the NCAA changed the name for 1-AA to the Football Championship Subdivision and I-A to the Football Bowl Subdivision). Kirk Herbstreit before the game on ESPN's *College GameDay* show would famously say there is no way Michigan should play a cupcake, FCS school like Appalachian.

"They had never played an FCS team and didn't have interest in playing FCS team, but they had to get a game," said Flynn. "It was February or March when that got done."

Many people thought the Wolverines scheduled the game with App State because the offense they ran was very similar to Oregon, who was coming to the Big House in week two, but it just worked out that way.

Pat Mills was a redshirt freshman offensive lineman in 2007 when he found out the game was scheduled.

"We were doing winter gym," Mills recalled. "Coach Moore would talk and said we would play Michigan at the Big House. It didn't seem like a big deal. We had played LSU [in 2005] and hung in there. It was Michigan, let's go. I don't remember any of us thinking, 'Oh my God, we have to play Michigan.'"

There was no way I could miss seeing App play that game, but it meant Stackow would get both of my tickets for the Notre Dame game (Spoiler alert: Tech got their revenge 35-3). Flynn's current position at Georgia Tech is Assistant Athletic Director for Media Relations.

"I get a lot of flak from people here because App State stole Tech's thunder that day!" Flynn said.

Stackow's day was ruined.

"That was going to be great," he said. "I met two of my brothers there. It was a new era of Notre Dame football. We were so pumped, and it's still got to be one of the worst losses."

Many of the App fans I know were very excited to make the trip to Ann Arbor.

"I was thinking we are going to get killed but I wanted to go," said Brian Hoagland, the former sports director of *The Appalachian*.

Jim Macholz is a 1991 graduate of Appalachian and was ecstatic with the news.

"We're going up there. No one knew we would win. We were going to have fun and see what happens."

Kirk Sherrill was a fraternity brother of Macholz. They had been attending games together since they were students and shared his enthusiasm for the trip.

"I was very excited. It was a must-go for me. Just being in the largest stadium and playing a big program was going to be great."

1983 App grad Jeff Owen knew he wanted to be a part of it.

"I had a friend who was a Michigan State grad and he said you have to go to a game in the Big House if you ever have a chance," said Owen. "It's one of those once-in-a-lifetime moments. I didn't think we would win, but I did put a bet on it."

Murray Griffin is a Georgia Tech graduate who was in Chicago for the Notre Dame game. His daughter had gone to Appalachian, and he had seen them play.

"I was telling people they are going to win. Everyone said I was crazy, but I knew they would give them a game."

After winning two consecutive national championships, Appalachian was brimming with confidence. They had a lot of returning starters, several of whom had played on the two previous championship teams. And of course, they had Armanti Edwards, the exciting quarterback who had a year of experience under his belt.

Edwards was from Greenwood, South Carolina. He was recruited by Clemson but not to play quarterback. He came to App and was not expected to play much as a freshman. Quality quarterback play is essential in the offense the Mountaineers were running.

Richie Williams was a junior quarterback for the 2004 team, the year Jerry Moore made the decision to switch to the spread formation. Richie excelled in the new offense, accumulating a school-record 3,393 yards of total offense. Wide receiver DaVon Fowlkes thrived as well. He led the nation in receiving with 103 catches for 1,618 yards and 14 touchdowns. Twice that year Williams and Fowlkes hooked up for 89-yard touchdown passes. Against Elon, Fowlkes set school records with 17 catches for 280 yards. It was only the third time an Appalachian player had more than 1,000 receiving yards in a season. Seven times Fowlkes had more than 148 receiving yards. Williams became the first Mountaineer player to throw for more than 3,000 yards in a season, finishing with 3,109. He had his most efficient game against Furman, completing 40 of his 45 passes, including 28 in a row. Williams set an NCAA FBS record for highest completion percentage during a game with a minimum of 40 passes attempted. Against Chattanooga, Williams set the school total offense record with 517 yards, 410 through the air.

But for all the flashy numbers the Mountaineers finished 2004 with a 6-5 record, Their fewest wins in 10 years. They were unbeaten in their six home games but were winless on the road. It was only the second time in 19 years App State would miss the playoffs in back-to-back seasons. Believe it or not, there was some dissatisfaction among the fan base about Coach Moore. The success he had was creating expectations and those expectations included not only making the playoffs but making a deep run. Heading into 2005, Jerry Moore had won exactly two-thirds of his games in his 16 years in Boone and had won more games than any other coach in school and Southern Conference history. He had given App State fans their only three Southern Conference Championships. But he had a new boss in first-year athletic director Charlie Cobb and how would Cobb put up with not making the playoffs?

"The first time I met him I told him, 'What I want to do is make you successful,'" said Cobb. "Before the Georgia Southern game that year [2005] I told him I wanted him back."

In 2005, Fowlkes had graduated, but Williams would be back and there was hope for the defense. They were unranked to start the season, but the only conference loss was at Furman. They played LSU at Tiger Stadium on November 5 and trailed 10-0 going into the fourth quarter but would give up two touchdowns in the quarter. They sealed a high playoff seed with two blowout wins to finish the regular season with an 8-3 record and number six national ranking. Williams had another great season, winning Southern Conference Offensive Player of the Year. The big difference in 2005 was that Williams didn't have to do it all himself. The Mountaineers had rushed for only 1,132 yards in 2004, their lowest total as a Division I program.

Kevin Richardson, a sophomore walk-on, was a versatile running back who ran for 1,433 yards with 19 touchdowns and also led the team with 52 catches and 588 yards. The team rushed for more than 90 yards a game in 2005 compared to 2004.

The playoffs started with two easy wins at home. That set up a showdown against long-time nemesis Furman for a trip to the national championship game in Chattanooga. For all the success Appalachian had enjoyed in football they had not only never won a national championship, but they had also never played for one. Before Moore came to Boone the Mountaineers advanced to the national semifinals in 1987, losing to conference rival Marshall at home. Moore made it to the semifinals in 2000 as a 13 seed but lost at Montana in overtime.

I feel like this was the most important game in Appalachian football history. I would have dedicated a chapter to it in this book if I had been there. I don't remember why I couldn't go but I watched it at home. Furman wasn't happy the game was being played in Boone because they had beaten us during the regular season. That year only four schools were seeded and despite Furman being ranked higher in the 1-AA poll, we had the number two national seed. Furman had defeated Nicholls State at home in round one and had to go on the road to beat Richmond in round two.

Furman led the series against Appalachian 21-11-3 going into that game. The regular season win by the Paladins ended the Mountaineers' first three-game winning streak in the series. Furman even led the series in Boone 8-7-2. Moore was 8-9 against Furman after the regular season loss. More than 15,000 people were able to make the trip to Boone that day. App was up 7-0 in the first quarter when Williams went down with an injury. On his first play off the bench, backup quarterback Trey Elder threw a 45-yard touchdown pass to Dexter Jackson to give App State a 14-0 lead. The Paladins battled back to take a 23-21 lead into halftime. The second half was a defensive battle. Midway through the third quarter Furman had a first and goal at the App 4. On third down, quarterback Ingle Martin slipped at the 1-yard line when it looked like he was going to run in for a touchdown. On the next play future NFL Pro Bowler Jerome Felton was stopped for a loss by Jason Hunter. It seemed to me that was the first time in four years Felton was held to a gain of less than three against the App defense. The Paladins held that two-point lead until Elder scored on a short run with just more than two minutes to play. Despite a penalty on the two-point conversion, Elder completed a pass to put the Mountaineers up 29-23. Could the defense hold? Would the Mountaineers finally get a chance to play for the trophy? Well, Martin had driven his team down to the 36-yard line with less than 30 seconds remaining. Martin was scrambling and looking down field for a receiver when Hunter hit him from behind, forcing a fumble. Omar Byron recovered, and the Mountaineers were headed to Chattanooga to play Northern Iowa. If App State hadn't won that game, I'm not sure any of the success the program has had since would have happened. Obviously, we wouldn't have won three national championships in a row and I'm not sure the program would have had the confidence to be able to win the close games it did the next few years. We had finally gotten over a big hump, making it to the national championship game.

It was a matchup between two of the best 1-AA programs that had never won the big one. My brother came to Atlanta and picked me up and we rode together to Chattanooga. We didn't really tailgate that afternoon but were bar hopping in the newly revitalized downtown and we walked to the stadium. There was so much excitement, but apprehension among the App fans. It was going to be doubtful that Richie Williams was going to be able to play because of the injury against Furman. The title game was the following Friday, so he had even less time to heal. Elder got the start but was ineffective. The Lions were in front 16-7 at halftime. That's when Moore made the decision to put Williams in. He was limping but was going to gut it out. Richardson scored his second touchdown of the game to pull the Mountaineers to within two. The overwhelming majority of the 20,236 fans in attendance were wearing black and gold and were hopeful the defense could pull off another big play. Despite Williams' gutty effort the offense just couldn't move the ball consistently. Then with less than 10 minutes left, it happened. Defensive end Marques Murrell stripped the ball from UNI quarterback Eric

Sanders. That man again, Hunter, picked up the ball and ran to the end zone to give the Mountaineers a lead they would hold on to and their first national championship. We had a long celebration after the game. It felt great to finally be number one at the end of the season.

Now back to Armanti Edwards. He was in the same class as Mills.

"When we came in as freshman we had tough conditioning tests," Mills said. "There's a lot of anxiety. We are all scared. Armanti has on a dirty T-shirt, takes off on a sprint, and smokes everyone. The seniors are telling him to slow down. He beat them all. We ran 30 100-yard sprints. He won them all and didn't say a word."

"I remember when they put him with the ones [first stringers]. I think he went four plays, and we scored every play and last one he had a 60-yard run."

It was assumed that Elder would take over as the starter for Williams like he had when Williams was injured in 2005. Elder was a former Mr. Football in the state of South Carolina at powerhouse Byrnes High School. He started the

2006 opener against N.C. State but didn't play very well and the Mountaineers lost. Edwards came in, but only for a few plays. The next week against James Madison, Edwards played a little more and Appalachian won the game. After the game, JMU Coach Mickey Matthews, old friends with Moore, told him he needed to play Edwards more. That just confirmed what Moore felt and Edwards got the start in week three against Mars Hill and had 252 yards of total offense. The next week he had his first 100-yard rushing game. The week after that he had his first 300-yard passing game completing 12 of 14 passes for 311 yards and didn't even play in the second half. He was truly settling into the offense. The Mountaineers were averaging more than 45 points in the four games he had started. After a close win over Wofford, the Mountaineers were headed to Statesboro, Georgia, and the annual clash against Georgia Southern. The week was known as "Hate Week" around the App State football complex. The Eagles had their six national championships and love to gloat about that. This year they were 3-3 and weren't ranked for the game against App for the first time since 1996, the last time the Mountaineers won in

Statesboro. Despite that, the Eagles played well, and the game was close. Edwards had one of his most famous plays, running over a Southern defender and knocking his helmet off as he scored a touchdown. The game went to overtime and Appalachian prevailed 27-20. The freshman had his most prolific game with 350 yards of total offense. That was the last time the Mountaineers were threatened the rest of the season. They had the number one ranking in FCS and cruised through the first three playoff games, all played at Kidd Brewer Stadium. The only team standing in the way of a second straight national championship was the third ranked University of Massachusetts. Again, the game was played at Finley Stadium in Chattanooga and there was another large throng of App fans in their black and gold. The atmosphere was so different from a year ago. While there was the nervous anticipation against UNI, we had Armanti, we had gotten over the hump last year and there was no way a team from New England was going to beat us. And they didn't. The Minutemen tied the score at 14 with less than five minutes left in the third quarter. People think the spread offense is a pass all the time offense, but not for the

Mountaineers. When they got the ball back, they had a 13-play touchdown drive that featured 12 runs. The next time they got the ball they ripped off a 14-play drive with only one pass again. Both drives were capped off with Kevin Richardson touchdowns. Richardson, the game's MVP, finished the game with four touchdowns and an NCAA record 30 on the season. Edwards again showed his fearlessness on the first play of the fourth quarter when the 155-pound Edwards collided with UMass safety James Ihedigbo. Edwards got up and was ready for the next play. Ihedigbo, who weighed more than 200 pounds and would go on to have a 10-year NFL career, stayed down on the field. That play to me tells you everything you need to know about Armanti Edwards.

"He could relax his body when he got hit like nobody I'd ever seen before," said Cobb, who had played football at N.C. State in the late 80s.

Richardson and Edwards each finished the season with more than 1,000 rushing yards, the first time App State had two players accomplish that milestone in the same season. Edwards passed for more than 2,000 yards and became the seventh

Division I player to pass for 2,000 yards and rush for 1,000 in a season. And he made the athletic academic honor roll to boot!

Expectations were high for the 2007 team and so was the anticipation of playing Michigan in the opener.

"We had the leaders," said Mills. "The confidence of that group. We never thought about it as something we couldn't do. Doesn't matter who they trot out there, we prepare, we play our game, play to our maximum potential."

Fox Sports South, a cable network based in Atlanta that carried Southern Conference games during the season, had the foresight to produce a special on Appalachian's preparations for Michigan.

"They were there all month for the fall camp," Flynn said. "Now you see those things all the time but then it was rare to have all that behind-the-scenes stuff. Coach Moore embraced it. That was a veteran team. They weren't distracted by anything like that."

"The coaches preached to us, 'what are we willing to do to be successful?'" said Mills. "What would you give up? It was never a focus on who we were playing. That was the culture day after day after day."

There were a lot of experienced veterans who had two national championships. That success had improved the quality of players that were coming to play at App. Mills said everyone was trying to prove themselves on the practice field.

"You had young guys like Armanti, [Brian] Quick, guys you knew would be good and that picked up everyone. We wanted to get out and do well. We always thought about these games as opportunity games to show our stuff. Go prove you belong. We were excited about the opportunity to show. Play our game, see what happens."

Flynn felt like it was a good camp.

"There was a quiet confidence leading up to it. I don't know that anyone thought we would win, but we may shock them and give them a game for a little while. No one was saying it out loud, but you felt it. When you are around a team long enough you can get a feel. They think they have a shot and there was that feeling with the coaches and players."

"I just remember the way we ran that entire camp," said Mills. "I don't think we took a day off. In other years, that was a little much. I'm not sure if it was to keep us from getting cocky after winning the two national championships. During two-a-days, we would go live, two and a half hours in the morning with shells, and same in pads in the afternoon."

When I worked at The Weather Channel, it was always tricky making plans for early season games because that's Labor Day weekend, right in the heart of hurricane season. I could ask for time off, but if there was a tropical system that we were going to be covering, I knew the off time would be rescinded and I would be at work. With that in mind, I booked an early afternoon flight to Detroit the Friday before the game and the first flight out on Sunday morning. That was the first time I had flown to an Appalachian game. A guy wearing an App shirt was sitting behind me and we started talking. His name was Brock Long and was the head of the Emergency Management office in Alabama. A guy I had worked with in Birmingham was the PR guy for that office and we talked about that. He is much younger than me, but we were in the same fraternity. After we landed, we walked into the bathroom together and a pilot from Northwest Airlines was in there and saw our Appalachian shirts and asked if we were up for the game.

"I've been a Michigan fan and season ticket holder for 15 years, but your offense scares the daylights out of me," he said. "We have always had a tough time with those types of offenses."

I responded by telling him, "I'll be very pleased if we can get a couple of touchdowns. We are so excited to be able to play in the Big House and it was quite an honor, and I wouldn't have missed it."

Long was the FEMA Administrator during the Trump Administration.

I had stayed at a hotel near the airport but had a rental car. I had hoped to drive to Detroit and see the city some, but as I headed toward town, the late afternoon traffic was picking up and I didn't want to get stuck in a traffic jam, so I headed back to my hotel. It was an early night for me because the game was kicking off at noon.

Meanwhile, the players had their walkthrough at Michigan Stadium.

"While we were having our walkthrough [Michigan running back] Mike Hart ate a whole pizza sitting on a stationary bike," said team video coordinator Jake Stroot. "They weren't taking us seriously at all."

Pat Mills' parents, Dean and Gail, both Appalachian graduates, had made the trip, but didn't think they would have the chance to talk to Pat until after the game. But he called them that evening.

"We had a ritual when Pat played high school," said Dean. "I would ask him how he felt about the game. When he would tell me they had a sloppy week of practice, they would have a close game. He was usually right on about that. After they had their walk through, he called us and we chatted and talked about the walk through, I said 'It's a big stadium.' He said, 'it's just a football field.' Before he hung up, he said, 'I've got a good feeling about tomorrow.' I told my wife. 'He thinks they can beat Michigan!' She said, 'He said that?' I told her, 'He didn't say that, but said he feels good about tomorrow.'"

"I think I told him we were going to win," said Pat. "We felt good. We had that Friday night player meeting. I could tell the way we traveled. We were almost breathing as one entity. It was quiet on the bus. We were locked in. We were ready. You are at the Friday night meal, all you hear was forks and knives clinking, nothing else."

Before the pregame player meeting the team would watch a motivational video put together by Stroot and his video team. He had started working for the athletic department while he was a student.

"When [strength coach] Jeff Dillman came back from LSU in 2006, he brought some of their motivational ideas. That was the first year me doing it, and I ended up sleeping at the office a lot."

He got a lot of ideas for things from movies: fight scenes, Braveheart, war movies.

"Before Michigan, Tyler Adams came up with the idea to use the speech from *We Are Marshall*," said Stroot. "His speech at the monument."

"They are bigger, stronger, faster and on paper, better. And they know it too. They don't know your heart. I know it. When you take the field, you have to lay down your heart today."

In the remake of the movie *The Longest Yard*, Adam Sandler reprised the Burt Reynolds role of Paul Crewe, the prisoner who was the former quarterback and wanted to play the game against the guards. He was explaining to the warden the idea of a tune up game: "In college we would start every season against Appalachian State or some slack Division II team and kick the living shit out of them. Get our confidence up."

"That really resonated with the players," said Stroot. "You could tell watching their reaction if the video was good or not."

"It was awesome," remembers Mills. "The coaches and Jake would leave after that. Then the real magic started with the players." Mills laughed as he said that.

Saturday morning, I got up and went downstairs to have breakfast at the hotel, several members of the App Band were there, already in uniform. I thought that was a great sign because the band usually didn't travel to road games. I asked about that, and they said someone had paid for their trip. Half were staying at my hotel and the rest were at another nearby hotel. After I ate, I bought some beer for the tailgate and headed to Ann Arbor. It was about 25 miles from my hotel to the stadium, but I was worried about traffic. It turned out not to be a problem at all. When I got to the stadium, it was very surprising. It wasn't that much above the ground. I was expecting this huge edifice that you could see for miles, but it wasn't the case. Across the street from the stadium is the university golf course is that where a lot of people park and tailgate for football games. If you wanted to park close to the stadium it was $40 and farther back was $30. I figured over the course of the season, the Michigan athletic department probably made as much on parking on that golf course as Appalachian's entire football budget. I found my group and parked. There were about a dozen of us who had made the trip, and several other groups of Mountaineers were sprinkled around the course. It was a lovely day. Warm and not a cloud in the sky.

I realized I had some catching up to do when it came to tailgating.

"We stayed at a hotel close by," said Hoagland. "We got to the tailgate at 6 a.m. as soon as it opened. Parked on the golf course. Cracking beers at 6 a.m. I remember talking to Michigan fans before the game, asked me where it was, and I explained to them, it's in Boone, North Carolina."

Brian Metcalf and Mike Wolfe, like Sherrill and Macholz, are guys that I tailgate with in Boone. All but Metcalf live in Charlotte, and they came along with some other friends. Another friend of theirs was in Detroit for business and had rented a van to get around in. Macholz wasn't sure he was going to be able to make the trip.

"My wife, Betsey, was going to go, but then as it got closer, we were having Mazy, our first daughter," said Macholz. "It got closer and closer. She had the baby seven days before the game. We had plane tickets, but we got home two days before we were going to leave and I asked Betsey, 'What are your thoughts?' She said, 'Our parents are here, you can go.'"

There was a pool going among those guys as to whether Macholz would make it or not.

"We went out the night before and the Michigan people were asking 'Who are you? What are you doing here?'" recalled Macholz. "They weren't rude, just wondering. We had the van and parked on the golf course. I remember Kirk telling everyone I was father of the year, because I had just had a baby."

"Tailgating on the golf course was neat," said Wolfe. "Everyone was nice and welcoming. They were very accommodating fans."

Appalachian's Alumni Association usually hosts a tailgate before big road games and I had signed up for that, so I went in there and ate something else and saw Hoagland and a few other friends. Everyone was discussing what would happen.

When we walked into the stadium, the field was way down below ground level. You could tell seats were added up as part of an expansion. All the first-time visitors to the Big House were surprised how it was down instead of up.

What was fascinating was the stadium was not as big walking in as you would think," said Sherrill. "You walk in, and most seats were down. The game seemed so distant at the time. But it seemed like there wasn't a bad seat."

Sherrill and I sat next to each other in the very last row of the stadium. The rest of the group was a few rows below us. It appeared there were a few thousand App fans there and we were all along the back few rows in the south end zone. I figured that's where they stuck us just because we were a smaller, non-conference team. But when I watched a Michigan game later in the season against a Big Ten team, and I saw the fans of that team were in the same spot we were. I thought that was unusual because in the SEC they give their opponent's fans a lot of tickets and some were even in the lower levels. That's where we sat when we went to Auburn in 1999."

Most of the fans that asked us about our school pronounced it App-a-LAY-chin. We [App State fans] hate that. The name of the school is pronounced App-a-LATCH-in, like most people in the Carolinas pronounce the mountain range. Whenever an official would say App-a-LAY-chin when announcing a penalty, he would get lustily booed by the Mountaineer contingent. At road games, when the PA announcer would say App-a-LAY-chin, he, too would be lustily booed. Up in the press box, Flynn was making sure that didn't happen today.

"That was a constant for me the 13 years I worked there," he said. "We would have it in the game notes. It's pretty standard procedure that a few hours before kickoff, you go and talk directly with the other school's radio crew and would go over pronunciation of players' names and I'd always throw in the App-a-LATCH-in. I'd also mention that to the PA announcer."

Michael Ladd was a 1978 graduate of Appalachian and spent a lot of time in Michigan working in the automotive industry. He took his wife, Bonnie, to the game so he could show her around a lot of the places where he worked. They stayed at a hotel near the stadium and the hotel had a van to drop fans off right at the stadium. They missed out on the tailgating. Ladd didn't get his tickets through Appalachian, so he sat on about the 40-yard line about 50 rows up.

"Obviously, sitting there we were surrounded by Michigan fans," said Ladd. "One of the guys sitting behind me wanted to bet. I told him, 'I don't think we'll win but I guarantee we'll score 25 points.' He couldn't believe I thought we would score 25 points on a Big Ten defense. We bet $50."

One of the iconic entrances in college football is Michigan running out of the locker room and the players jump up and touch the M Club banner as the fight song plays. It was something I definitely wanted to see, and it was something to hear the band playing the Michigan fight song and the crowd going crazy.

Meanwhile, in Bristol, Connecticut, at the ESPN Headquarters, Rece Davis, Lou Holtz, and Mark May were settling in for a day of watching all the top games in the country. The three were the hosts of *College Football Final* that aired after all the games on the network had ended. Also, they would do halftime reports, scoreboard shows in between games, and break in with news from games around the country.

On the field, Michigan won the toss and took the ball straight down the field to score in six plays. App State got the kickoff and was faced with a third and 6 from their 32-yard line. Edwards dropped back to pass and hit Dexter Jackson on a short post pattern. Jackson, a track star, outran the Michigan defense for the touchdown and we were tied 7-7. I had a camera with me and had taken a picture as Jackson approached the goal line and it just so came out that it was right as he crossed the goal line. Another of my favorite Armanti moments came after I got home and looked at the pictures on my computer and I saw Edwards was at the 15-yard line when Jackson crossed the goal line. So, Edwards, too, outran the Michigan defense. It was awesome to hear the Appalachian fight song in the Big House.

"Dexter's touchdown was the biggest play," said Cobb. "We showed them our speed and it relaxed our guys."

Pat Mills said that play gave the Mountaineers confidence.

"I had been watching so much tape on their defense, and you could see they were big, but not fast. That play by Dexter validated what we thought; we could beat them. That was the catalyst."

The Wolverines weren't impressed and scored another touchdown to take a 14-7 lead into the second quarter. The Mountaineers exploded for three touchdowns in the quarter to go in front 28-14. Edwards hit senior receiver Hans Batichon for a short touchdown pass, Jackson again for 20 yards and took one in himself from eight yards out. Michigan rallied to kick a short field goal as the first half ended. Edwards finished seven for seven passing for 129 yards and another 41 yards on the ground. I got a call at halftime from Jon Nese, a friend who was on the faculty at Penn State. They were also playing a game that kicked off at noon against Florida International. He told me every time they announced the score of our game at Beaver Stadium, the place was erupting. He asked me what was happening, and I told him we were just playing our game. It wasn't anything special we were doing, and Michigan wasn't turning the ball over or really helping us. The defense had settled down after the two touchdowns and were stopping the Michigan offense. The Michigan offensive line was huge, as you would expect, and featured Jake Long at tackle, who would be the number one pick in the NFL draft the following spring. Chad

Henne was the quarterback, who would finish the season as Michigan's career leader in passing yards and touchdowns. Throughout the quarter, I kept taking pictures of the scoreboard showing Appalachian was tied with Michigan, then leading late into the second quarter.

Among my friends in the stands, we couldn't believe what we were seeing. App State had the lead at the Big House. Could we hold on for 30 more minutes?

"I was thrilled with the first half," said Sherrill. "Talking to the Michigan fans at half time, they said, 'We are just biding our time. We will take over.'"

Macholz recalled, "We got some people yelling at us at halftime. Pregame, they were nice, at halftime they weren't so nice!"

Wolfe didn't have much confidence we'd leave with the win.

"Nothing really changed for me," he said. "No way we would win. I kept taking pictures of the scoreboard throughout the game because we had the lead. I kept taking picture after picture. I have the picture of the final score hanging in my office. It was like the players weren't intimidated at all, which was much different from me. It looked like they were there to win. We had enough athletes to make plays and we were doing that."

"It was surreal the way it started," Ladd said. "At the half, I felt we had a good chance. Hart was banged up and that played to our favor."

As we would later see on the Fox Sports show, Coach Moore was calm in the locker room, telling the team they were about to get the best shot Michigan had. The shot they would give to Ohio State, to Notre Dame, to Penn State, and the many other teams that had ventured into Michigan Stadium and lost. The Wolverines didn't become the winningest college football program by lying down when they were behind at halftime.

"He always said that," said Pat Mills. "You are about to get their best shot. It wasn't a rah-rah deal. Most coaches not as experienced as coach Moore would act like they were just happy to be there. We are supposed to be there."

In the press box Flynn wasn't surprised, but things were starting to get busy for him.

"When we got out front, I don't want to say we knew we were going to be there, but I wasn't falling over with shock," he said. "In was in the second quarter when my phone started buzzing. Family and media guys. People were starting to reach out and say, 'If you keep this up, I'm going to want an interview.' And I started to jot all those down."

In Bristol, one of the eight monitors Davis and his team used to keep up with all the games around the country was not moving from the Big Ten Network.

"Mark, Lou, and I were completely locked in," said Davis. "It looked like one of those games, the giant gets caught sleepwalking but eventually wakes up."

Appalachian got the second half kickoff and Coco Hillary had a nice return and it looked like the Mountaineers would be able to build on the lead. But after the perfect first half, Edwards' second pass of the half was intercepted. However, despite the good field position, the App D held Michigan to a field goal and the score was now 28-20. Needing a good drive to run some clock, Appalachian's offense looked like it did in the first half. Facing a third and 10 at the Michigan

41, Edwards hit Hillary for 27 yards to the 14. On third down true freshman wide receiver Brian Quick was wide open in the end zone but couldn't hold on to Edwards' pass and the Mountaineers would have to settle for a field goal. The Apps now led 31-20 halfway through the third quarter. The App fans in the stadium started the popular Kidd Brewer Stadium "App" "State" chant. The west side of the stadium yells, "App!" and the east side replies, "State!" In a road game situation, in the tailgate lot or leaving the stadium, people usually take part in the chant based on were they sit at Kidd Brewer Stadium.

Michigan was tackled at their own 10 on the kickoff return and after a short pass on first down, the maize and blue crowd was beginning to express their displeasure. Believe it or not, people were leaving the game. Sitting in row 92 (the last one) of the stadium, I could turn around and see people leaving. I took a picture of them.

Mike Hart, their All-American running back, had missed significant time because of injury. The Big Ten network telecast kept showing him riding a stationary bike on the sideline. With 6:56 remaining in the third, Hart's replacement, Brandon

Minor, fumbled and senior linebacker Pierre Banks, who had been outstanding all game, recovered for App State. However, the offense couldn't get a first down and Julian Rauch's 46-yard field goal attempt hit the upright.

Appalachian's defense was back on the field and held the Wolverines to another three and out. On first down following the Michigan punt, running back Kevin Richardson broke loose for a 15-yard run and the Apps seemed to have some momentum as the third quarter wound down. However, Edwards fumbled while scrambling and Michigan recovered at the Mountaineers 31-yard line. Hart re-entered the game and scored on a 6-yard run with 25 seconds remaining in the third quarter. Michigan lined up to go for two on the conversion, but Henne fumbled the snap and defensive back Leonard Love smothered him. The Apps were holding on at 31-26. Could the offense run some clock?

Back at ESPN, one of the *College Football Final* crew was beginning to believe in the Mountaineers. Davis is a life-long college football fan who grew up in Alabama. Holtz is a Hall of Fame coach and May was an All-American at Pitt and one of the "Hogs" for the Super Bowl Champion Washington Redskins.

"Lou more than anyone, can feel a game," said Davis. He was the first among the three of us to say that App was going to win. He said Appalachian looks like a better team. He gave us that quote he likes to use, 'You don't have to be the best team in the nation, just the best team in the stadium that day.'"

"Coach Moore loved that quote," said Flynn. "It was on the hallway leading from the locker room to the field. It was just behind the 'Today I Give My All For Appalachian State' saying at the door. He would especially use that in the playoffs when it was important just to win. 'We just need to be the best team in the stadium today' he would remind the team."

This game was the first game televised by the Big Ten network. They had just signed on the air that morning. It didn't have a wide distribution on cable networks, even in the Midwest. A lot of the guys I worked with at The Weather Channel were from the Midwest and several were graduates of Big Ten schools. Most of them were also big NFL fans and had Direct TV satellite service, primarily so they could see their NFL team play. One of them, Jon Erdman, was from Wisconsin and Friday, before I left, I asked him to record the game for me. He said he would. If the game wasn't great, you just record over it. I also like to see on TV any questionable plays from the game.

One of the anchors of the show I produced, Marshall Seese, grew up in Chicago and graduated from the University of Illinois. His son, Marshall Junior, had grown up in Atlanta and got his undergraduate degree at Georgia, but got a law degree from Michigan. Marshall had probably never heard of Appalachian State until he met me. Once it looked like it was going to be a game Marshall started recording it for me on DVDs. He started midway through the first quarter and gave me the DVDs on Monday at work.

In the press box, Flynn was communicating with his assistant who was back in Boone. There weren't many bars in Boone in 2007. There were a few that had satellite TV and they were getting popular as the cable company in Boone didn't carry the Big Ten Network and a bar was the only place to watch the game.

"That was the last year we only traveled one person from our office for a football game," said Flynn. "My assistant was back in Boone, and we were texting, if we pull this off, here's what's going on. He told me that the bars were starting to get packed. The fire department was going around telling the bars, they couldn't let anyone else in there."

Flynn thought that was an interesting note and texted that to Charrisa Thompson, the sideline reporter for the game. She relayed the information to the announcers in the booth, Thom Brennaman and Charles Davis. They mentioned it on the air.

As the game entered the fourth quarter and we held a narrow lead, it was deja vu for many App fans. So often, like Ed Boyd mentioned about the Wake Forest game (Chapter 1), we played hard, but we just didn't have the depth to battle for four quarters.

"Auburn was the one that really depressed me," said Sherrill.

He was referring to the 1999 game. Auburn was supposed to play Florida State to open the season and that was going to be Bobby Bowden, the Florida State coach, facing off against his son, Terry, the head coach at Auburn. However, Terry Bowden resigned during the 1998 season and Auburn bought the game out, knowing Bobby was likely going to take things out on the school that got rid of his son and run up the score. With the late opening on the schedule, Appalachian agreed to go to Auburn in Tommy Tuberville's first game as Auburn's coach. The game was Saturday night of the opening week of the season. Hunter, my brother, joined Wolfe, Sherrill, Macholz, and several other of their fraternity brothers in renting an RV and going to Auburn in it. The Friday night before the game was my last day at WXIA. I drove down and tailgated with those guys on Saturday afternoon. During the game, we dominated, but missed several kicks and the score was tied at 15 with less than two minutes to go. App State had a fourth and a little more than a yard at midfield and Coach Moore decided to punt it. Probably not his best decision, although if we didn't obviously make the first down on a big run or pass, there was no way the SEC refs were going to give us a good spot. Auburn took the punt, went 77 yards in just more than a minute and won the game with a Ben Leard 33-yard pass to Ronny Daniels. That was one of my toughest losses to take, especially given my history at Auburn.

"I was thinking we had played a good game, but here we go again," said Sherrill. "But we kept playing App state style football. We were doing whatever it took. Some of the best players we ever had were on that team."

Now may be a good time to remind everyone about the main difference between FBS and FCS. It's primarily the number of scholarship players. FBS teams have 85 players on scholarship; FCS schools have 63. I remember thinking we didn't sub a lot on defense. I know the four DBs didn't take any plays off. Linebacker Cam Speer subbed a few plays with true freshman DJ Smith, and we subbed a few players on the defensive line. Flynn has heard the stories Coach Moore says we played 14 guys on defensive during the game.

"I can't confirm that," he said. "We rotated at least six or eight guys on the defensive line."

"Could we hold on?" wondered Macholz. "You knew they will impose their will. The crowd got so loud when they needed to. Just like their ability to flip the switch and they were coming back."

On the second play of the fourth quarter Appalachian was guilty of delay of game, setting up a third and 10. Edwards threw behind an open Hillary and the Mountaineers would have to punt. Appalachian committed a face mask penalty on the punt and that gave the Wolverines their best field position of the day. But the Mountaineer defense made another huge play. A blitz from Banks forced Henne to throw across his body, and Love intercepted it. After the return, the Apps had the ball at the 41. But this time, Michigan's defense rose up and forced the Mountaineers into a three and out.

Michigan had the ball at their own 21 still trailing by 5. Hart was better and Coach Lloyd Carr decided it was time to flex the Michigan muscle with an offensive line that vastly outweighed their counterparts from North Carolina. Hart ran for 5, then 16 yards. Minor came in and gained 2, then Hart gained 6. An incomplete pass gave Michigan a third and 4. Henne hit receiver Greg Matthews for 5 to convert the first down. But with 7:08 remaining Michigan had a fourth and 5 and

Henne couldn't complete the pass. But all the magic the Appalachian offense had earlier disappeared. It was another three and out and with just under five minutes remaining Michigan had the ball at their own 46. At this point in the second half, the Mountaineers had only gained 74 yards in the half. All the three and outs weren't giving the defense much time to catch their breath either.

The Appalachian offense was dealing with something no one away from the Mountaineer bench knew about.

"Armanti was hurt and hurt badly," said Flynn. "He was hurt in scrimmage before that game and hurt during the game. For him to do what he did as hurt as he was so special."

In fact, Armanti's injured shoulder would keep him out of the next two games for the Mountaineers.

On first down, Mike Hart showed why he was fourth in the Heisman voting the year before. He broke a number of tackles through the App defense and took it to the house, finally giving the Wolverines the lead and seemingly making everything right in the world.

"That run he made to put them ahead was a great run," said Flynn. "He was a really good player. We didn't have an answer for him all day."

If Hart had been totally healthy, he may have stayed in the game for the two-point conversion, but Minor came in and slipped so the conversion was no good. And with four and a half minutes to go, it was Michigan 32, Appalachian 31. The reality had set in for the fans in black and gold.

"All right, there it is, fun while it lasted," lamented Wolfe. "You knew that was that. I didn't expect us to come back from that."

For the first time since early in the second quarter, the crowd finally had something to cheer about. And that place was loud. Attendance was announced at 109,218, still the largest crowd the Mountaineers have ever played in front of. For Michigan, they had had crowds at the Big House larger than 100,000 every game since "only" 93,857 showed up for a Michigan blowout win over Indiana in October of 1975. Two weeks later, 102,415 showed up to see a win over Purdue and the Big House hasn't had fewer than 100,000 people at a game since then. For another measure to show the disparity between the two programs, Appalachian had never drawn more than 100,000 fans to home games for the entire season until 1986 and '87 and that was a result of having extra home games because of the playoffs. It wasn't until 2005 more than 100,000 fans regularly came to Kidd Brewer Stadium for an entire season. Now it's commonplace and I'll get into that a little later.

On first down Armanti threw his second interception of the day and that totally seemed to erase any doubt that the valiant effort of the Mountaineers would go for naught. 4:25 remained in the game and Michigan had first down at the App State 43. Four runs had Michigan at the 25 with a third and 5. A delay of game penalty backed them up 5 yards. After a pass gained only 4 yards, Jerry Moore called the Mountaineer's last time out. Carr sent Jason Gingell out to attempt a 43-yard field goal. Freshman receiver Brian Quick, a 6'5" high school basketball player who dropped a touchdown pass earlier in the game, blocked the field goal. There was still a chance.

Wolfe said, "If Quick didn't block that kick, I don't know. Leading and finally falling behind. They played like they expected to win. They didn't seem to get rattled at all."

Mills confirmed that was the case.

"We were never rattled," he said. "There could be three minutes left and down three touchdowns, we felt we would win. We are not going to lose this game. With that kind of team, something good is going to happen. We don't know what, but it will. It wasn't just the talent. It was the culture and the mindset; we just knew we were going to win."

It was the Mountaineers ball at their own 27 with 1:37 to play and no time outs. After hitting all seven of his passes in the first half, Edwards was six of 12 for only 43 yards and two interceptions in the second half. But they had the ball, and it was time to make history. Edwards ran for 18 yards on the first play. The next play was a lateral to Hillary. He was going to try and pass but was tackled for a 4-yard loss. One of the unheralded plays of the game came next. Edwards hit receiver TJ Corman near the sideline. Corman looked like he was going to step out of bounds and as the Michigan defender relaxed, he cut inside and gained 20 yards. Edwards then hit Batichon for 7 and got a first down on a short pass to Jackson. There were 50 seconds remaining and App State was on the Michigan 30, right about the limit for kicker Julian Rauch's range. Remember he had missed from 46 earlier in the game. The 109,000 or so in maize and blue had gotten quiet again and the folks in black and gold had their swagger back. We knew what Armanti could do and we had seen these guys pull out plenty of big wins the last two years.

"I think conditioning was a big part of that game," said Wolfe.

"They didn't have Armanti," said Stroot.

Armanti dropped back to pass and was bottled up. He rolled to his left (he's a lefty) and saw Hillary break into the clear. He threw across his body to the right, but the pass was high. Hillary had to stop and jump about as high as he could to make the catch at the 22-yard line. He turned, saw he had some space and made a great run down to the 5-yard line. Michigan called a time out to settle their defense. The App fans were going crazy again. I asked Sherrill what we should do. I knew we needed to kick now, even though there were 30 seconds remaining. If we didn't score on that play and with no timeouts, I wasn't sure the officials would try very hard to get the ball spotted to get off the field goal attempt. Penn State lost a game a few years before that when that happened to them and if the officials screwed Joe Paterno, they would surely not try very hard for App State. Some of the coaches were pleading with Moore to run one more play.

Ladd agreed. "I thought we could have run one more play. I was worried we were leaving time on the clock."

A Michigan fan who had been sitting next to Sherrill and I got up and shook our hands and said, "I don't know how this game is going to turn out, but you guys played a helluva game."

He then walked out of the stadium. Moore sent Rauch out for the 24-yard field goal.

"I think you take the score," said Wolfe.

The kick was a low, line drive but was good, and the Mountaineers had the lead again. Surely, we couldn't lose now, could we?

"After we took the lead I was still skeptical," said Sherrill.

"It was the best I had felt all game," said Wolfe.

Rauch's kickoff didn't go very far, and Michigan returned it to the 34-yard line with 21 seconds remaining. On first down, Henne overthrew a receiver on a deep ball. After that incompletion he was 18 of 36 for 187 yards, one touchdown, and an interception. On second down he went deep again. Receiver Mario Manningham was well covered by senior cornerback Justin Woazeah, but he caught the ball at the 20-yard line, and he was tackled immediately. An official threw a flag. There were six seconds left.

"After the big pass that was it, here we go again," said Sherrill. "Oh well. All they need is a field goal now."

Wolfe said, "Manningham pushed off. I thought we were done. Maybe he would miss it."

"We were celebrating," said Macholz. "I just remember, he pushed off, that's so home cooking."

"The fourth quarter was such an emotional roller coaster," said Ladd. "But I thought the game was over then. We hung with them and gave them a game, but it was over."

It turned out the flag was a pass interference on Woazeah. The penalty was declined, so Gingell would get another field goal attempt and this one would end the game. I had my camera out and was focused on the holder. It was at the opposite end of the field, so even zoomed in all the way, you could see plenty of things. We were screaming, not that it would do any good, but maybe it did. Corey Lynch broke through a seam in the Michigan line and blocked the kick. I got a great shot of it from my camera. The ball bounced up, and Lynch grabbed it with one hand and began to head for the goal line. He ran about 50 yards before he started to cramp up and Gingell tackled him. It didn't matter, time had expired, and the Mountaineers, as App State play-by-play announcer David Jackson declared on air, "... HAVE JUST BEATEN THE MICHIGAN WOLVERINES!!!!" Pandemonium ensued in the Appalachian section.

"Words can't describe it," said Sherrill. "It was unbelievable exhilaration, just hyper excited."

The team had run across the field and piled on top of Lynch, who was lying on the sideline.

"When Manningham caught that pass, I was at the end where Rouch had kicked the field goal," said Stroot. "I had to sprint to the other side after that pass. I had a side view of the block and then I had to sprint to the dogpile on Corey."

"They were lined up to kick," said Macholz. "Did I think we would block it? No. I thought we were done. We gave it a great effort, but I just thought we had missed a great opportunity."

"Not only was it the greatest game I've ever seen but just the way we won," said Hoagland. "We had it won, then we had lost, and we won. Lynch came through that gap and blocked it. We went crazy, the stadium was silent."

"I was sitting at the desk," said Davis. "We were doing something for postgame or updates. When Michigan lined up for the field goal and you had the sense they were going to pull it out and there was the block and the return, and we all went crazy. Not because anyone had anything against Michigan, just the unlikelihood of Appalachian State going into the Big House and beating Michigan. I have the best job hosting *College GameDay* now, but that was great. To be in the middle of it and delivering it to everyone was great. You were the conduit."

Sherrill and I high-fived with each other and everyone around us.

"I never thought we would win," said Brian Metcalf. "I wanted to see Ann Arbor, I wanted to see 100,000 people. Even though we had played teams close never thought it would come to that. When you think of the scholarship difference, it's even more incredible."

"I remember how loud it went to quiet so fast," said Wolfe.

"I can't even tell you the amount of pandemonium everyone was feeling," said Macholz. "I remember looking at one App fan and he had his hands on his knees. He was so happy and crying so much it filled up his sunglasses!"

"They weren't intimidated," remembers Cobb. "People think it was a bad Michigan team. It wasn't. We made plays and weathered the storm."

I asked Ladd what the guy he made the bet with said.

"I got my $50 and he congratulated me," said Ladd. "When we blocked the kick, he had his head buried in the knees. I didn't say anything to him."

Hoagland still remembers the emotional swings.

"The up and down of that game. The range of emotions from elation to bitter disappointment to elation. We won on a blocked kick and that was a miracle."

It was the first time a ranked FBS team had lost to an FCS team. The Wolverines were ranked number five. Michigan was also the winningest program in the history of the sport.

"It was all about trust, respect, sacrifice, and it was all put together for a cause," said Pat Mills.

After graduating he coached college football until 2018 and now works in recruiting for IT companies.

"If I could take the mentality of those App football teams and put it with my company, we would be a billion-dollar company."

I was taking a lot of pictures and was sure to get one of the scoreboard with the final score. I had an idea to go down to the field and get some pictures of me with the scoreboard behind me, so I climbed down all 92 rows of Michigan Stadium to get to the field. Most of the Michigan fans had left by then. I got someone to take several different pictures of me. One of them, I remembered to take my sunglasses off and I was signaling number one. I wanted to use one of those pictures in some form for a Christmas card that year. I had a great picture and on the inside of the card said, "I hope there are no upsets for you and your family in 2008." It was very well received. I was actually surprised Michigan left the scoreboard on as long as they did. I took a picture of the guys still up in the same spot of the stadium and headed back up there.

On the field, the work was just starting for Mike Flynn. Flynn was on the App sideline for the last several minutes of the game. Regardless of the outcome, TV was probably going to want to do some interviews and he needed to be there to get them what they needed. He dealt with more than professional responsibilities.

"My mom was in Columbus, Ohio, at that time," he said. "She didn't have Big Ten network and was calling me every five minutes to get an update. I love my mom, but I had to tell her, 'Mom, I'm trying to work!' She called right when we made the field goal. I told her, 'We just went ahead. Assume we won unless you hear different.' Then she calls again. They are lining up to kick the field goal to beat us. 'Oh my God, we blocked it! I've got to go.' There's a picture of the sideline as everyone is starting to run on the field and you can see I have the phone to my ear, and I was talking to her."

His first responsibility was to get Moore to Thompson for the post-game interview.

"When Coach did his interview, he didn't take his headset off. That's on me. I remember thinking I did such a horrible job, and I was feeling bad."

"I commend the Michigan folks for how gracious they were," said Cobb, now AD at Georgia State University. "They let us celebrate the moment. We were there in the locker room longer than we needed to be. We won at Tennessee [in 2019] and they couldn't get us out of there fast enough. We get on the bus. [University Chancellor] Dr. [Ken] Peacock is there with his wife Rosanne, and he can't get enough. 'It's the greatest day in my life!' he says. His wife looks at him and says, 'What about our wedding or the day our kids were born?' He thinks for a minute and says, 'This is the greatest day of my life!'"

While Stroot was happy with the win, he was mad about the way the Michigan folks acted toward him.

"They were very condescending. 'That's cute; we're glad you showed up.' It was surreal. I shot all the celebration, the locker room stuff. Getting all that video on the pile. But I was still mad. I was the first person on the bus ready to leave."

We had finally gotten back to the golf course and our cars. Everyone's phone had gone crazy with voicemails. We were just beginning to realize what a huge story this was becoming. Jon Nese had called me back from State College and said their game had ended before ours and on the big screen in the stadium and all the TVs in the concourses were switched to our game on the Big Ten network and everyone was glued to the monitors.

I had gotten notes from Stackow from Notre Dame. He has been a Notre Dame fan all his life.

"It was amazing the cheers when they announced the App-Michigan score," said Stackow. "There was such a reaction. I hadn't realized how much Notre Dame fans hated Michigan and how invested they were in them losing. The buzz in the stadium was the App game." (I don't think he intended that pun.)

Murray Griffin, the Tech fan who had confidence in the Mountaineers, was hearing it from his buddies.

"After the game, everyone said 'how did you know, how did you know?'" said Griffin. "I'd seen App play and knew they could play with anyone."

One of the companies Ladd did a lot of work with was run by an Ohio State grad who was at their game that morning against Youngstown State.

"He called me. You could hear in the background the Ohio State fans chanting 'App State!'" Ladd said.

Most of the Michigan fans congratulated us on the win and were nice.

"Some Michigan fans were excited," said Owen, recalling that fans told him, "'Thanks. We've been trying to get rid of Lloyd Carr for years!' I saw another guy with a camera around his neck and I told him I bet he got some great pictures He said he did and told me to give him my email address. He sent them to me, and they were incredible. My family and the Rauch family had been friends and I sent them the pictures and they passed them along to the players. Several of them had them framed they were so good."

Hoagland has this to say about the Michigan fans: "To this day, I like Michigan, not just because we won but because of how their fans acted. That was a devastating loss for them."

"They were still very cordial even though they were victims of an upset," recalled Wolfe. "I think they underestimated us and didn't appreciate our athletes."

"We tailgated a little more then went to the hotel," said Sherrill. "There was a lot of sitting in traffic. We were riding from stadium to the hotel in that van and had the door open celebrating."

"I have so many memories about that day," said Dean Mills. "That whole Michigan weekend was just crazy."

It was a beautiful day and was warm but wasn't overly humid. I was exhausted and wasn't looking forward to sitting in traffic, which hadn't died down much, but that's what happens when there are 109,000 people in a tight space. I remember listening to the radio recapping the game as I drove back to the hotel. I took a shower and fell asleep. When I woke up, I was hungry, and the hotel next door had a restaurant so went over there to get something to eat. When I got there, I was amazed. The lobby and the adjacent restaurant were packed with App fans, ESPN News was on the TV and kept talking about the game, and all the App fans would cheer when they showed a highlight.

Obviously, media from all over the country were calling Flynn to set up interviews. ESPN in particular had been talking to him about trying to get more coverage when the team arrived back in Boone. After the team left the stadium, they were on the tarmac at Ypsilanti airport waiting to go through security. Flynn's phone, as well as several other phones, were being used for interviews. This was before smart phones. His phone died and fortunately the pilot heard about that and had a charger in the cockpit, so he had a freshly charged phone when they got back.

ESPN had done its *College GameDay* show from Blacksburg, Virginia, that day and were going to send the satellite truck they had used to Boone to do live interviews. They were badgering Flynn when they were going to get back. Boone is very hard to get to by air. There is a small airstrip, but that will only accommodate small aircraft. When the team was flying to a game, they would usually fly out of the Tri-Cities airport near Johnson City, Tennessee, or Greensboro. This time the charter would land in Johnson City and under normal circumstances it would take about an hour and a half to get to the Appalachian campus.

It was around 9 p.m. when they landed. Things were fine on the buses driving home from the airport, except for the people at ESPN who were getting impatient waiting on the live shot from Boone. Flynn said despite the police escort, the traffic as you got to Boone was very heavy and it was almost impassible as they got closer to the stadium.

"My assistant was on the phone with ESPN and he said they are wearing me out wondering where we were," said Flynn.

The scene on campus was as chaotic as the postgame celebration in the App section at the stadium.

"It was a little scary with the crowd as we got to the stadium," he said. "It was all students, and they were so excited. They weren't doing anything malicious, but I was a little afraid they may tip over our buses."

"We should have let everyone in the stadium and had the buses drive in on the track in the stadium," says Cobb. "We were afraid of the damage the buses may do to the track."

"We finally got up there and ESPN wanted someone live when we got off the bus to be live on Sports Center," said Flynn. "After all that when we finally got there, ESPN killed the live shot."

The reason ESPN killed the live shot was because Clay Buchholz of the Boston Red Sox threw a no-hitter against the Baltimore Orioles.

At the hotel next to mine I met Owens and his friend Paul Joyner.

"At the stadium everyone wanted to get back to the hotel to watch the highlights on TV," said Owen. "Larry Hand kept buying appetizers, wings, chips for everyone at the bar. After about two or three hours we said let's go back to Ann Arbor."

Hand was the first Appalachian player to play in the NFL. He played 13 years for the Lions in the 60s and 70s and lives in Winston-Salem now.

Their hotel had a shuttle that ran between the hotel and Ann Arbor. The driver gave us a great tour of the campus and dropped us off downtown. We went to a restaurant and sat on the patio and cheered when someone walked by wearing App stuff. After my nap, I had my second wind and we didn't have to worry about driving. I called Macholz to see what they were doing, but he said they weren't going out. I kept getting notes from Stackow, not only a Notre Dame fan, but a diehard Red Sox fan. Stackow had salvaged a tough day with Buchholz's gem. He was sending me, a big Orioles fan, almost pitch-by-pitch updates the last few innings. I was disappointed the Orioles lost, but that wasn't going to mess up my night. I had fun with those guys. Owen is good friends with Jeff Horne, a fraternity brother of mine and a guy I lived with my senior year. A few years later Horne and Owen had their season tickets at Kidd Brewer Stadium moved right in front of me. It was a fun evening, but I had an early flight the next morning back to Atlanta.

At the airport I bought all the newspapers, and they all had the game on the front page. A year ago, the App State athletic department had a sale of a lot of game worn uniforms for several different sports, not just football. I happened to be in Charlotte that weekend, so I drove to Boone, to see what they had. I have always loved uniforms and wanted to have a nice jersey to wear to games. There was a crowd when I got there, but I found some good things. I got a black number 96 jersey in the style we were wearing then. I bought another, older jersey to give my brother for Christmas and I found a white jersey, from several years ago that was number two. It was kind of buried at the bottom of the pile, but I felt very lucky to find it. Two is my favorite number. I figured out it was the jersey Dexter Jackson wore as a freshman. I wore the white jersey to games when we wore white and the black jersey when we wore black. It was what I had worn to the game, so I wasn't planning on wearing the jersey on Sunday, but now I wasn't sure I was ever going to take it off again! The airport wasn't very crowded, but several Michigan State fans were sure to say thanks and way to go. At the gate, a couple game up to me and said, "I think that's our son's jersey." It was Dexter's parents (they also live in Atlanta) and I told them I agreed and congratulated them on the game he had. They were very proud, obviously. It was a nice flight home with a few other App fans.

The Charlotte guys had an early flight as well, but I didn't see them, since they were on a different airline.

"All the fans from other Big Ten schools were giving us high fives at the airport," said Sherrill.

"We had an early flight," said Wolfe. "We were all still wearing the same clothes. We were treated like celebrities. The flight attendants made an announcement on the plane, and everyone cheered."

Even though they were back in North Carolina, they were still part of the celebration.

"When we got home, I went straight to the neighborhood pool," said Sherrill. "I was a hero at the pool. That whole Sunday afternoon was high fives. There were a lot of App grads there and they all said they wished they could have been there."

"I went to Lake Norman that day," said Wolfe. "I flew an App flag on the boat, and everyone was hollering and honking at us."

Hoagland had always enjoyed going to Ann Arbor. He worked in NASCAR for several years and always stayed there on Michigan race weekends. This time it was a little different.

"We had an early flight Sunday, but we paid the penalty to get on a later one," he said. "We didn't want to stay and talk crap to people, we just wanted to soak it in. We knew it was something special that wouldn't happen very often."

It was an early morning for Flynn, but Appalachian was getting publicity it had never had before.

"I didn't sleep at all that night," he said. "ESPN kept that truck there all week. They sent Tom Rinaldi on Sunday, and he stayed several days. They were doing live shots on Sports Center that morning."

"We knew we had done something special," said Cobb. "ESPN wouldn't let the story die!"

Because of the media demand Coach Moore was going to have a news conference at 2 p.m. They had decided to hold it in the team room at Owens Field House. The usual media facilities weren't nearly large enough to accommodate the expected crowds. ESPN decided they wanted to carry it live on ESPNews. Most of the bigger schools ESPN usually deals with have in-house infrastructure to accommodate live, satellite TV interviews already in place because they do so many live broadcasts. One of my jobs in Birmingham was to coordinate live coverage or at least work to get satellite feeds set up to get video from the location to our station. It was rare for any outlet to do anything more than just a live shot from Boone with their own satellite truck so it wouldn't have been a great investment with the limited resources Appalachian has. The people on the ESPN assignment desk didn't know that.

"They were asking if the room was prewired," said Flynn. "I laughed and said no. 'What do you do when people carry them live?' they asked me," Flynn said. "I said, 'they don't carry them live!' So, they were going to run the wires from the camera to the sat truck through the windows. Those windows had been painted so many times, we couldn't get them open. They had to use a putty knife to cut through the paint to get the windows open. I think John Feinstein [of the *Washington Post*] drove down for it. The *Orlando Sentinel* drove up. Everyone from driving distance was there. Atlanta, Chattanooga had people there. It was something."

"The news conference was scheduled for Sunday, but no one could find Jerry," said Cobb. "He was home cutting his grass because that what he did on Sunday, go to church and mow his yard."

"On Sunday I was with coach Moore, and I told him, 'I'm going to prioritize the interviews, we can't do them all,'" said Flynn. "He said, "Mike, we're going to do all of them. If someone wants to talk to us, then we're going to do them.' So, for five days I would hand everyone a list with phone numbers and what they wanted. It was organized chaos getting it all done."

Monday morning, the game was the lead story on the front page of most of the nation's biggest papers. App alum Stephen Dubner, the co-author of the best-selling book *Freakonomics* and probably the university's most famous alum at the time, had written an article on the front page of the *New York Times*. Feinstein wrote in the *Washington Post* that the win was the biggest upset in American sports history. He proclaimed that the winners of the other two games that are considered the biggest upsets: Chaminade over Virginia in basketball and the U.S. Olympic Hockey team over the Soviets in 1980, played at home. Appalachian accomplished their win on the road, in the most storied venue in the sport.

All the sports websites still had pictures and articles about the game on their home pages. I did my best to capture those sites and articles. I was able to record a lot of the post-game coverage too. I had recorded the Tech-Notre Dame game and the entire halftime report was Bob Costas and Chris Collinsworth talking about Appalachian beating Michigan. It was even more impressive that they pronounced Appalachian correctly! I was able to burn a lot of that stuff from my Tivo to a DVD. I had a lot of stuff from ESPN too, including the guys on *Pardon the Interruption* and *Around the Horn* talking about it. It was such a feeling of pride not only for the school, but for the players and everyone associated with the team. We were nestled up there in our corner of the state ignored no more.

Applications got a huge jump from all the publicity the school received after the historic win. People who had never even heard of App State before or had no idea even where it was suddenly wanted to come to school there. Becky Zupcic was a year behind me in high school. Her son Tyler was a promising high school baseball player and was in Boone the weekend of the Michigan game for a baseball tournament. He was so captivated by what happened in the aftermath of the game on campus he decided that's where he wanted to go to college. He was a star baseball player for the Mountaineers. He was the leadoff hitter for the team in 2012 that came within one win from the NCAA super regionals.

Flynn got a call from *Sports Illustrated* a few days before the issue came out to let them know Appalachian would be on the cover. It was a profile shot of Dexter Jackson and a great view of the helmet. I thought that was about the biggest thing that could happen for Appalachian State University. Magazine covers don't have the cache they used to, but in the sports world in 2007 the *SI* cover was seriously big time. I had my mom put together a collage for me of some of the pictures I had taken (I had several blown up) the *SI* cover, and my game ticket. It's a prized possession. Hoagland has the cover framed and is hanging on the App State wall in his man cave. I was a subscriber so got one in the mail but bought three other copies.

"That was something else I never thought I'd see," said Wolfe. "I went to buy my copy the day it came out. I have it framed along with the ticket stub and some newspaper articles from the game."

Despite all the interviews and attention, the program was getting, there was still another game Saturday the team had to prepare for. Edwards would not be able to play because of his injuries. Lenoir-Rhyne, a Division II team from nearby Hickory was the opponent. The two schools had played 45 times before and were once in the same conference. However, as App's program had moved to Division I the once close series had become lopsided. In fact, this was the first matchup since 1982. Lenoir-Rhyne won for the last time in 1974, but in the seven games since, App had scored fewer than 45 points only once. Tickets were selling quickly. There would be an overflow crowd.

Not only would there be an unprecedented number of fans at the game, media members from all over the country wanted to see for themselves what all the excitement was about and see the team that took down the mighty Wolverines.

"*USA Today* was there; *Sports Illustrated*, all these major outlets," Flynn said. And we didn't have a press box that year! It kind of played right into the story."

The reason there wasn't a press box was because the stadium was being expanded and a whole new football building was being built, that had club seats, luxury boxes, new team locker, and meeting rooms as well as a state-of-the-art, pre-wired press box. But that was a few years away. A makeshift media area had been set up in the east stands.

Appalachian beat the Bears 48-7 in front of a school record 28,802 fans. And so ended the craziest week of Mike Flynn's life.

"It was invaluable experience for me personally and professionally," he reflects. "We were able to put a good plan in motion. I feel good about the job we did."

When the AP poll was released after week one of the season Appalachian didn't appear at all. The reason was that FCS schools could not receive votes in the poll. A lot of voters complained because they felt the Mountaineers were one of the best 25 teams in the country based on their win against

Michigan. So, the AP changed their rules (and it's still called the Appalachian State Rule) and any Division I team was eligible for the poll regardless of their subdivision. In the poll released on September 9, after the Lenoir-Rhyne win, they received 19 votes. Michigan lost to unranked Oregon in week two and didn't get any votes. After the Mountaineers beat Northern Arizona in week three, they got five, then didn't get any more votes until the final poll of the season.

The following week against Northern Arizona the Apps won handily in front of another big crowd despite Edwards being out. In a game-time decision, He started against Wofford. However, he re-aggravated the shoulder injury on the second play of the second half and Appalachian lost the game 42-31. Edwards missed the next two games, but the Mountaineers won them both despite his absence.

He returned at home against arch-rival Georgia Southern. The Eagles took the opening kickoff and scored. On the next drive for the App offense, Edwards threw maybe the worst pass of his life. It was intercepted by Georgia Southern and returned for a touchdown. App trailed 14-0 and could never catch up. Edwards rushed for a career high (so far) 220 yards against the Eagles but was only 10 for 21 passing with two interceptions. Trailing 38-35 with time running down, the Mountaineers ran out of time and had two conference losses on the season. That would be this senior class's only loss at Kidd Brewer Stadium.

Edwards' health improved and the Mountaineers finished the season on a four-game winning streak. Against The Citadel, Edwards set a new career high with 291 rushing yards. Against Western Carolina, Edwards only played three quarters, but had his best completion percentage in a game, going 26 for 31 for 295 yards and three touchdowns. The Mountaineers won 79-35, the most points Appalachian had ever scored against their oldest rival. (A personal note about the Western-Appalachian series: the Catamounts were our biggest rival when I was in school from 1981-85. We lost all four games against them in the four years I was in school. It was only the second time in the series history Western had a four-game winning streak in the series. Once I graduated, the Mountaineers went 27-2 against them until the series ended when Appalachian moved to FBS after the 2013 season. The two games Western won had future NFL star Brad Hoover rushing for 250 yards in 1998 and in 2004 when App lost all its road games. Western scored two late touchdowns to rally for the 30-27 win.)

Because of the two regular season losses, the Mountaineers didn't receive one of the top four seeds in the playoffs and would host old rival James Madison in the first round. The way the schedule worked was the opening weekend was on Thanksgiving weekend. Despite the playoff success and people had learned there was a high likelihood of a game that Saturday, those games didn't draw well.

James Madison and Appalachian had a long-time rivalry. When I was in school, we were in the middle of a 12-game series. The 1992 game ended with App quarterback DJ Campbell hitting Craig Styron in the end zone with a Hail Mary pass as time expired. In 2006 James Madison came to Boone in a matchup of the two most recent national champions. The Mountaineers had prevailed 21-10 in the game that Coach

Moore realized Armanti Edwards should be the starting quarterback.

I was in Charlotte with my family celebrating Thanksgiving so rode up to the game with Macholz, Sherrill, Wolfe, and others. When we arrived at our tailgate spot at 8 a.m., the temperature according to the thermometer in the car was 14 degrees. We had heaters with us and used plastic to seal off two sides of the canopy. That was a cold tailgate even by Boone standards, but we were prepared. The game kicked off at noon and the official gametime temperature was 22 degrees.

This was one of the most incredible games I had seen in Boone. If I wasn't doing so much already on this season, I would dedicate a chapter in this book to it. The Dukes were ranked 12th in FCS and had controlled the game. They had more than 40 minutes of time of possession. However late in the fourth quarter with a 27-22 lead, they had a third and 1 on their own 31. Gaining a yard would allow the Dukes to run out the clock and end the Mountaineers championship run. The defense stepped up big and held JMU to no gain on two successive plays and gave the ball to the offense in great field position. Devon Moore made a diving catch to convert a fourth and 3. Two plays later Edwards scored his third touchdown of the game on a 5-yard run with 1:10 to go to give the Mountaineers a 28-22 lead. But just like in the Michigan game, the defense was looking like it wasn't going to be able to hold the late lead. James Madison drove the ball 62 yards in only four plays and was in range for a chip shot field goal to win. Would the season that started with such promise and all the national attention fall short of the ultimate goal of a national championship?

This was a special year for a special team. Playmakers make plays and just like in the Michigan game; the Mountaineer defense made the big play. Instead of kicking the field goal like coach Moore did at Michigan when he had the chance, JMU Coach Mickey Matthews decided to run one more play. Linebacker Jacque Roman hit the Dukes' Jamal Sullivan hard in the hole, popped the ball loose, and Pierre Banks made another huge play by recovering the fumble. The App fans erupted, and it seemed nothing now was going to be able to stop the team from the third consecutive national championship.

Round two would have the winner of the first-round game between the number two seed, undefeated McNeese State and Eastern Washington. If McNeese won, the Apps would have to hit the road in the playoffs for the first time since the 2001 quarterfinals. But Eastern Washington blew out the Cowboys and the Eagles were coming to Boone. Appalachian won that game 38-35. The Eagles scored two late touchdowns to make the score closer than the game was.

The Richmond Spiders would be the opponent in the semifinals at Kidd Brewer stadium. I would not be able to make this game. It was played on Friday night, and I must not have been able to get off work that day, because I didn't go and it's one of the three games I regret not going to (The Miracle on the Mountain game against Furman in 2002, the 2005 game against Furman in the semis, and this one). Edwards stole the show. He rushed for an FCS playoff record 313 yards on 31 carries and scored four touchdowns. He completed 14 of 16 passes for 182 yards and three touchdowns. For the game he had 495 yards of total offense and was responsible for seven touchdowns. He was just so good. But despite Edwards' heroics, a Richmond touchdown with nine minutes left in the third quarter tied the game at 35. The Spiders wouldn't score again, and App scored three times and advanced to the final with a 55-35 win.

The opponent in the Championship game was the 11-3 Delaware Blue Hens. Ironically, Delaware has the same iconic helmet design as Michigan, except Delaware's helmets are a lighter shade of blue. Joe Flacco was the Delaware quarterback and was being touted as a top pro prospect. It appeared Appalachian had decided they had had enough close games for the season and stormed out to a 21-0 lead early in the second quarter. Delaware seemed to have regained a little momentum when Flacco hit Mark Duncan for a 38-yard touchdown pass with just over a minute remaining in the half. But the Mountaineers weren't content to run out the clock and Edwards hit Jackson for a 72-yard touchdown 26 seconds later. The lead was back to 21 and the Apps would never be threatened as they cruised to a 49-21 lead.

Edwards was pulled in the fourth quarter and backup quarterback Trey Elder exploded for a 53-yard touchdown run. As he scored, the entire App bench ran on the field to congratulate the popular backup quarterback. By the end of the game, App fans had come out of the stands and surrounded the end zone at one end of the field, ready to storm the field and celebrate being the first FCS team to win three consecutive national championships. In the four playoff games Edwards had accounted for 1,387 yards of total offense (727 passing and 660 rushing) and was responsible for 16 touchdowns. Not only did the Mountaineers have the historic three-peat, but they also lead the FCS in attendance for the first time, averaging 27,140 fans per game.

In the final AP poll of the season after the bowl games, Appalachian received five votes. Michigan defeated Tim Tebow and the Florida Gators in the Citrus Bowl to finish the season 9-4 and ranked number 18 in the final AP poll. The Citrus Bowl was Lloyd Carr's last game as coach of the Wolverines.

The 2007 college football season is regarded as one of the best ever. One of the reasons is the result in one of the first games played that season: What happened in the Big House, when "THE MOUNTAINEERS HAVE JUST BEATEN THE MICHIGAN WOLVERINES!" On October 6 Stanford beat

Southern California at the LA Coliseum 24-23. The Cardinal were 41-point underdogs, so the result was the biggest upset by point spread in college history. The "mainstream" sports books didn't set lines for games between FBS and FCS teams so there was no "official" line on the Appalachian-Michigan game. Many people at the end of the year were saying the USC-Stanford game was the biggest upset of all time in college football, not the App win. Hearing anyone say that makes me mad. First of all, USC and Stanford were in the same conference and had been playing each other almost annually since 1919. They have the same number of scholarship players. That win would kick off a streak where the Cardinal would beat the Trojans five times in the next six years. Sure, USC has the great tradition and was ranked higher that year, but there is no way these upsets could be considered equal.

It's been more than 15 years since Appalachian's victory over Michigan, and it still gets talked about. Before the 2022 season, Andy Staples, then of *The Athletic,* listed the 20 most influential games in the 2000s. This game was listed as number two. Anytime there's an upset, it's measured against that game. Even in basketball season it comes up. After all the upsets in the NCAA tournament in 2023 someone asked *The Athletic* college football writer Stewart Mandel his top upsets in college football since 2000 and of course, this game was number one.

Michigan got a chance to get its revenge in 2014. The Mountaineers went back up to Ann Arbor and lost 52-14 in what turned out to be Appalachian's first game as an FBS team. I didn't think we should have given them the rematch. I liked seeing 0-1 against Appalachian showing up in perpetuity in the Michigan media guide.

Cobb explained his decision to grant the rematch.

"It was a few years later and they reached out to us about coming back," said Cobb. "I said, 'If you pay us $1 million and put it on national TV we would do it.' Everyone remembers the Miracle on Ice. The U.S. and Russia have played many times since, but everyone remembers that one. I'm not sure I would do that now. App's program stands on its own now, but for building a program we needed the money. Not now."

Everyone who is associated with Appalachian seems to have a story about that game.

Mike Flynn: To this day, if I meet someone who doesn't know I worked at App and it comes up, the question is: Were you there? Fifteen years later. It's just crazy. It has slowed a little, but I still get asked about it.

Brian Hoagland: The thing that sticks with me is every year when I start talking football and someone asks who I pull for and I say App State, they say, "They were the ones that beat Michigan!" That game will never be topped even if we win a New Year's Day bowl game. It was a pivotal point in App State history.

Mike Ladd: I worked in the automotive industry and made frequent trips to the Detroit area. There was a LA Fitness in Auburn Hills where I worked out and I was wearing my App State stuff. Usually, you had to pay a $5 guest fee. There was a lady at the desk, and she said, "My dad went to Michigan State and you can get in free tonight."

Jim Macholz: I have this great picture of Armanti going over the top to score against Michigan. One of my neighbors was over at the house and we didn't know each other really well then. He had walked through my den downstairs from the pool, and he saw the picture. When he saw me, he said, "Why do you have that picture?" I told him, "I went to that game." He said, "You went to that game? I went to Michigan, and I was at that game."

Ed Boyd (App State offensive guard 1981-84): I was at a bar in Fort Mill, South Carolina (just outside of Charlotte), and a guy game in wearing a Michigan cap. I went to my car and got my App hat and sat beside him. We talked and he was a good sport.

Mike Wolfe: It comes up pretty frequently. When they find out I went to App they say, "I remember you beat Michigan." Everyone is surprised I was there.

Kirk Sherrill: If I see someone with Michigan stuff to this day I ask them, "Do you remember that game? I was there. I was there when we beat Michigan." That's sort of died off now, but I mention it to them if I see them around Charlotte.

Dean Mills: The new CEO of the company I work for was a dedicated Michigan fan. His first week on the job he came to meet all the sales guys and I said, "I want to tell you. My son played in the App State-Michigan game." He said, "I hate you already!"

Alex Johnson and Charles Haynes co-host the *Black and Gold Podcast* about App State sports. Every year they host a raffle on September 1 to raise money for the Yosef Club. They call it 34-32 Day. They started the raffle in 2019.

"I think our fan base has arrived at a place where we have appropriately appreciated the Michigan game," said Johnson. "We don't talk about it all the time, but it's still so vital to our history and success. I thought we should spend at least one day a year to 'celebrate' and then move on to the rest of the season. I used the Twitter account to generate a bunch of donations. In 2020 we switched to a raffle [of App State athletics memorabilia] because I thought it would generate more money and it did. This past year we did $7,000 and over the four years have roughly raised $30,000."

Over the years, many people, even App fans, seem to have forgotten just what a great game it was. Everyone remembers the Lynch blocked kick and thinks it was a fluke. But there was the Quick blocked field goal a series earlier. There was the drive that set up App's winning field goal. There were so many times in the second half when it looked like Michigan was going to take over, but the Mountaineers wouldn't be denied. I would have been heartbroken if I hadn't made that trip. There are only a few places that I would have passed up the trip to Notre Dame for, like the Rose Bowl, the Coliseum for a USC game, maybe Ohio State, but not many. It's such a sense of pride for everyone who not only went to Appalachian but has some association with the school. Fortunately, we've been able to maintain success as a football program, not only in FCS, but even after we made the move to FBS in 2014. It's nice not to be just a one-trick pony.

Chapter 8: Wofford's Nightmare
Wofford at Appalachian State
October 31, 2008

When I was in high school, Appalachian was frequently referred to as "Happy Appy" and had a reputation as a party school. I'm not sure it was deserved. When I was there a lot of students, especially freshmen, went home on weekends. There weren't any bars in Boone. Watauga County was dry, except in the city of Blowing Rock. In 1981, my freshman year, the road from Boone to Blowing Rock, U.S. 321, was a two-lane road. I joined Sigma Phi Epsilon fraternity as a freshman so after that, I nearly always had something to do on the weekends. But the Greek system at App State was fairly new. Most of the fraternities were less than 10 years old. Only one had a house in town. The campus did provide a floor in a dorm for each sorority, but membership in fraternities and sororities was less than 10 percent of all students. Students would drive to the package stores in Blowing Rock and bring beer back to drink in Boone. Police would patrol 321 for drunk drivers. The relationship between the Town of Boone and the student body was not always a cordial one.

All throughout my four years at App, there was talk about a vote to allow beer and wine sales in Boone. Finally in May 1986, there was a referendum to allow alcohol sales in Boone. It passed and students didn't have to drive to Blowing Rock any longer. Brian Metcalf, who graduated in 1985, wanted to take part in the historic vote.

"I left my voting registration in Boone," said Metcalf. "I went back so I could vote."

Before 1984, in North Carolina the legal drinking age was 18 years old for beer and wine, and 21 for liquor. That year the federal government had raised the drinking age nationally to 21, but at least older students could drink. Several package stores opened in town. My younger brother, Hunter, was a freshman at Appalachian in the fall of 1985 and when I went to Boone to visit him after the referendum had passed, I bought a can of beer in Boone for the first time. I labeled it and still have it on my shelf of mementos.

Tailgating wasn't a priority for football games. Some people did it, but it wasn't that big of a deal. Usually, some guys would get together and have a few beers and some Bojangles chicken or something else to eat. When I was in school, the fraternities, sororities, and other groups would have canopies set up on the Duck Pond field, close to the stadium and that was basically what consisted of student tailgating. Our fraternity would set up a canopy, but usually just for homecoming when a lot of alumni would be there.

I graduated in the spring of 1985. Hunter was a freshman at App that fall and joined the Sig Eps too. Eventually, Mike Wolfe, Jay Hellinger, Jim Macholz, and Kirk Sherrill all joined the fraternity. I met those guys through Hunter and have been tailgating with them since around 2006. Our group has gotten much bigger over the years.

"Back when we were in school, we tailgated on Duck Pond Field," said Wolfe. "As the years went by, we started getting more organized. Nobody did anything in advance. You woke up that morning and had to get drinks. Games were at 1 p.m. so it was tough to get all that done."

"Back then the games were just a reason to drink and party," said Hellinger.

Mike Nauman is a 1984 graduate who wasn't a Sig Ep, but his younger brother was friends with Wolfe. That's how he got involved in our tailgate group.

"I was working a lot at school but went to every game I could," he said. "We tailgated in the dorms."

"After we graduated, we parked in the stadium lot," recalled Wolfe. "That was the only lot there was any payment for parking, and you got assigned parking. The last two rows at the back of lot were first come first served and we would park there."

"We would leave Charlotte about 6am to get there by 8 a.m. to get our spots," said Sherrill.

I remember parking in the stadium lot for the playoff games in 1987 when Appalachian made it to the semifinals but lost to Marshall after beating them in the regular season. I moved to Birmingham in February of 1988, so didn't regularly make it back to Boone for many years. Life, work, and family responsibilities started to affect Sherill and the group, and they just couldn't make as many games as they once did.

"In the early 90s we parked there in Stadium [Lot]," said Sherrill. "There were several years we didn't go to any games."

"I started traveling and would maybe make one game a year," said Wolfe.

Charles Haynes graduated from Appalachian in 2003. He lives in Boone now and is the Clerk of Superior Court in Watauga County. He is the co-host of the *Black and Gold Podcast*, which started in 2015. He's a big guy and is best known as "Big C" and is introduced on the podcast by co-host Alex Johnson as "the world's most famous App State fan." He's been a regular tailgater since he graduated.

"I met a buddy about halfway through college," recalled Haynes. "His parents were big Georgia fans and tailgating is a big thing there. We thought, there is no reason why we can't do that here. We started in what is now Peacock [parking lot]. My first year out, it was nothing but a cooler and a card table, a couple of tailgate chairs, and a couple of portable grills. It wasn't a big deal. But I always felt that if you show a commitment to something, people will show up and they'll pay attention."

"I came to the game against The Citadel in 2004," said Charlie Cobb. "I couldn't believe how few people were there."

I looked it up and there were only 8,931 people in attendance at that game in September 2004. I don't know what the weather was like, but that's the last time Appalachian has had an announced attendance for a football game of less than 10,000 [except for the COVID restrictions of 2020].

"Back then it didn't cost a dime to park in Peacock," said Haynes. "It never filled up. People didn't show up until an hour before kickoff. We stayed down there looking ridiculous for a reason. We had something going on here."

But at that time there were a lot of changes at Appalachian. As I've mentioned, the football team didn't make the playoffs in 2003 or 2004. In 2004, Dr. Kenneth Peacock was hired as chancellor of the university. The hiring was a little unusual because he was already at Appalachian. He was the provost of the business school. One of the things I liked the most about Dr. Peacock is that it appeared to me that he ran the university as a business and not so much like a university. He went to Board of Trustee meetings and fought for Appalachian like no chancellor had ever done before. He made presentations that showed the discrepancies in state funding per student for Appalachian compared to other schools in the system. When he took over, App's state funding was one of the lowest in the system, and he changed that.

In 2005 Peacock hired Cobb as AD. Cobb's parents were both teachers and had earned their masters' degrees at Appalachian. Charlie had an older brother Patrick, who graduated from App with a degree in communications and had some classes with me. Cobb was an offensive lineman at N.C. State. He was impressed with Dr. Peacock when he met him.

"He was an incredible ambassador for Appalachian," says Cobb. "After we won our first national championship, you only got one trophy. We had to order another one and pay for that so we would have one for the trophy case and one to show. Someone made him a case to carry all of them. He would take them to Board of Governors meetings because we were the only school in the system to have won a football national championship. He would set them up before meetings and play dumb about how they got there. He was genuinely excited about the attention that brought to the university."

Cobb said another thing was a passion for Peacock was the student experience.

"The basic theory is fall Saturdays should matter," said Cobb. "In an academic world, it's not the most important, but it is the most attended. Those fall Saturdays get all the stakeholders involved."

And one of the ways he wanted to do that was change the tailgate culture.

"I give credit to David Jackson and Kindsay Green Reeder that spring and summer," said Cobb. "They were already working on it. I kind of walked into it."

Jackson, an Appalachian graduate, was best known at that time as the Mountaineers radio play-by-play voice. His call of the Michigan win helped him win Sportscaster of the Year in the state of North Carolina in 2007. But then, athletic department employees wore a lot of hats. Green Reeder was working for the alumni association and the two departments were trying to coordinate their efforts to get people back to visit and to financially support Appalachian.

"We were trying to build something," said Green Reeder , another App graduate. "We had some ideas and knew the passion was there. Charlie had the vision to do what we wanted to do. There had to be a vehicle to push that forward. Dr. Peacock's willingness to lead and do that. It all came together. And the winning helped."

"Our personalities were different, but he understood the athletics experience," said Cobb of Peacock. "If you are a fan, you don't understand role ... [a] college president plays in making things happen. Some like that and some run from it. He valued what athletics brought to the school. What it meant for alumni and student engagement. He was so big on the student experience."

Dr. Peacock would practice what he preached. I'm sure many university presidents looked down their noses at what he did. It was wonderful for the university, and I don't think it's a coincidence the university had its biggest period of growth during his tenure as chancellor. Every home game he would wear a jersey over his shirt and tie and climb on the director's tower and lead the band in the fight song between the third and fourth quarters. When there was an alumni function off the mountain in Charlotte, Greensboro, Atlanta, or anywhere else, he would pack those three national championship trophies in that specially designed case and take them to the meeting where grads could pose for pictures with them. He would say that everyone associated with the university was responsible for those trophies and their fingerprints should be on them.

"Chancellor Peacock came to campus, and he wanted to celebrate game days," says Haynes. "He said 'we need to let it all hang out.' And that's where it took off. For so long at App State it was frowned upon to drink a beer in the open."

"We set up the story of what we were trying to create," said Green Reeder. "Working through the red tape we knew it may be a challenge. But with the administration's support, everyone bought in. The chief of police and the director of parking, they were phenomenal helping us."

"The biggest credit goes to Ken [Peacock]," said Cobb. "Before then they were issuing open container citations and there were a lot of restrictions. He was able to get some of that stuff relaxed."

Before the 2005 season, the athletic department released a list of guidelines for tailgating before football games. There were time limits installed and restrictions against liquor and underage drinking. Also, in 2005 Appalachian only had four home, regular season games.

"The first game against Coastal we had 22,000 and I was very surprised," said Cobb. "We had success and people wanted to be a part of it."

"By 2005 it was getting full mid-morning," recalled Haynes. "Still at that point you didn't have to pay. Twenty-two thousand showed up for the Coastal game. People just showed up because the chancellor said to. To me, that was when it kicked off. By 2006 you had to have a donation."

Wolfe said his group started going more in 2004 and would park in what was then called the Raley Lot because it was the parking lot for Raley Hall, the home of the Walker College of Business. The building and the lot were re-named for Dr. Peacock after he retired as chancellor. When I was in school, Raley Hall didn't exist and the lot was called the Driving Range Lot because that's where the Watauga County schools did their driver's education classes. Wolfe has a picture of the lot from a game in October of 2005 and there's a big crowd, but there are very few Appalachian flags or canopies with Appalachian markings on them.

Cobb also announced that kickoff time for all home games would be 3:30. That's still the preferred starting times for games even now, although there is a better chance now that TV may move the start time.

"We thought it was best to play at 3:30 and it was the model that works," said Cobb. Once you find something that works you don't change it. We got tremendous support from the town. One of my first days in Boone, I talked about the economic engine. My goal is that a football game and the other events around it become part of that environment. And we accomplished that. On the field results helped with that."

It was nice to see the university and the town be at peace with one another for the most part. When I was in school, that wasn't always the case. There were only a handful of restaurants in Boone in the early 80s, but after the vote to allow beer and wine sales, more started to pop up. King Street, the main drag through downtown, is close to campus. When I was a student, there were only a few restaurants; it was mostly retail stores, and I didn't really have a need to go there very often. Now there are more restaurants along the strip, and on side streets too. I don't go to restaurants on game days. I enjoy the tailgate environment so much and that's where so many of my friends are. I do know several people, especially ones without a parking spot, who do their pregame at the places downtown. I really enjoy the rare days when I'm in Boone not on a football day, because there are some really nice places to hang out.

In 2005 TV wouldn't change the start time because the Southern Conference only had one game a week televised, and that window was at 3:30. That certainly made a big difference for me driving the five hours from Atlanta to Boone. We could leave at 7 and get to the lot at noon. If the game ended by 7, we could be home by 12:30 a.m. or so. People thought we were crazy for driving up and back the day of the game. I didn't want to spend money on a hotel room, and if you did you wouldn't get back until mid-afternoon and Sunday was shot at that point. There were usually others in our group and once we got satellite radio, it was great listening to other games on the way home.

"People could come from two to three hours away to tailgate and get home at a decent hour," said Sherill.

"3:30 kickoff was huge," said Hellinger. "No one is as amped with an early kickoff."

"What [a] difference it was," said Wolfe. "For two reasons. One, we could get there a little later. And students were able to get there too."

"App football brought me and my roommate together," said Nauman. "We hadn't seen each other for years, but now we sit together, and it brings us together. The most important social time for me each year is football. I cherish football season in the mountains."

One of the other changes made was to allocate about 150 spaces in the Raley Lot for students to use for tailgating. The Raley Lot wasn't very wide. There was an aisle that separated the two sides. One was about 10 rows deep and the other side, where the students parked, was about a dozen. It really created a great vibe.

"Get students to come and others would come," said Cobb. "The vast majority of people give emotional support, so we were dependent on people coming up there."

"There was so much positive energy having half students and half alums," said Sherrill.

"The cheerleaders and the band would come through and play and get everyone fired up," said Wolfe.

It could have created some awkward moments for Nauman. His daughter Emily came to Boone as a freshman in 2008. He was the first one in our group to have a child at App and to come by the tailgate.

"We had a rule when Emily would come to the tailgate," he said. "I would not serve her, but if the other guys did, I didn't see it."

"My freshman year, I was living in the dorm," said Emily Pegues. "We would hang out there, maybe have a drink or two, then go by the tailgate. I didn't want to drink in front of dad. My dad has always been the fun one! People love it when I post things on social media with him, and they always get the most engagements of all my posts. All four years, we always went by dad's tailgate."

Currently, Wolfe has a son, Jackson, and Sherrill has a daughter, Paige, who are students at Appalachian as of 2024. One of Hunter's sons, my nephew Sam, graduated in 2024. It was nice to see him at the tailgate. Their experiences at the tailgates as kids is one of the reasons they wanted to go to school there.

I was talking to Mike Wolfe about the second generation of App students taking part in our tailgates, and how neat it is. Jackson grew up with App football and going to Boone on fall Saturdays.

"As long as I can remember I was going to games there," recalled Jackson Wolfe, who was a freshman in the fall of 2022. "Dad brought me up a lot, depending on if I had baseball games or not. All the games I went to I would see the student section and it looked like a good time to me."

When Nauman, Metcalf, Mike Wolfe, and I were students, very few of us and our fellow students grew up on App football. My dad went to Lenior-Rhyne College (now University) in Hickory, and we never went to any football games. Dad was a dedicated UNC fan, where he did some postgraduate work. So many of our fellow students had grown up as fans of the sports teams at UNC, N.C. State, or another "bigger and older" school. Most of those schools have three or more generations of families that have been going to games at the schools and the season tickets and seats in the stadium have been passed down for those generations. The University of North Carolina after all has been around since the 18th century. That's the kind of engagement with the alma mater Dr. Peacock was trying to grow. Seeing these kids who grew up with App State coming to school there just strengthens their tie to the school.

"It's so cool to see the evolution of our kids coming through the tailgate," said Nauman. "Emily still tailgates with us along with her husband [Lanier Pegues]. She's passionate about it like I am. She gets fired up like her dad and we share that. My wife, Martha, is proud that Emily and I have gotten to share that bond. My son-in-law went to Winthrop, but now he's the biggest App fan! I wouldn't change it for the world!"

"My mom buys matching App Christmas presents for my dad and my husband," said Pegues. "It's so cool."

In 2007 Wolfe was at the game in Charleston against The Citadel and saw someone there with a trailer that had a grill on it, a place to mount speakers and poles to put flags in. The sides had a tabletop or bar where you could put a plate to eat. They had bar stools for people to sit on. There were spots to put magnets on it, so you could change out what team you were supporting that day. Many of those guys also had tickets for the Carolina Panthers so they put Panthers magnets over the App stuff on Sunday when tailgating.

"That trailer was a focal point in the Raley Lot for a while," said Hellinger. "We must have had a hundred people ask where we got that. Students were interacting with us because of the trailer. The student and alumni mix and interaction helped that lot grow and improve the atmosphere."

Johnson, the co-host of the *Black and Gold Podcast* with Haynes, was a sophomore in the fall of 2008 and was a big fan as a student.

"I never tailgated in the student area," he said. "I had family friends who were big App fans and tailgated in the stadium lot. When he found out I was going to App, he always invited me to their spot. The greatest thing about that was that he was there to share. That's all he was there for, to share the joy of App State. And when I think about what I do now, that's what I do, is share. I spend most of my time cooking. I wouldn't do anything else. We have people that show up and we share the experience."

On the field, Appalachian was still basking in the success of the 2007 season. They had won three national championships in a row and star quarterback Armanti Edwards was only a junior. However, there were some significant losses to graduation in 2007. On defense, all four defensive backs would need to be replaced, including Corey Lynch, who had made several big plays over his career, not just the blocked kick at Michigan. The biggest loss on offense was record-setting running back Kevin Richardson who was the school's all-time leading rusher and scorer. Two wide receivers and three linemen had to be replaced. ESPN was good to Appalachian after the Michigan win and wanted to show them to the nation. The game against Wofford was originally scheduled for Saturday, November 1, but was moved to the night before and would be shown on ESPN2. It would be the first home, regular-season game televised on ESPN or ESPN2 since 1979, a game against Western Carolina that was the second college football game ESPN ever televised.

"Dave Brown worked for ESPN scheduling games," said Cobb. "He called and said we have a slot on Friday night, would you play? You are the only FCS team we would approach."

Cobb agreed to it but knew there would be some push-back from the high schools, who saw Friday night as their night. He went to work on that.

"The high school association was critical of ECU a few years before," said Cobb. "We knew we had to walk a fine line.

They said, 'We understand what you have to do, but Fridays belong to high schools.' When we looked at the calendar Watauga [the high school for Boone and Watauga County] was to play in Charlotte. Watauga got their game moved to Thursday. Ashe and Avery [nearby counties] were off that week. Winston-Salem schools were on break and didn't have games. Things worked out pretty well for that."

"We tried to be a good partner and do things for the community," said Cobb. "Little things like kids getting on the field to run around after the game. A few local kids on the team now were running around back then with my kids. We would have games on Monday nights where youth teams in surrounding counties would play at the stadium. Ran that for a long time, the Mighty Mountaineers program. We tried a lot of different things to get the community engaged."

The 2008 season didn't get off to a very good start. The opener was against the defending FBS national champion LSU in Baton Rouge. The game was scheduled for a 4 p.m. kickoff on ESPN. LSU was coached by Les Miles, a Michigan graduate, who wasn't going to let Appalachian sneak up on his team. Tiger

Stadium (I can't call it Death Valley. To me, Death Valley, the stadium, is in South Carolina) was at the top of my bucket list for stadiums to visit. When I worked in Birmingham, I made it to Athens, Gainesville, and Knoxville, but never got to go to a game in Baton Rouge. I couldn't make the trip when Appalachian had played there in 2005 and was really looking forward to checking that off the list. I had booked two nights in Baton Rouge and had a flight to New Orleans and would rent a car and drive to "Red Stick." I knew when I made the reservations, they would be dependent on hurricane season. I was still at The Weather Channel and knew any time off would be cancelled if I was needed for tropical weather coverage, which was basically all hands-on deck.

Mother nature was not going to make things easy. Hurricane Gustav had already devastated several islands in the Caribbean and was headed toward the Louisiana coast. This was the first hurricane that was forecast to hit the Louisiana coast since Katrina in New Orleans in 2005. I knew the state and local governments would be very diligent about safety and wouldn't hesitate to cancel a football game. When I was driving to the airport in Atlanta on Friday, August 29, I heard a report that the kickoff would be moved to 10 a.m. local time in Baton Rouge. Instead of a prime slot on ESPN, the game would be shown on ESPN Classic, a channel that most people didn't have. ESPN was not going to pre-empt *College GameDay*, and other games couldn't be moved on such short notice, so ESPN Classic was the only option. I was disappointed, but at least the game would be played. One of the main reasons I wanted to go to a game at LSU was for tailgating and with a 10 a.m. kickoff, it wouldn't be the same. Also, I was concerned with the mood of the crowd, because I knew after Katrina, the good folks of Louisiana weren't going to mess around.

When I arrived in New Orleans and was on the shuttle to the rental car place, it was announced that I-10 would be on a contraflow (all lanes in one direction for evacuation purposes) Saturday evening. I was able to book a room at a hotel near the New Orleans airport for Saturday night and decided I would leave Baton Rouge after the game and hunker down in the hotel there. I was already on the first flight out to Atlanta on Sunday morning.

I had a great time in Baton Rouge with my friends Friday night. We got up early to tailgate a little before kickoff. The game wasn't very good. LSU was ranked number seven in the nation and won 41-13. I got to my hotel in New Orleans and nearly everything was closed. The local stations were doing coverage of the storm so were pre-empting coverage of college football. The only game I could see was on ESPN and that was the game that was added at the last minute because that was supposed to be the slot for the LSU-App game. I drove around and finally found a Subway that was the only restaurant open. Most of the buildings were boarded up and the roads were deserted. Many people had already left. It was eerie. When I got to the airport Sunday morning, it was jam packed with people who had slept there. Everyone was trying to get on flights. I felt very fortunate I was able to make it back to Atlanta when I did. Many people who had flights later in the day canceled, drove their rental cars back home, but struggled to find gas stations. It turned out to be the largest evacuation in the history of the state of Louisiana. Gustav came ashore in Louisiana as a Category 2 hurricane on Monday, September 1.

Forty-eight people died in the state as a result of the storm. Baton Rouge was particularly hard hit. There were two fatalities there and more than 85 percent of the city lost power.

Appalachian easily defeated Jacksonville 56-7 in week two. That game was significant that the crowd at The Rock that day surpassed 30,000 for the first time. The next week the Apps had a 21-0 halftime lead at James Madison in week three in a rematch of the first-round playoff game from the previous season. This time, the Dukes rallied to win 35-31. Despite the loss, the Mountaineers were still ranked number three. With a 1-2 record it was time to rely on that culture and leadership.

"I'm not sure if it was because of the mountains but we were able to go full speed all camp," said sophomore offensive lineman Pat Mills. "We could push harder; we were in game shape game one. In the summer we had organized workouts on our own. Coaches never had to tell us to do that. During the season we would have a closed-door player meeting on Thursday at 7 p.m. At 7, we would bolt the door. If you weren't there by 7 you couldn't play. Players would keep you from playing. That was our time. The players would tell the coaches,

'This guy isn't ready because they didn't want to show up.' You can't help but be good. Every position group had a leader, and it was a magical study with talented people and leadership."

In their next four games, all lopsided wins, the offense averaged more than forty points a game and climbed back to number two in the nation. This set up the revenge match against Wofford who had beaten the Mountaineers 42-31 the year before.

"I wanted revenge from Wofford," said Alex Johnson. "They were the ones who beat us and who took the luster off the Michigan game. I wanted blood. I wanted it bad!"

"You knew it would be rocking," said Mills. "This is going to be wild. We fed off that. We were the show."

Wofford came into the game ranked number three in the nation. Another sellout crowd was expected. But Appalachian hadn't hosted a game on a "school day" before. On Friday nights, lots that are used for game day parking on Saturday are cleared by students that park there during the week. However, some of the lots used for tailgating were used during the week by professors who were teaching class on Friday afternoon. That could be a problem.

"Someone with the university asked me what time we should open the lots," recalled Haynes. "I told them I wanted to be there at noon. What we did was we parked on the street, which you could do then, and set up in the grass."

I don't remember what time they ended up opening the Raley Lot. A lot of students parked there, but there was some faculty parking there too. I rode up to the game with Sid Moore, a former colleague at The Weather Channel who went to a lot of games with me then. We stopped in Shelby at Red Bridges BBQ and met my parents, who had driven over from Charlotte, for lunch. After we left Shelby, we drove up through Marion and got on the Blue Ridge Parkway to drive in Boone that way. It was such a beautiful day, and Sid was a photographer and had never been on the Parkway before. Driving up on a Saturday, we wouldn't have time for that. Even though it was late October, there was plenty of fall color at the lower elevations. We checked into the hotel and got to the lot around 4 p.m. The place was already going crazy.

"I know [my friend] Kelly and I dressed up," said Pegues. "Everyone was dressed up. It was really fun. I'm pretty sure I didn't go to class that day. We were looking at everyone's costumes. That was when they had the trailer. Kirk had people in costumes dancing there we didn't know. People would stop by the trailer because the vibe was so good."

"I remember a bunch of lead up to that game," said Wolfe. "It's one that still a lot of people keep talking about. It was just a different atmosphere for sure."

"I remember there was a lot of Halloween stuff at the tailgate," said Macholz, another one of the guys we tailgated with.

"My friend Brian Hester met his now-wife that night while he was dressed as 'App Man,'" said Hellinger.

"I remember the tailgate," said Brian Hoagland. "Everyone is dressed in Halloween costumes and there were a lot of scantily dressed students. We got there early. I had that great parking space across the street from the stadium."

"It was Halloween. I'm not a Halloween guy, I didn't dress up," remembered Haynes. "Halloween is cool and all, but this is game day. We've played other games on Halloween, and it does not come close to matching the energy that was in that stadium, that town, that street, that lot, you name it, wherever. Every time you turned around the next costume that would walk by outdid the one you just saw 15 seconds before. It was incredible."

"I was there midafternoon," said Johnson. "The quality of the students dressing up was incredible. The weather was perfect. It was just a perfect storm."

That was how Mills described the scene too. On the night before games, video coordinator Jake Stroot would show a video he had put together to get the team ready to play. In the 2007 game at Wofford Stroot had video of some Wofford frat guys saying "F--- Appalachian." He put that in the video.

"Typically, on games I was shooting highlights," said Stroot. "If we lost, I would take off my App stuff, if I was wearing it, and go into winner's fan section. I would act like I was from a local TV station and get the fans' reactions. Sometimes I would have to egg the fans on a little, but most of the time I didn't. I would use that for the motivational video the next year."

After the video was over Mills said Coach Moore addressed that specifically.

"He pointed at his heart where a Polo shirt logo would be. 'Those guys, with that ol' horse on their chest, that ain't us.'"

"We loved him as players," said Mills regarding Stroot. "He was so talented. He put in the time, and we knew he worked all night to make those things for us."

Kickoff was at 7:30 p.m., so the sun had gone down. The kickoff temperature was 52 degrees and the commentators mentioned it could get to the 20s. But the offenses started hot. In September, Wofford was trailing South Carolina by 3 points midway through the fourth quarter before the Gamecocks scored a late touchdown to win by 10. They had scored 153 points in their previous three games. The Terriers had beaten App the year before and ended the Mountaineers' 17-game winning streak. Edwards had re-aggravated the Michigan injury and didn't play most of the second half, but the Terriers rushed for 291 yards. They were confident they could compete with App State, despite the raucous environment at Kidd Brewer Stadium.

Mills remembers the scene. "Kidd Brewer at Night, national TV, Halloween night, and we have a score to settle. We were going to kill them," said Mills. "We didn't need extra incentive, but we had it. I was so proud of that. You had a team that was motivated. We were pissed off. If you played at 11 on Sunday morning it wouldn't matter. We were locked in and then to walk out into that environment. It was a night you'll never forget."

"I sat on the Hill that night," said Pegues. "The student section was already packed when we got in. I don't remember much of the game."

Coco Hillary had a nice return of the opening kickoff across the 50 into Terrier territory. On third and 8 from the 23, Edwards hit tight end Ben Jorden on a seam pattern to give the Apps a 7-0 lead. Wofford runs an option attack, so they fooled the Mountaineers with a long pass on their first play from scrimmage. They would score a few plays later.

On App's next drive, Edwards had a 25-yard run and hit Jorden for a 49-yard touchdown pass. Wofford answered with a long run that set up another touchdown. There were more than seven minutes left in the first quarter and the score was 14-14. In less than eight minutes the two teams had run 18 plays, had nine first downs and four touchdowns.

Mountaineer running back Robert Weldon scored on a 5-yard run to put App State back on top. This time the App defense would respond. Mark LeGree, who was replacing Corey Lynch at safety, intercepted the first of his three passes on the night. App converted five third downs on the next drive and Edwards capped it with a 1-yard run.

The defense was fired up and turned in the first three and out when Wofford got the ball back. After the punt, Appalachian had a 3-yard run on first down. It was second and seven on the App 42 and Edwards dropped back to pass, he was on the 35 and threw off his back foot and hit Brian Quick in stride at the goal line for a 58-yard touchdown. The Mountaineers led 35-14, the Kidd Brewer crowd was going crazy, and the rout was on.

"It almost got out of control," said Mills. "You could watch them deflate and that was great. It was pretty cool to look up there in the stands and see everyone dressed up. Like a professional wrestling event."

There was 10:58 to play in the second quarter and Edwards was eight for nine for 208 yards and three touchdowns, plus a touchdown rushing. Wofford was moving the ball again and had driven to the App 22. On third and 6 LeGree stopped their running back for a 2-yard loss. Wofford coach Mike Ayers had to go for it. The Mountaineers put great pressure on the quarterback and his pass was incomplete. With less than five minutes to play in the half, Devin Radford scored from 47 yards out to make it 42-14. The App defense got another three and out, but the Mountaineers were forced to punt for the first time when a third and 17 couldn't be converted. The half ended 42-14. Edwards was 12 for 13 with 233 yards passing and three touchdown passes, as well as the rushing touchdown. App State had 372 total yards, was five of six on third down and had eight plays of 15 yards or more. It was about as perfect a half of football as you get.

"I just remember we played so well," said Cobb. "I get anxious about games and the second half we had more than control of the game. So many people and especially students got into it. Armanti was on fire and the rest of them were as well."

Appalachian's band, "North Carolina's Band of Distinction," plays a big part in the environment inside The Rock. That night, they were as much a part of the night as the football team. Going with the Halloween theme, they played Michael Jackson's hit "Thriller." The performance was a hit, and the students were going crazy. YouTube videos have been seen by thousands.

Wofford took the second half kickoff and drove into Appalachian territory, but LeGree picked off a pass inside the 10. App punted, and the Terriers kicked a field goal. The Wofford onside kick went out of bounds at mid-field, so the Mountaineers took over there. On the first play, Edwards hit a wide open Quick who scored. The 6'5" high school basketball player dunked the ball over the cross bar and was called for unsportsmanlike conduct. No one on the App State sideline cared. Kidd Brewer Stadium and the Mountaineer sideline was going crazy. Mills said the players were feeding off the coach's aggressiveness.

"[Scott] Satterfield [the offensive coordinator] called smoke. That was two wide on each side and they all went vertical and the running back went up the middle. Quick caught it and dunked it and we were going crazy. As a player, when that's the coaching staff's mentality. We loved that. If your leadership is that way, we got excited about that."

Edwards' day was done with a final line of 17 of 19, 367 yards, and five touchdowns passing, plus 73 rushing yards and a touchdown. Quick had only four catches for 172 yards and the three touchdowns. Quick made his presence felt as a true freshman by blocking the first of the two field goals the Apps blocked against Michigan. He was injured in the next game and got a medical redshirt for 2007.

"I'll always remember it as the Brian Quick game," said App State SID Mike Flynn. "It was so special. Such a special athlete and hard worker."

Quick was perhaps the most physically gifted player at Appalachian, at least during the championship era. He was tall with big hands and could run. He really grew as a player.

But the backups weren't finished. DeAndre Presley replaced Edwards and led the team to two touchdowns. The defense got two turnovers to set up the offense. The last touchdown came with 1:37 remaining to make the final score 70-24.

"I was so enamored with Armanti Edwards and watching him play," said Johnson. "He is my favorite all-time player to watch. To see him throw 19 passes for five touchdowns. There wasn't a throw he couldn't make. Brian Quick, who is he? He is so big and so good."

Edwards and Quick weren't the only stars. LeGree not only had three interceptions, but he also had eight tackles, including one for a loss and a forced fumble. Edwards was named the Southern Conference Offensive Player of the Week. He received the weekly honor from the conference 12 times over his career. LeGree was named the Defensive POW and Quick was the Freshman of the Week. It is extremely rare for players from one school to win more than one of those awards, but that's just how dominant the Mountaineers were. Edwards and LeGree were named National Players of the Week by both organizations that honored FCS players.

"It was electric," said Macholz. "We couldn't do anything wrong."

"Armanti was great. They had no answer for him running or passing," said Wolfe.

"I think we ran the score up and it was appropriate we ran the score up," said Johnson, laughing. "I have never been a part of a game, ever, that felt more like a party than that game. It was great, I loved it."

"That was as good as you could play," said Mills. "Even after we won, when we went over the film, you could still get ripped by [offensive line coach] Shawn Elliott. But after that game, the execution was close to perfect. He would say, 'great execution.' All of it combined for a bad night for Wofford. It was a satisfying game. It was a good night to be a Mountaineer!"

Johnson and Haynes still refer to that game and the tailgate on their podcast. At least until 2022, it was my favorite regular-season home game. When Wake and Miami came, that was great, but we lost those games. It was really just a great day from getting to meet my parents and having Bridges BBQ, to the beauty on the Parkway, the tailgate, the game, the halftime, everything was perfect.

It was magical, being on national TV," remembers Cobb. "The only negative there was a high school coach who complained and made a big stink about it, but some of our coaches said he just wanted his son to be recruited by App and we didn't so he complained."

The attendance was announced at 30,931, a single game record that stood until 31,531 showed up to see the Apps beat Elon in 2010.

Stroot watched a replay of the ESPN2 telecast and he got an idea for the next week's motivational video.

"We are watching the TV replay and they were talking about Quick and Armanti and said, 'those are video game numbers.' We recreated the plays on the NCAA video game. We recorded that and we had Armanti using the controller and shot that. It cut from him on controller and to video game and to the video highlights of the game. The players really bought in to those videos. Anytime they had a chance to get involved they loved it."

I'm not sure if the blowout over Wofford gave the team a big head or not. They were unbeaten in the Southern Conference and ended the regular season ranked number two in the nation. They lost at home in the playoffs to Richmond in the second round 33-13. The Spiders would go on to win the national championship.

"Armanti got hurt again," said Flynn. "He wasn't the same in the playoffs. And Richmond was good, and they beat us."

It was a disappointing end to a season that showed so much promise. It was the first time Appalachian had averaged more than 25,000 fans per home game over the season.

The athletic department was taking advantage of the popularity of the football program. The Wofford game, and all the televised games from the season were broadcast from a makeshift press box on the east side of the stadium. The new Appalachian Athletics Center was under construction on the west side of Kidd Brewer Stadium. It would provide club seating, luxury boxes, a new press level as well as new locker rooms, coaches' offices, and player meeting rooms. You could see the building towering over the stands during the Wofford game.

"The building we started in 2005," said Cobb. "Ken's leadership, getting the student fee increase, helped build that. The Michigan game added second deck on east side and the softball field too."

"Seeds were planted in 2005," recalled Green Reeder. "Because of what happened then, there's been continued growth."

"One of the first meetings I had after being hired was with Tommy Sofield to put his family's name on the indoor practice facility," remembered Cobb. "We needed that for all sports. Tommy made that first initial gift and others came after that, but that was very important. I don't think he gets the credit he deserves. The university fundraiser, Jerry Hutchins, was trying to get people excited about giving."

Green Reeder came to work in the athletic department in 2005. Cobb hired former All-American wide receiver Rick Beasley to work in the department. Beasley is very outgoing and was a good foil to Cobb's more business-like personality. He also provided some experience for a group of twenty-somethings that were full of dreams for the department. People like Green Reeder, Jackson, Flynn, Suzette Mauney, and Jay Sutton. They even got the University Development Office involved in the projects. Part of that was establishing fees for tailgating lots.

"We had all those meetings after hours around the dinner table," said Green Reeder "Wouldn't it be great if we could do this? Engage alumni. It's humbling to see where things have come because we had so much fun but did a lot of work."

"I will say there was a core group, and you usually have turnover, and your people move," said Flynn. "Frankly, I didn't want to move. We were so young, and there was a core group of us. I'm having a lot of fun and don't need to move right now. It was special."

The tailgate at App games has continued to grow with the athletic department. Our group has grown too.

"All four years, me and my friends came to dad's tailgate we knew it was there," said Pegues. "I didn't have other obligations, so we always went. My best friend Kelley and her husband Jordan are parking with us now. This will be something they hand down to their kids. Our best college memories are tailgating with my dad's friends."

During the 2022 season the group chipped in and bought a TV and a portable satellite dish we could use to watch *College GameDay* when it was there. We always have at least one generator and are prepared to deal with whatever weather gets thrown at us be it sun, wind, cold, or rain. Despite the elements, there's no place we'd rather be. We are Mountaineers.

As the demand for tickets for games has increased, finding parking spots for those ticketholders has gotten more difficult. New dorms have been built where the old stadium lot was, so that's a big parking lot that's not available any longer. A deck has been built to accommodate parking for those dorms, but tailgating on a deck just isn't the same to me. I have a friend who has a spot there and I like to stop by on my way to the stadium to see some folks. I'm glad I don't park there.

It has been amazing to see the growth in the athletic facilities as well as everything else at the university. Those kinds of experiences for App State fans are one of the reasons they keep coming back and are buying more tickets and paying more for parking than ever before. Seeing more second and third generation legacy students enroll who already have App State in their blood when they get there will be more willing to follow in the family tradition of donating back to the school. Between the grand plans for the future of the football program and facilities for the players, and still another year to watch Armanti Edwards, Appalachian fans were anticipating an exciting future. On this night, the Mountaineers turned Wofford's dream of a win against a huge rival into a nightmare, something App fans hoped defensive coordinators from across FCS would notice.

Chapter 9: The End of an Era
Appalachian State at Montana
December 12, 2009

Christmas 2008 was the first time in four years Appalachian fans weren't getting national champion gear as gifts. But the gift of being able to watch Armanti Edwards for another season was coming up in the fall. Spirits were high. In addition to Edwards, six other offensive starters were back. On defense, linebacker Pierre Banks, who was the heart and soul of the defense for four years and was the NCAA's record holder with 62 games played, graduated, but nine starters from 2008 were returning.

Edwards finally won the Walter Payton award in 2008, given to the best offensive player in FCS. In three years, he had already set school and conference records for total offense and touchdowns responsible for in a season. He also holds App State and Southern Conference records in those categories for a career. One of the people blocking for Armanti would be redshirt junior Pat Mills. Mills had played on special teams against Michigan and had rotated as a backup at both guard positions in 2008. He wasn't listed as a starter in the pre-season media information but earned a starting role in camp.

"I had a good off season and was faster," said Mills. "I had a good camp and worked my way up as a starter. I had split time at both guard spots. It was my time to step up."

The defense would be led by senior linebacker Jacque Roman who was the returning Conference Defensive Player of the Year. Mark LeGree was a first-time starter at safety in 2008, replacing legendary Corey Lynch. All LeGree did was set school and conference records with ten interceptions and was third in voting for the Buck Buchanan Award, given to the best defensive player in the FCS.

There were several other reasons for the excitement of the 2009 season. One was the opening of the Appalachian Athletics Center, the grand new building on the west side of the stadium that had a new press box, club seating, luxury boxes, and a locker room for the players. The facility is 120,000 square feet. It has a 9,000 square foot football locker room; a 9,000 square foot athletic training room and hydrotherapy center; and a 9,000 square foot strength and conditioning center. It also provided new coaches' offices, meeting rooms, and a player's lounge.

"It was something else," said Jake Stroot. "[Head football coach] Jerry [Moore] had his fingerprints all over it. It had never been done at that level. Meeting spaces were state of the art. It was incredible at App State."

"It was amazing," said Pat Mills. "You felt like you had a part of that. When we got here, it looks like the way it did when Shawn [Elliott, his position coach] played [in the 90s]. We built something. I was proud of it. You are seeing some of the fruits of your labor. You see an *SI* cover and $40 million building coming up and being proud of that. It didn't change us."

It gave video director Stroot some ideas. He worked on the audio-visual layout for the building. He knew it could really pay off when recruits came to town.

"Getting Florida and Atlanta folks to Boone in the season was tough because of the distance," said Stroot. "When you got them there in the cold Boone winter, we made videos to show them the atmosphere of what the fans were doing, tailgate, and the atmosphere at Black Saturday. It helped paint the pictures of App and set us apart. We did photo shoots when guys got there on Friday. They would put on a jersey, you toss them a football and I would take different pictures and edit them with different backgrounds, around campus and games. I would edit it all together and play the loop on all the TVs in the building as they went around with their families. Then on Saturday night, when they met individually with the coach, guys would sit on the balcony of the complex, and we would play video on scoreboard in the stadium with the lights off. That was a lot of hours, and no one was doing stuff like that."

There were a lot of special, mountain-themed architectural details in the locker room. The players had pictures of themselves in action on their locker and it was something the upperclassmen appreciated.

"Everyone says we're great but walking into that, we weren't recruited to that," said Mills. "It was ours. Have respect for it. 'Freshman, don't leave your Gatorade cup lying there,' 'Don't throw your tape down.' That was the way we thought."

One of the reasons for excitement for the upcoming season was that the Mountaineers would play East Carolina for the first time in 30 years. The two schools had much shared history. Appalachian was founded as Watauga Academy in 1899. In 1929 the North Carolina legislature authorized the Appalachian State Teachers College as a four-year program. In 1967 it was renamed Appalachian State University. In 1971 the University of North Carolina System was created, and it was named as one of its regional campuses.

East Carolina first opened in 1909 and became a four-year institution in 1920 and changed the name to East Carolina Teachers College. My mom always called it E-See Tee-See. Like App it was given university status in 1967 and became one of the regional campuses of the UNC System in 1971. Athletically, the schools first played one another in football in 1938. They were both members of the North State Conference from 1940 until the Pirates left in 1960. East Carolina joined the Southern Conference in 1964 and they left in 1976. Appalachian joined the SoCon in 1972. Appalachian had won the first 10 games and leads the series 19-10. However, the Pirates had won the last four games. East Carolina had a large enough stadium and had the attendance to remain a FBS program, whereas Appalachian was moved down to the FCS with the rest of the Southern Conference in 1982. That was one of the reasons the schools had gone so long without playing.

The summer of 2009 had some big changes for me personally. There were some significant changes at The Weather Channel. In September 2008, just days before the collapse of Lehman Brothers, Landmark Communications sold the channel to a group consisting of two equity firms and NBC. The firms paid NBC to run The Weather Channel. There was a lot of benefit to us at The Weather Channel. We had access to NBC's stable of reporters and when they were covering weather stories, we could get live shots and video from them. More importantly for me and the morning team, we could have access to the NBC-owned stations for their live video and tower cameras to help us show what was going on in the big cities around the country. Also, it gave Weather Channel reporters the opportunity to appear on NBC programs and it was great exposure for them.

But the NBC folks are news folks, and they are used to covering news. The Weather Channel has meteorologists, and they are used to doing weather. They are not news reporters and most of them didn't want to be news reporters. Management's insistence that the on-camera meteorologists report on news stories began to create some problems. In the spring of 2009, I had spent 25 years in TV. Most of the time had been fantastic and I loved it. I wasn't enjoying going to work much any longer and reached an agreement with management to leave.

My dad was dealing with some health issues so having the time off, I was able to get up to Charlotte to see him and my mom. I started making plans to see Appalachian play a lot that fall.

When I first got to Birmingham, Ron Grillo was the weekend sports anchor, and I was the producer of the weekend newscasts. We had a lot of common interests and really hit it off. He is several years older than me and had some great stories that I enjoyed hearing about, especially the sports history of the state of Alabama. Grillo was very well read and used a lot of big words in his sportscasts. He referred to an Alabama football win as a Pyrrhic Victory because of the injuries suffered by two running backs during the win. I had never heard that term before. When he would use a "big" word in his sportscast he would add the phrase, "And for those of you who went to Appalachian State, that means …" It caught me off guard at first, but thought it was funny and I don't think in the late 80s there were many people in Alabama who had ever even heard of App State before. Grillo said he got a call once from a grad who didn't like it.

Grillo's wife, Ronnie, was an advertising account executive in Birmingham and got a job in Rocky Mount, North Carolina, so they moved there in the mid-90s. I had stayed in touch with Grillo and had wanted him to come to Boone for a game, but Rocky Mount is east of Raleigh so a long way from Boone. In 2006, I had driven to Rocky Mount and spent Friday with him, and we went to the UNC-Georgia Tech game at Chapel Hill. Rocky Mount is close to Greenville, North Carolina, where ECU is so I asked him if he wanted to go to that game. He said yes. I would fly to Raleigh, and he would pick me up from the airport Friday afternoon. I was looking forward to the game. I had only been to ECU once, when I visited the campus when I was a senior in high school and was considering enrolling there. Grillo had basically retired but was writing a sports column in the Rocky Mount paper that ran on Mondays.

But with all the high hopes for Appalachian's season, something happened that could quickly derail it. During the summer Edwards was mowing the grass at the house where he and wide receiver Brian Quick lived and cut his foot. Quick called the head athletic trainer, Justin Smith.

As Mills remembers, "Justin asked him why he called me. [He] said, 'take him to hospital.' I remember seeing him [Edwards] in the locker room and people were saying, 'What were you doing? I would have cut your grass for you!'"

Edwards wouldn't be ready to play for the ECU game.

"We knew we had guys to replace him," said Mills. "It was always next man up. We would figure it out."

There was a great crowd for the game. A sellout crowd of 43,237 fans was on hand. A good group of App fans had made the trip East. The ECU fans knew Edwards wouldn't be playing.

"Their fans had lots of signs with lawn mowers and feet," said Mills.

D'Andre Presley got the start at quarterback but was ineffective. The Pirates were up 24-0 in the middle of the second quarter before App got things going. Travaris Cadet, a transfer from Toledo, replaced Presley and led a valiant comeback. Appalachian had the ball trailing 29-24 with about a minute and a half left but couldn't get into the end zone.

"I think we would have won the game with Armanti," said Mills.

Stroot said, "I wish I could have mowed his grass for him, and we would have beaten East Carolina."

Edwards returned the following week against McNeese State, a powerhouse from the Southland Conference. The game was played at night and the Cowboys won on a field goal with 18 seconds remaining. A safety on the kickoff made the final margin 40-35.

But after that the team got on a roll. They were feeding off the positive leadership of their senior leader.

"You could miss a block and he wouldn't care, just say, get them next time," said Mills. "He was so powerful, but he had a weird body type. He would get hit and just pop up."

But despite having Edwards back and the team winning, the season was taking a toll on the senior quarterback.

"Me and him lived in the training room that year," said Mills. "It was the way he played. He was all out. You wouldn't see him slide and that kind of led to some injuries. The training staff did a great job just getting him to Saturday."

Almost every year in the early 2000s, the Southern Conference schedule had the Mountaineers facing the three best conference teams they would play in back-to-back-to-back weeks. Those traditional powers were Furman, Wofford, and Georgia Southern. But 2009 was a down year for the conference overall. That season was the first time none of those three teams were ranked when Appalachian played them since Wofford joined the conference in 1997. The Mountaineers won the three consecutive games by a combined score of 148-77.

Elon was the school that would stand in the way of Appalachian's fifth straight conference title. The two schools would face off at Elon in the penultimate (Grillo word!) week of the regular season. In 2008 Elon was ranked number 11 when they came to Boone but lost the game 24-16. This year they were ranked number six, one spot ahead of the Mountaineers.

That was a wet week in North Carolina. Boone had more than three inches of rain, but it was even wetter in the Greensboro area, where nearly five inches fell. I asked Mills if having that indoor facility helped the team's preparation that week.

"Coach didn't like it," said Mills. "We would look at it, standing there in the rain, in 35 degrees wondering why we weren't in there. Coach said you will be outside because that's an advantage. Then after you got used to it, you bought into it. We have the nicest facility because we never use it. We would use it in the spring some. When there was lightning, then we would go in."

There was a lot of trash talk between fan bases the week before. Elon's athletic website "accidentally" put 2009

Southern Conference Champions on their website. It was talked about a lot on the App fan groups. Despite all the hype among the fans, it was just another game for Coach Moore and his Mountaineers.

"Part of the magic of Coach Moore was it was never about other team," said Mills. "Just us, we do what we do, we play our game, we'll be fine. I carry that with me now. If it's important enough to do, do it to your best. We prepared that way all the time. It wasn't that big of a deal. He had the standard of preparation. We operated above the line regardless of the opponent. We do what we do and we do it at a high level."

"I knew we would win then as Coach always focused on beating Elon," said App State AD Charlie Cobb. "They were trying to win a title. It was the same story with Delaware in the national championship game. They were playing to win a title. We played to beat Delaware."

I was in Charlotte that week and had tickets to the game. None of the Charlotte guys in our group wanted to go. Brian Metcalf came over from Raleigh and met me there.

I parked on campus not far from the stadium. Everyone from Elon I saw was wearing a maroon T-shirt that had "BEAT APP" in huge letters on the front. I laughed and walked down to a parking area where all the App fans were going to be. I couldn't believe all the App fans that were there. I was pumped for the game. I met up with Brian and we tailgated for a while and then headed to the stadium. We got in early as did a lot of the App fans. The whole visitors' side was packed with folks wearing black and gold and making a lot of noise. I thought how disheartening it must be for the Elon players to come out for the biggest game in their program's history and their own stadium is half full of their opponents' fans.

"We had the crowd and that made you feel good," said Mills. "Sometimes fans wonder, 'do they know if we are here?' We do and we did. Your chest gets broader coming out of the tunnel."

App struck early and often on both sides of the ball. The defense picked off Elon three times in the first quarter and Edwards' third touchdown of the game on the first play of the second quarter gave the Mountaineers a 21-0 lead. They went on to an easy 27-10 win. Most of the Elon fans were gone when the game was over.

"We shut them down," said Mills. "That was such a good feeling."

Armanti was shaken up during the game and there was a lot of talk about a bounty being placed on Edwards by the Phoenix. A coach on that staff I met a few years later said they were trying to get him out.

Cobb didn't like the hit.

"A cheap shot on Armanti when we were up 21-0 cost us a national title," he said. "He couldn't run afterwards."

I asked Mills about that.

"Every D wanted to knock him out of the game. We would always hear that. I thought every team would. You better want to hurt him and get him out."

That was about as satisfying a win in a conference road game I attended. I loved it because the App fans really turned out for that game. It's not surprising because so many graduates live close to Elon and obviously knew what was at stake. To see the players execute so perfectly and break Elon's spirit so quickly was great. I was worried about Edwards and his health and there was still a lot to play for. App's win streak was now at eight and would get to nine after a win over Western Carolina to close out the regular season. The Apps were seeded fifth in the playoffs and that meant they would likely have to go on the road twice to make it back to Chattanooga.

"One of the things I enjoyed about the FCS playoffs was another month of football!" said Metcalf.

The opening round of the playoffs was a closer than expected win over South Carolina State. Edwards played but wasn't great. Next up was Richmond, which App would be playing for the third year in a row but the first time at Richmond. The Mountaineers won in 2007 behind Armanti's 313 rushing yards and 495 yards of total offense and seven touchdowns responsible for. Richmond shut down Armanti in 2008 and ended App's 13-game playoff winning streak and went on to win their first national crown.

A guy in Charlotte put together a bus trip that would leave Charlotte early Saturday morning and stop in Greensboro and Durham to pick up folks and get to Richmond about two hours before kickoff. I decided to do it. All the seats ended up selling out. Metcalf got on in Durham. I had brought a cooler with a 12-pack of beer, and the drinking started when we stopped in Greensboro. The van had a DVD player, and someone had brought a copy of the Michigan game. I brought the DVD I had made with a collection of media clips talking about us in the aftermath of the Michigan game. It was a blast. I had consumed a lot of beer by the time we got there. The Richmond stadium was away from campus in a city park and was also used by high school teams. It didn't have a very large capacity and it was a cold, wet night. A few of us from the bus walked a few blocks to a restaurant to get some food in us. Some snow was beginning to mix in with the rain.

"I remember the locker room was leaking. We were getting soaked in the tunnel," said Mills. "It was a messy game. That field wasn't great. Wasn't well lit, we couldn't get anything going."

Because of the weather, I stood for most of the game. The father of star linebacker DJ Smith was standing next to me.

With 9:23 remaining in the game, the Spiders kicked a 27-yard field goal to take a 24-14 lead. It was Armanti time once again.

"We were all beat up," said Mills. "That game was another one, we found a way to win."

Edwards completed passes of 32 and 27 yards to put App State at the Richmond five. Moore scored on the next play to cut the lead to 3.

The defense got their first three and out since the first quarter and gave the Mountaineers the ball back. Moore was the star of the drive, picking up 67 of 73 yards on the drive. Edwards capped it with a three-yard run and Appalachian had their first lead of the game with 4:32 remaining. Things looked good when the defense turned in another three and out. On the punt, Cadet had the ball stripped by a Richmond defender who ran the ball into the end zone and the Spiders were back in front 31-28.

There was 3:26 remaining when Edwards got the ball. The Apps were facing a second and 20 on their own 20. Edwards hit Quick with two passes to give the Mountaineers a first down near midfield. Two more completions plus a 15-yard penalty gave the Apps the ball at the 18. Three runs set up a first and goal at the 8. Two runs picked up four yards and it was third and goal from the 4. The Mountaineers, trailing by three, were out of timeouts. Edwards found Matt Cline for the touchdown with 10 seconds left. The winning drive was 12 plays and 70 yards. In the final 9:23 of the game Edwards was seven of eight passing for 106 yards and had 20 rushing yards. Moore carried the ball 22 times for 175 yards and two touchdowns. The win was the 11th straight for Appalachian. That was a great win. Everyone slept on the way home and after we got back to Charlotte I drove back to Atlanta.

The win set up a trip to Missoula, Montana, to face the number one Montana Grizzlies. The Griz had won national championships in 1995 and 2001. They were the runner-up to Richmond in 2008. They had won 118 games during the decade of the 2000s. Despite Appalachian's recent dominance, the Mountaineers had won only 101 games. Montana hadn't had a losing season since 1986 and was in the midst of a streak of playoff appearances for 17 consecutive years.

Appalachian visited Washington-Grizzly Stadium in the 2000 semifinals and lost a 19-16 heartbreaker in overtime. The next week, Georgia Southern beat the Griz for the national championship.

They were 12-0 and had scored 132 points in their previous two playoff games. I knew this was a game I didn't want to miss. The Yosef Club had announced there would be a charter out of Greensboro and I quickly signed up. During the week, Grillo interviewed me about the trip for his column that wouldn't run until the Monday after the game.

The team was going about its business as if it was any other week.

"We tackled on Tuesday the week of the national championship game in December," said Mills. "We weren't going to prepare any differently because of the time of the year."

Our flight left Greensboro early on Friday morning and we stopped in Des Moines to refuel. We got to Missoula about mid-afternoon. Steve Stroupe was a guy I had met a few times before and was on the flight. He graduated from Appalachian a few years before I got there. His younger brother Scott and I lived together for a while in Birmingham. Scott was a year younger than me, and we had gone to the same schools. Steve was traveling with Dean and Gail Mills, Pat's parents. He knew he would have more fun going out with me, so we went out to grab a bite to eat, then hang out around town.

It was a lot of fun. Everyone was so happy to see us and welcome us to town. They were treating us great. After we ate, we went to a bar and watched the other semi-final game between Villanova and William and Mary. We didn't have to buy a beer all night. All the Montana fans were saying whoever won our game would win the title. They were looking forward to having us experience the environment at their stadium. Dean and Gail Mills were experiencing the same thing.

"Everywhere we went the people we saw said we are so glad you came, can't wait to see Armanti play," Dean Mills said.

There is a mountain above Missoula and the campus, Mt. Sentinel, which has an "M" on it 620 feet up. The peak of the mountain is more than 5,100 feet above sea level. I wanted to climb the mountain Saturday morning, but we just didn't have time. The weather wasn't good on Saturday morning either. It was windy and cold, and snow was forecast for the afternoon. Kickoff was at 2 p.m. local time. As part of our trip package, the Yosef Club had provided a tailgate for us. It was in a big tent that was heated. I wanted to get to the stadium about 30 minutes before the game, even though I knew it would be cold. I was wearing long johns, which I rarely do. I thought about not wearing them, because I wouldn't be able to change out of them and I was afraid they would be too hot on the flight. We had checked out of the hotel and had our luggage on the buses that took us to the stadium and would take us to the airport right after the game. I was wearing a thermal layer shirt, with a sweatshirt on top of that and a pullover windbreaker over that. At that time, I always wore a jersey in the color App was wearing. The only white one I had was the one I wore to Michigan. I put it over everything else. I had mittens, ear warmers, and a wool hat. I felt pretty confident I would stay warm.

The tailgate scene was pretty good. I didn't walk around there as much as I would have done now. I'm sure there were some interesting meats being cooked out there.

"When we got off bus to the tailgate, the fans urging us to come and have food and a drink with them," said Dean Mills. "Even at the stadium, fans would walk up to us, and say we're so glad out are here. It was a recurring theme."

Appalachian had about 300 tickets and we were on the same side of the stadium as the press box. To get to the stadium, we went through an area that highlights the great teams and players in program history. It was very impressive.

The App group was down on the 10-yard line, and we had about 10 rows all together down to the field. The first thing I noticed at the seats is how close the stands are to the field. All stadiums have a dotted line that's a yard behind the painted area of the sideline outside of the bench areas. That line is for safety, as a buffer to keep the media and other folks on the sideline out of the way of the players. At that stadium, there wasn't very much room behind that dotted line. That can be a problem for photographers.

"That's my fear," said Stroot. "That there's nowhere to go if the play is coming toward you."

The bench areas had storage space cut out under the stands because there wasn't the usual amount of room on the sidelines to store the big equipment trunks teams have. We had a great view of Mt. Sentinel, and I was disappointed I didn't climb up there. You could see several people on the mountain near the M and several other people who looked like were going to watch the game from there. According to the broadcast, it was 17 degrees with a wind chill of 15, but I know that wind chill was wrong because when the temperature is that low, almost any wind will create a wind chill several degrees cooler. The way that wind was blowing, I think the wind chill had to be at least in the single digits. The stadium sits at the mouth of Hellgate Canyon, and yes, it's aptly named. The stadium was packed, and it was very loud. Capacity there is just more than 25,000 and it seems smaller because it's so compact and close to the field. But between the proximity of the field, the mountains around the stadium, and the passionate fans in the seats, it is very loud.

"That was my favorite stadium," said Stroot. "I want to shake that architect's hand."

The Mountaineer offensive linemen weren't wearing any sleeves, as they won't do for games at Boone, but most of the other players were wearing long sleeves. I had a camera with me and took a few pictures of the stadium before the game, but it was too cold to keep my hands out of my gloves for long.

The crowd was quickly having a big impact on the Apps' offense. The Mountaineers took the opening kickoff and in eight plays had moved 49 yards to the Montana 37. On third and one, they were flagged for the first of four false start penalties in the first half. The third and six play was an incomplete pass. Before the fourth down play the offense huddled because of the crowd noise, something that hadn't happened much in the past five years.

"I don't remember a louder environment," said Mills. "We had several false starts. We went silent which we never did."

The Griz responded to the fourth down stop by taking the ball down the field and scoring on Chase Reynolds' 39-yard run. When the Mountaineers got the ball back, the running back was helping Armanti communicate with the linemen on the play that was called. But early in the second quarter, Devin Moore scored a short touchdown and nine minutes later, Jason Vitaris booted a 46-yard field goal through the wind. Thirty yards of penalties against the Mountaineers on the drive forced the field goal.

Midway through the second quarter, a winter storm warning was issued by the National Weather Service and right before halftime, the snow picked up considerably. The Apps took the 10-7 lead to the locker room at halftime.

I wanted to take some pictures of the snow, but I didn't want to take off my gloves. The visibility had been reduced so you couldn't see the M on Mt. Sentinel any longer. Montana lets fans return to the parking lot during halftime and most of the App fans went to stand in the museum area to warm up. I didn't think that would do me any good, but I did walk around the concourse.

When the teams returned to the field, they were joined by a coating of snow. Some of the yard lines were being cleared, but not the entire field. Reynolds scored again less than two minutes into the half to give the lead back to Montana. Appalachian answered with a nice drive into the red zone combining running and passing.

"They didn't mind being cut blocked," said Pat Mills. "Some teams if you cut their D linemen, they would get up and complain. The Montana players, they would say 'good job.' You are supposed to be mad. That kind of messed us up a little, I think."

But the drive stalled, and Vitaris' field goal attempt was blocked.

The Grizzlies drove the ball inside the App State 25, but senior linebacker Jacque Roman picked off a pass and returned it to midfield. Edwards led the Mountaineers to the four-yard line, but they faced a fourth and two. Edwards picked up the first down with a three-yard run and on the next play, Moore took it in, and the Mountaineers were back in front.

Once again Montana answered with a nice drive. On third down at the 15, two App State defensive backs had their hands on a pass but couldn't make the interception. It did force the Griz to try a field goal and they were going into the wind in the fourth quarter. The kick was good, and the score was tied with 14:50 to play.

When the Mountaineers got the ball back, they had a nice drive going. Edwards hit Quick to convert a long third down. But on the Griz 32, Edwards threw an interception. The defense responded with a three and out highlighted by a Roman sack on first down. The punt into the wind only went 33 yards. Once again, the Apps were moving the ball, mixing the run with short passes. A 13-yard run by Moore gave Appalachian a first down at the Montana 22. The Mountaineers committed their first penalty of the second half and their fifth false start penalty of the game. It seemed to take them out of their rhythm. Edwards threw three straight incompletions, and a 44-yard field goal attempt had no chance, despite the wind.

The Grizzlies took over with 3:45 remaining. Three runs by Reynolds, aided by an App State face mask penalty, got them to the 15 with the score still tied. On first down, the Griz were called for holding, only their second penalty of the game. On the next play quarterback Andrew Selle threw a beautiful ball to the sideline in the end zone and Jabin Sambrano hauled it in despite great coverage from Appalachian's Ed Gainey. Coach Moore challenged the call, but it was upheld. The lines at the edge of the end zone had been scraped and you could see he made the catch. The extra point gave the Grizzlies a 24-17 lead with 1:31 remaining. Washington-Grizzly Stadium was the loudest it had been all day.

Travaris Cadet returned the kickoff to the 40-yard line, but a holding penalty was called on the Mountaineers (their 10th penalty of the game for 86 yards) and the drive would have to start at the 25. There was 1:21 remaining and the Apps had two time outs.

"We never thought we were out of the fight," said Mills. "That was the mindset, and it was because of Armanti. We just play and do what we need to do. We knew how to win. We are running red 40 and I've got to block the NG. We never thought we would never win. We were trained for that moment and when you get to that moment and if you do it right, you win."

Edwards' first pass was incomplete under heavy pressure. The next play he completed a pass to BJ Frazier that went for 30 yards. Then he hit Quick for 11 and Cline for 10. Suddenly the Mountaineers were down to the Grizzly 24 with 48 seconds to play. In the stands we knew Superman was going to pull it out, again.

But three straight passes were incomplete, and the season was down to a fourth and 10. Moore called the second time out to talk about the play. Edwards threw a jump pass to Quick who caught it right at the line to gain. A measurement gave App State the first down, but Montana's coaches challenged the spot. It was upheld. First and 10 for Appalachian at the Montana 14 with 18 seconds remaining. Edwards was looking for Quick, who had 10 catches for 135 yards, but they couldn't hook up. Devin Moore got open out of the backfield and Edwards found him and he was tackled at the four with 6 seconds left. Coach Moore called his final timeout.

How many plays could the Mountaineers run? On first down, Edwards looked for Cline on a quick slant and it was batted away. If Edwards had waited for another instant, Cline was behind the defense and would have been wide open. But Edwards didn't have an instant, and fortunately, there was still one second on the clock. Cline was a clutch receiver all year and was on the receiving end of a brutal hit in the first half. He left the game for a while but caught seven passes for more than 100 yards in the game. As Edwards took the snap for what would be the final time in his college career, he looked at Quick who broke to the outside, away from his defender, right at the goal line. The pass hit him in the hands and fell to the snowy turf. The crowd erupted and Quick fell to the ground.

That play happened right in front of where we were seated. I will always remember that play and looking back at Edwards after he threw that pass. It seemed to me that he slumped his whole body. It seemed that he realized that that was it. His college career was over. This time, the Mountaineers would not win. There was no joy in Boone. Mighty Armanti had thrown an incompletion.

The App fans, many of whom were parents of players, cheered the team as they slowly made their way back to the bench and to exchange greetings with the Montana players on the way to the locker room.

"It was just one of those games we didn't execute," said Mills.

Stroot, who would go into opposing fans' stands and video them celebrating the rare win over Appalachian, knew he had to do something he didn't want to do.

"I have to go to Brian Quick's face and get his eyes when he's lying on the ground after dropping that ball," said Stroot. "It's the worst part of that job. That's the motivation for next year. I don't want the guys to have that feeling next year. I'm not proud of it, but I have to get his eyes."

Stroot didn't play for Coach Moore, but from being around him so much had picked up on his favorite saying: Always do more than what is expected.

"That's what we did," said Stroot. "That's still what I do and what I tell my staff today."

After working at Appalachian for 14 years, he went to Louisville and then Georgia. He's been the video director for the Atlanta Falcons since March of 2021. Doing more than what is expected earned him a game ball after a Falcons win over the '49ers.

"Quick thought he should have had it," said Stroot. "It was a long walk to visiting locker rooms and that was awful. I felt bad for him, he would have caught that nine of 10 times."

"There were a lot of tears in the locker room," said Mills. "We wanted to send those seniors off right. That was the thing about the playoffs. You had a chance to win, and it hurt to lose."

It wasn't just the tears in the locker room for the Mountaineers. After playoff games, the NCAA picked a few random players for drug testing. Because the players were so cold and dehydrated, they couldn't pee a sample to be tested. Most of the team was sitting on the buses waiting for the players to give a sample.

"The NCAA decides to drug test and guys just couldn't go," remembers Mike Flynn, the Mountaineers' SID. "And we had to wait for them to go. Kind of added insult to injury waiting for that."

The game was a classic emotional, nerve-racking game that makes the playoffs so special. Appalachian hadn't been on the losing end of too many of those games. In 2002, Maine won in Boone 14-13 and the 2000 overtime loss in Missoula were the only one-possession playoff losses the Mountaineers had since the mid-90s.

"As much as it hurts if we score at the end. We win the national championship," lamented Flynn.

"There was nothing like the playoff games," said 1984 Appalachian graduate Mike Nauman. "The finality of it. It's more devastating than a bowl loss. It's different now. You are king of the mountain, or you go home."

"There's no real pain like a playoff loss," said Alex Johnson. "It wouldn't have been quite so painful if it wasn't Armanti's last game."

And while the Grizzly fans were having a big party for beating Appalachian, the following week, they would feel the heartbreak Mountaineer fans were feeling. They lost the national championship game to Villanova 23-21.

"I think Montana expended all their energy against us," said Flynn.

I know so many of the fans I talked to felt like the Montana-App State game was going to be for the championship. It had to be hard to come down after that win, then travel to Chattanooga to play again in just six days. Several of the Appalachian fans who had bought tickets for the national championship game went anyway and pulled for the Grizzlies.

Despite the result most of the App fans were glad they went.

"I played at Michigan and LSU and coached at Auburn and Alabama and Montana is the best football environment in the country that I've experienced," said Mills.

"It was an awesome atmosphere," said Flynn. "It was an awesome game. Two great teams. I hate the outcome, but it was as good as it gets."

"As fan of college football, it was a great experience," said Kindsay Green Reeder, an athletic department employee. "Minus the loss of course, I had a really great experience."

"If there's a game you could change, that is one," said Cobb. "Armanti deserved to win a championship at the end. They didn't have a way to clear the field and it was to negate our speed advantage."

"I loved the playoffs," said Appalachian graduate Mike Wolfe. "I'm glad it's finally been adopted in FBS. It's like March Madness in football."

But having played 17 playoff games in the previous five years had taken a toll on the players. That's an extra season and a half. Not only do the games and the practices take a toll, but it cuts the rest and recovery time to get ready for the next season. It's one reason it's so hard for teams at any level of sport to repeat as champions.

"It was the finality of the playoffs: win or go home," said Pat Mills. "It was hard for us, you go back to that you can't lose mentality and when you do, it's hard to take. All the games we played began to take a toll, I think. We played NFL seasons most of our career. Especially Armanti."

"We had a ton of joy watching him play and it was great how well they did," said Dean Mills. The run they had was incredible. Obviously, you live with it a little bit, but for me, we were there to support our son and our school. Any game can go anyway. I don't think people realize how many games these kids were playing, and the physical wear and tear was taking a toll. I never dwelt too much on losses, I felt bad and hated to see it, but didn't crush me."

After the game, we got on the bus and after waiting a while for traffic to dissipate eventually made it to the airport. There was a little concern that the weather may keep us from taking off, but after waiting for the plane to be de-iced, we were able to leave. We stopped in Rapid City, South Dakota, to refuel on this leg. I wasn't bothered in the least with the long johns I had on during the flight. I slept most of the way and still had to drive to Atlanta once I got to Greensboro.

For several months after that game, when someone would see me wearing Appalachian stuff, they would say they saw that crazy snow game we played. When I told them I was there, they were surprised and asked if it was as cold as it looked. I always say, "Yes, it was."

"I still say person for person, there may be some stadiums as good, but I'm not sure there are any better," said Flynn. "They are awesome people. That home and home series we did was born from the trip out there."

Appalachian finally was able to beat Montana in week two of the 2012 season. The 11th-ranked Mountaineers won 35-27 over the 12th ranked Griz. That game is perhaps best known for the spectacular sky over Kidd Brewer Stadium. There was a rainbow over the east stands that was photographed and sold as posters in the bookstore. I sit in the east stands so couldn't see the rainbow, but the sky over the west stands was an incredible orange, purple, and white. The picture I took of it was the background on my phone for more than 10 years.

After the team arrived back from Missoula, the next day Armanti Edwards made his final appearance as an Appalachian State student at his graduation.

"When Armanti's name was called at graduation the ovation he got was something," said Cobb. "I remember that like it was yesterday."

He set 64 school records as a player, was a Dean's List student and earned his degree in three and a half years. I'm not going to list all his records here, but only Steve McNair had more yards of total offense in FCS football in a career. He was the first Division I football player to rush for 4,000 yards and throw for 10,000 in a career.

The athletic department retired his number 14 at halftime of the Georgia Southern game in 2023. This will be the last time the school retires a number. Edwards was also elected to the College Football Hall of Fame in his first time eligible as part of the class of 2024.

"For the coaches' video, he was hard to follow because he could fake you out," said Stroot. "He was a quiet leader, but you could get him laughing, especially around other players."

"I've yet to see a QB that was as electrifying as he was for us," said Hellinger. "The way he could escape, extend plays, create mismatches, and use his talents to almost will wins was incredible."

"He was one of the most exciting players I've ever seen play the game," said Wolfe.

"I've seen a lot of football and the best college QB I ever saw in person was Armanti," said Brian Hoagland.

"Holy cow, what he could do," said Dean Mills. "Just how special he was. He was fun to watch."

He was drafted by the Carolina Panthers with the 89th overall pick in the third round of the NFL Draft. Supposedly the Panthers coach, John Fox, who was in the last year of his contract, didn't want Armanti to be taken with that pick. Armanti didn't play much that year. I did go to a game with Stroupe, and it was the first game Armanti was active all year. He was only in for a few plays.

The Panthers finished 2-14. The next year, Ron Rivera took over as coach and Cam Newton was drafted by the Panthers. I felt Armanti would be a perfect backup for Newton because that offense was more in line with what he was comfortable with from college. I also thought he could be a valuable "slash" type player at receiver or running option plays. But that off-season had a lockout and players couldn't practice with the teams. I think the missed meeting and practice time to install those kinds of plays hurt Edwards. He ended up playing for four years in the NFL. He signed with the Canadian Football League in 2016. He played strictly receiver in the CFL and had several good seasons and won a Grey Cup with the Toronto Argonauts in 2017. Not long after he left the NFL several smaller quarterbacks who could run started having an effect in the NFL.

"It's a shame he wasn't given a chance at the next level to play QB," said Hellinger. "I'm not saying he would have been successful, but I think a lot of people wished he were given that opportunity."

"Even though we've moved on, we stay in touch," said Greene Reeder. "He was so dynamic. He was the people's quarterback. Those teams in the years we won were a magical time. All those guys have a special place in what we created here."

"There were times during his freshman year when he looked like a freshman," said Haynes. "There were other times during his freshman year, and you wondered how did he make that happen? He was the show. Tailgating was taking off, but we weren't putting 30K fans in the stands for Elon in the sleet because we had a good defense. They were there to see Armanti Edwards. He was the difference. We were the circus. During his era, past that, and even now. You could get a ticket to Wofford and The Citadel for $15, but when App came to town it was $35. We were everyone's homecoming, and they didn't care if they won or lost. In the SoCon it was easy. One year you went to South Carolina and the other year you went to Tennessee and Georgia. People showed out to see Armanti play. Somehow, they still showed up to see the circus. We were blessed to be where the circus called home. In my opinion. You knew he and that team were going to do something special and you had to see it with your own eyes."

"He had a way of making stuff happen and he had such great instincts," recalled Johnson. "But the cool thing was, I was on campus the same time he was. He was a year ahead of me. But the thing about him was how he carried himself, so low key, unassuming. He represented himself so well on campus. When

I was walking up stadium drive to go into the game, the question wasn't whether we were going to win, but were we going to get 40, 50, how much are we going to score? It wasn't just him of course, but there is just something about having your all-time best player not just doing it physically, but in big moments and always coming through. Armanti lost two conference games in four years, and they were within about 30 days of each other. I wish more people could have experienced in real time what it was like to have those players and those special teams as we did in the championship era. As we are talking about the Halloween game with Wofford that we were living the good old days and didn't realize it. I kind of see that was the good old days like, we had such a great culture, conference, recruiting classes, stars, bowl games. It was about winning the game, getting to the playoffs, and winning championships. And it was all anchored by the greatest player I've ever seen at App State, ever, Armanti Edwards. I'm blessed to say that I was in school when he played, and I was able to see him front and center."

I echo all those sentiments. I hope Appalachian is lucky enough to have another player who will take the GOAT at App State away from him, but I'm not sure it is possible. I would put him as one of the top five players ever in I-AA/FCS football along with names like Rice, Payton, and McNair. It was such a blessing to be able to watch him play for four years.

Chapter 10: A Pair of Power 5 Wins

Appalachian State at North Carolina September 21, 2019

Appalachian State at South Carolina November 9, 2019

Armanti Edwards graduated after the 2009 season, but the Mountaineers still made the playoffs the next three years. Although they never made it past the second round those years, there was plenty of talk about how long the program should stay at the FCS level. In the late 90s a committee was formed to explore making the move, but they decided it wasn't a good time. Several of the programs App State had played in the playoffs, Boise State, Middle Tennessee State, and Western Kentucky, had all made the jump to the BCS.

This was a topic of discussion even before the Mountaineers won their first national championship. Charlie Cobb raised the question when he was interviewing for the AD job with Chancellor Dr. Ken Peacock in the spring of 2005.

"He wanted a recommendation from the athletic director," said Cobb.

"It was a topic as soon as I stepped on campus," said Mike Flynn, who had worked in the sports information office since 2003. "Around 2010 when Charlie formed the feasibility committee everything was pointing to it. I was on the committee. It was the right time."

Said Cobb, "What else do you have to prove at this level?"

In the summer of 2011, after seven months of work, the committee recommended to Dr. Peacock that Appalachian should seek out membership in an FBS conference. A news release stated, "The committee found Appalachian is best suited for FBS as an institution and an athletics department ... its academic philosophy and its strategic vision going forward more closely mirror FBS institutions than its current FCS counterparts. The committee has worked to develop a blended financial model that ensures that the move would not be made on the backs of students."

Dr. Peacock took the recommendation to the Board of Trustees and that was approved. But that was the easy part. It was now out of the university's hands.

"At that point it was getting that elusive invite," said Flynn who was promoted to SID in 2004.

That invite had to come from an existing FBS conference. With conference realignment happening at the higher levels of college athletics, was Appalachian State remained hopeful some of the trickle-down effect may open up a spot for them. One of the most likely conferences to extend an invitation was Conference USA.

Conference USA (C-USA) was founded in 1995 with the merger of the Great Midwest and the Metro conferences, primarily because of men's basketball. The conference didn't sponsor football when it was founded and most of the members didn't even have football teams. UAB was one of the schools that didn't have football then. The Blazers had been in the Great Midwest. I saw all this first-hand when I was working in Birmingham. The conference had started sponsoring football in 1996 but had seen several members come and go. After the 2013 season, four schools left for the American Athletic Conference so C-USA would need replacements and Appalachian was hoping to be one of the schools invited.

"We tried getting into C-USA," said Cobb. "They wanted big media markets. I told the commissioner, 'You are ignoring programs that have had football success.' History has proven C-USA was wrong."

The invitation didn't come. C-USA got North Texas (Dallas market), University of Texas-San Antonio, Old Dominion (Norfolk), UNC-Charlotte, and Florida International (Miami). It was particularly galling for App fans to see Charlotte get an invite when they hadn't done anything as a football program. The program played their first game as an FCS program in 2013 and was going to be able to move up to FBS in 2015 because of the membership in Conference USA. Residents of Charlotte had no interest in what was going on at the campus northeast of uptown Charlotte in Harrisburg unless they had gone to or had some kind of tie to the school. Many students there who had grown up in the state were fans of UNC or N.C. State or even Clemson or some other, proven football program. UTSA had only had football since 2011. ODU started their program in 2009. FIU had only had football since 2002. The conference thought that having the schools from the major media markets would mean more money when TV contracts were being renegotiated.

A year later Western Kentucky was invited to C-USA and left the Sun Belt. That was five schools, WKU, Middle Tennessee, North Texas, Florida International, and Florida Atlantic, that had left the Sun Belt. The Sun Belt was down to only eight football playing members, the lowest number permissible by the NCAA. They needed some new blood and fast. On March 27, 2013, Commissioner Karl Benson offered an invitation to Appalachian and Georgia Southern to join.

"When the Sun Belt approached us, we said yes," said Cobb. "We were tied with Georgia Southern."

It's kind of ironic that the two schools who were the biggest rivals on the field had joined up to enter the new conference, but it made sense. App and Georgia Southern had become bitter rivals and with the Eagles' six national championships and the Mountaineers' three they were by far the most successful programs in the Southern Conference. It would allow them to continue the rivalry in the new conference.

There wasn't universal acceptance of the move by App State fans. On the message boards online, some people complained about the expense of FBS and the increased expense of travel to go to road games. The Southern Conference was very compact, and it was an easy drive from Charlotte or even Atlanta to most of the road games. But most Appalachian fans knew that if they wanted to stay relevant as a football program, the move would need to be made.

There would be growing pains. For one thing, there was a two-year transition period. In the final year in FCS, Appalachian and Georgia Southern would be ineligible for the playoffs. Also, in the first year of FBS, the schools would likewise be ineligible for post-season play. Since the Sun Belt didn't have a championship game, that just meant bowl games. An advantage of being an FBS program would be that bigger schools could come to Boone. No FBS school would go on the road to play an FCS team, no matter the crowd or environment.

The 2012 season ended up being the last for Jerry Moore. The team went 8-4 and shared the Southern Conference championship. The last game was a heartbreaking loss to Illinois State in the first round of the playoffs, when senior Sam Martin, the only kicker Jerry Moore offered a scholarship to as a high school senior, missed a point after touchdown in overtime. Martin excelled at both kicking and punting as a Mountaineer and has probably had the best NFL career of any App State player in the 21st century.

Former Mountaineer Quarterback Scott Satterfield was named as Moore's replacement for the 2013 season. Satterfield led the Mountaineers to their first undefeated and untied regular season as a senior in 1995. After graduating, he joined the football staff and worked in various positions. He was the quarterback coach for Richie Williams and Armanti Edwards and left for Toledo after the 2008 season. He spent a year there, then worked for Mario Christobal at Florida International for two seasons before returning to Boone and serving as the offensive coordinator in 2012.

2013 saw the Mountaineers suffer through the program's first losing season in 20 years. Some blamed that on the fact that the playoffs weren't an option, and the players didn't have anything to play for. Some felt there was a funk because Coach Moore wasn't there any longer.

One of the main differences between FBS and FCS, which I outlined in the Michigan chapter, is that FBS schools can give 85 scholarships while FCS schools only have 63. At that time, you could only have 25 people in a single recruiting class so it would take the Mountaineers a few years to get to the 85-scholarship level.

The Mountaineers' first game as a FBS program was the rematch with Michigan Cobb scheduled for the million-dollar payoff. There was no upset this time. A blocked punt return for a touchdown late in the second quarter gave the Wolverines a 35-0 halftime lead. Appalachian didn't even convert a third down until midway through the third quarter. The final was 52-14. The following week Appalachian routed FCS Campbell 66-0.

Even with the rout, Satterfield made the decision to replace quarterback Kam Bryant with freshman Taylor Lamb for the game at Southern Miss. It was notable when Lamb signed with the Mountaineers. His father, Bobby, was a quarterback at Furman and later the head coach of the Paladins. It was in his first year as head coach in 2002 when Appalachian pulled off the "Miracle on the Mountain" (more on that later). Three years later he was still the coach of Furman when they lost to the Mountaineers in the national semifinals. He resigned as coach of the Paladins after the 2010 season after the fourth consecutive year of not making the playoffs.

Taylor Lamb played well, but a blocked PAT with six seconds left gave the Golden Eagles a 21-20 win. The first two Sun Belt games didn't go well for the Mountaineers. They were blown out by Georgia Southern in Statesboro and lost at home to South Alabama. They got a break in the conference schedule with FCS Liberty coming to Boone, but the Flames left Boone with a 55-48 overtime victory. Satterfield's record was 5-13. The luster had come off the Mountaineer program. Boos were heard at The Rock. The people who were opposed to the move up where screaming "I told you so!" at the top of their lungs on the internet "fan" boards.

It wouldn't get any easier for Appalachian the next week with a trip to Troy. The Trojans were struggling in what would be Coach Larry Blakeney's final season. Under Blakeney, a former assistant to Pat Dye at Auburn, the Trojans had made the move from FCS to FBS and had won five Sun Belt titles. Troy's last game as an FCS team was an upset loss to the Mountaineers in the 2000 playoffs.

I decided to go to the game with Mike Ladd and Eric Race, two grads from Atlanta who I frequently went to games with. Race met us in Montgomery with a friend of his and the four of us got to the stadium. We had bought some fried chicken and were going to tailgate a little. We ended up parking at a church across the street from the stadium so didn't drink much. There weren't very many people there. None of us had tickets and as we were walking up to the stadium from the church, a woman came up to me and asked if I needed a ticket. I said yes, but we had four we needed tickets for. She had four, and just gave us the tickets. As soon as I walked into the stadium, there was a man in an App shirt was holding two beers and said to me, "They sell beer here!" It was $5 for a 16 ounce can of beer. That was the first time I had seen beer sold on a college campus for a football game. We all bought a beer and went to sit behind the App bench. There were only a few thousand people in the stands. It was a beautiful day. The student section didn't have many people in it. Troy got the ball first and on their opening drive moved right down the field to score a touchdown. To make matters worse, the only senior who started the game on defense, cornerback Joel Ross, was ejected for targeting on that series. We didn't think things could get any worse and went to get more beer.

But Taylor Lamb showed why he earned the starting quarterback job on the Mountaineers' first offensive play by airing out a long pass that Malachi Jones hauled in and took for a 59-yard touchdown to tie the score. The play energized the Black and Gold. The Mountaineers upped their lead to 21-7 and Troy returned a kickoff for a touchdown. The offensive onslaught didn't stop, and the Mountaineers left Troy with a 53-14 win. Their first Sun Belt win, as well as their first win over a FBS team since the Michigan win in 2007. It also provided a much-needed jolt of confidence for the entire program. App State didn't lose another game the rest of the year. We were proud to say we went to that game at Troy to support the team and help them get on the run that would last for years.

The following week they began to show that they were regaining their swagger. It was November 1st and snowing and very windy as the Mountaineers were hosting Georgia State. The Panthers had a new program and were playing their home games in the Georgia Dome and had a pass-heavy offense. Their offense couldn't handle the wind and cold in Boone. The Mountaineers had a 20-0 lead and had sent the field goal team on the field on a fourth and goal with seconds remaining in the first half. Georgia State had all three of their time outs and called all three of them. Satterfield didn't like that, so he called a fake field goal. It was converted into a touchdown, and it was 27-0 at half. The only question was whether Georgia State would come back out after halftime. I was watching a video stream, but you could see their spirit had been broken in the Boone cold. The final score ended up 44-0.

After a win over Louisiana-Monroe in Boone, the team won back-to-back road games against Arkansas State and Louisiana-Lafayette, the two preseason conference favorites. A win over Idaho in week 12 gave the Apps a 7-5 overall record and a 6-2 record in the conference. Because the Apps beat Lafayette and Arkansas State, Georgia Southern won the conference title. The Eagles didn't have to play either one of them. Although the Mountaineers won seven games, they weren't eligible for a bowl game because of the transition period. But the confidence had been restored, both with the players and the fans. The Mountaineers showed they could compete in the FBS. There were a lot of players returning for next season, too.

The Sun Belt had some expansion news of its own; before the 2015 season kicked off. Coastal Carolina located 11 miles from the coast in Conway, South Carolina, would join the conference to play football in 2017. After the 2017 season, Idaho and New Mexico State would no longer be a part of the Sun Belt. App State and Coastal had played several times in the FCS days, including a playoff game in 2006.

One of the advantages of being an FBS program is the payouts for playing "guarantee" games against bigger programs are much higher. The athletic department would make more than $1 million in those games now. They had assembled quite a list of opponents too. In addition to the Michigan game in 2014, Clemson was on the schedule for 2015, Tennessee in 2016, Georgia in 2017, and Penn State in 2018.

On the field, the strong finish to the 2014 season had fans optimistic for 2015. This year a bowl game was possible if the team won six games. The season started off with a 49-0 win over Howard. Then they went to Death Valley to take on number 12 Clemson. The Tigers won 41-10 and would end up in the national championship game, losing to Alabama. Appalachian went on a roll winning six games in a row. One of the games in early October was in Boone against Wyoming. It poured the whole day and was one of the wettest days I've ever experienced, not just at a football game. Another highlight was a win over Georgia Southern on a Thursday night. There was a great crowd and an impressive performance by the Apps. The win also clinched bowl eligibility for the Mountaineers for the first time.

Two weeks later the Mountaineers had another home Thursday night game against Arkansas State. When the schedule came out, I was worried about this game for several reasons. I didn't think fans would come in big numbers to two Thursday night games and given the choice, most fans would pick the Georgia Southern game. That was the team they were familiar with, and the one we had had the rivalry with for years. I felt like we would need the home field advantage more against the Red Wolves. They had a good team and had revenge on their mind after our win the year before ended their run of conference titles. The Georgia Southern game drew a crowd of more than 24,000, an excellent crowd then for a Thursday night game. But there were more than 5,000 fewer people in The Rock for the Arkansas State game. The Red Wolves went on a 23-6 run in the second half to pull away with a 40-27 win. Arkansas State went 8-0 in the Sun Belt and won the conference title. Appalachian ended up second with a 7-1 conference record and 10-2 overall. They would be matched up with 8-4 Ohio University in Montgomery's Camellia Bowl.

There was a great group of App fans there. I rode down with Ladd, and we met up with a lot of the guys I tailgate with in Boone. It was a fun afternoon of tailgating, but the game didn't start well. Appalachian was trailing 24-7 midway through the third quarter. But an explosion of 21 App State points in less than two minutes gave the Mountaineers the lead. But the Bobcats scored five points and had a 29-28 lead with 1:47 to play. Lamb was brilliant throwing and running in moving the Black and Gold into field goal range. Zach Matics kicked a 23-yard field goal as time expired and went on a sprint around the Cramton Bowl with his teammates chasing him.

The 11 wins gave the Mountaineers the record for most wins by a school in their first season as a full member of FBS. It was also the first time a school won a bowl game in their first season as a full member of FBS.

2016 was a big year because in week three of the season, the Miami Hurricanes would be coming to Boone. Finally, a Power 5 school would be coming to App State. In all those close losses to the "big boys" we always said, let's just get them to The Rock.

Cobb had left Appalachian to be the AD at Georgia State, and Doug Gillin took over the position in the spring of 2015. Gillin felt like his biggest challenge taking over the job was to increase the number of season tickets sold. There were only about 4,500 season tickets sold when he took over. I think most App fans didn't really feel like they needed to get season tickets because there had never been the demand. You could always just come up that day and get a ticket to the game. There were some big crowds for Georgia Southern and for homecoming, but if you couldn't get a seat, there was always The Hill you could sit on.

"From a season ticket standpoint it wasn't growing," said Gillin. "How could we get more tickets sold? We decided we need to get creative with scheduling."

Mike Flynn was promoted to assistant AD. In addition to his role as SID, he was the point person for non-conference scheduling. Flynn was calling around looking for money games.

"I got the guarantee game against Penn State," said Flynn. "I reached out to peers about a home and home. But I called Miami looking for a guarantee game. Their scheduling person said we need something for next year. This was winter of 2015-16, and they need a game in 2016. I basically said we are full and couldn't come down there, but what about coming up here for the front end of a home and home? He said, 'Yeah, that's something we could talk about.' From that point, I turned it over to Doug."

"He came in and said, 'We may have Miami.' I said, 'Whoa!' said Gillin. "It came to fruition. We got them here."

"Sometimes it's better to be lucky than good," said Flynn. "I don't even think it was public that they were short a game that fall and it just worked out for us."

But week one would be at Tennessee. The SEC moved the game to the Thursday before Labor Day. The Vols were ranked number nine. It was the first time the two schools had played. My wife at the time had family near Knoxville and we were going to spend the weekend with them. I had worked with Emily Stroud in Birmingham and her husband, Greg, at The

Weather Channel and they were now living in Knoxville. I had been given four tickets to the game from a friend who was a Tennessee booster, but they couldn't make the Thursday night game. I asked Greg, an Alabama graduate, if he wanted to go and I was surprised he said yes. We didn't tailgate, but instead did some bar hopping. Greg, a bourbon fan like me, took us to a neat place that had great burgers and a big bourbon selection.

Neyland Stadium was always one of my favorite stadiums and I had been there several times for Tennessee games against Alabama and Auburn. I was there for Peyton Manning's last game there. Auburn was going to play the Volunteers in the SEC Championship game the following week and I went there to get a jump on interviews from Tennessee players and coaches about their first trip to the championship game. There are several cool traditions Tennessee has. First, the stadium is right next to the Tennessee River and a lot of fans come to games in their boats and dock near the stadium. The band plays the fight song of the visiting team before the game as a way of welcoming them. And after the band plays the national anthem, they line up in a big T from the locker room to the bend and the players take the field through that as the band plays "Rocky Top." Neyland Stadium has always been among the largest stadiums in the nation. During the game, Appalachian lead most of the way, but lost another heartbreaker in overtime.

After a win over Old Dominion, it was time for the number 25 Hurricanes to come to town. Kickoff was moved to noon and it would be televised on ESPN. With the early kickoff, I got a room and drove up there Friday. Eric Church had hit it big as a country music singer and had attended App State. He had finally done a few things with the athletic department and was going to be in Boone for the game. He didn't sing the National Anthem but was there for the coin toss.

The Mountaineers got the ball first and after one first down had a third and short at their own 48. But a false start penalty backed up the Apps and they didn't convert the third and seven. After the punt, Miami took over at their 20.

The Rock was so loud. The announced crowd numbered 34,658. That's more than 3,000 people that had ever been there for a game. On their first play, Miami running back Mark

Walton took the handoff and was popped in the hole by App State safety A.J. Howard.

The crowd erupted with the hit. Kaiden Smith was a freshman safety who was being redshirted. During the game all the redshirts are supposed to run along the area behind the benches in front of the student section and wave towels and keep the crowd fired up.

"That crowd was insane," remembered Smith. "AJ hit him, and I turned to the crowd to celebrate, and I saw everyone get quiet and realized what had happened."

What had happened was that Walton bounced off the hit, broke into the clear and went 80 yards for a touchdown. All the energy was sucked right out of the stadium. The final score was 45-10 and it was obvious how far the Mountaineers needed to go to consistently match up with the nation's best. But the game showed that App State and Boone could handle a big game. The pre-game environment was incredible.

Despite that loss, the team didn't hang their head. They ran off a six-game winning streak and were set up for a showdown with Troy for the conference lead. Both teams were unbeaten in the Sun Belt. I couldn't go to the game because of work and was really disappointed. I did watch it on TV and the Trojans prevailed 28-24 with a last-minute touchdown. The win earned the Trojans a number 25 AP ranking. The following week they were blown out by Arkansas State. The Red Wolves lost at Louisiana-Lafayette on November 26th. There was a three-way for first between App, Arkansas State, and Troy. The Trojans lost the following weekend at Georgia Southern, so the Mountaineers and Red Wolves were declared co-champions. Appalachian was headed back to the Camellia Bowl, this time to face Toledo, from the Mid-American Conference. It was not a real popular decision with the App fans.

    I went to the game again with Ladd. It was an easy drive for us. None of the folks from Charlotte came and there wasn't that great of an App crowd this time. The game was a back-and-forth affair. Appalachian kicked a field goal with a little more than five minutes remaining to take a 31-28 lead. The Rockets drove inside the App 10. On a third and two, the Mountaineers stopped Toledo for no gain, forcing a field goal. For some reason, Toledo took a delay of game penalty before the field goal, backing them up to the 13-yard line. The kick was no good and the Apps became the first team in college football history to go to and win bowl games in their first two years of eligibility. On the way back to Atlanta we stopped for gas and there was a car with Atlanta plates at the pump beside us. We were talking to the guy while he filled up his car. He was the brother of the Toledo kicker who missed the field goal.

In February of 2017, the Mountaineers made the biggest announcement in the history of the athletic program. The University of North Carolina at Chapel Hill would come to Boone to play a football game. It was part of a three-game series. Two games would be played in Chapel Hill in 2019 and 2023. In 2022 the Heels would come to Boone. Soon after, South Carolina and App State announced they had a series that would see the Gamecocks come to Boone. The scheduling reflected a change in philosophy in scheduling.

"We didn't want to play anymore 'buy' [guarantee] games," said Gillin. "Scheduling is far out. Some of those games are getting more difficult to get. Some schools may not be paying. We've grown our fan base so big. We want to get home and homes, North Carolina, South Carolina, and N.C. State, those games become more appealing. We reached out to Bubba Cunningham [the UNC AD] and asked if there would there be interest. They were interested and we got it worked out. We did the same with South Carolina. I can't say enough about Ray Tanner [South Carolina AD] and Bubba. What I've always said is that those games are good for fan bases and the state; it keeps money in the state. The South Carolina game keeps it in the region. They certainly agreed; they believed that too."

Adam Witten had just finished his first season as play-by-play announcer for the Mountaineers. The 2004 App graduate grew up in the Tampa Bay area but knew how big this was for his alma mater.

"It's not just playing an ACC school; it's playing the big in-state school," said Witten. "App has a goal to be the best program in North Carolina, and for that to happen, you have to win games like that. To have a legit multi-year series was a big deal. The UNC series was the change in philosophy in scheduling. Play in-state and regional teams. These series that make sense. Fans will flock to that opportunity. That is what it was going to take to build ticket sales and sustain success."

I couldn't believe North Carolina was going to come to Boone to play a football game. I saw Gillin and told him what a big deal I thought that was. It wasn't just me. Former App State coach Mack Brown was working at ESPN at the time. Brown had a home in the Boone area and had helped with fundraising for the Mountaineers. That part of the contract surprised Brown too.

"I called Doug [Gillin]," said Brown. "I can't believe that Carolina would agree to that. He told me, 'You are a part of that!'"

Jeff Owen, who I met at Ann Arbor, was another of the long-time App fans who couldn't believe the news.

"I was floored. I thought that would never happen," said Owen. "Miami was a fluke. I never thought we could get UNC or [N.C.] State to come to Boone."

It would be several years until the Tar Heels came to Boone, but during the 2017 season another, in-state, ACC team was coming to Kidd Brewer Stadium. This time it was Wake

Forest in week four. The Mountaineers were opening the season at Georgia. I felt pretty good about our chances against the Bulldogs. A good friend of mine, Roger Manis, was a big Georgia fan and was pretty well connected with the program. He had heard that freshman quarterback Jake Fromm was trying to get the receivers to play catch with him while the starting quarterback, Jacob Eason, was enjoying campus life a little too much. It was Kirby Smart's second year and was still trying to find his way as a head coach. We had a senior-laden team, starting with Taylor Lamb. His top target was Shaedon Meadors, who was also a senior and had averaged nearly 17 yards a catch in 2016. We also had two good running backs in Jalyn Moore and Darrynton Evans. Evans had dynamic speed and the coaches had talked about getting Evans on the field at the same time as Moore. If Evans was in the slot and could get the ball in different ways, his speed and elusiveness could be deadly for a defense. It was much the same way Georgia had talked about using their two dynamic running backs, Nick Chubb and Sony Michel, the same way. I gave us about a 20 percent chance of winning. I thought maybe Meadors would make a catch to convert a third and long and keep a drive alive and if Evans got the ball in space and someone slipped or missed a tackle, he had the speed to outrun an SEC defense.

My wife and I went with Ladd and a friend of his, Mike Smith. Smith was at App with Ladd in the 70s and worked with the training staff for four years as an undergrad and for two years of grad school. A lot of App fans had bought spots in the same parking lot to tailgate in and that was a lot of fun. When we were literally walking into the stadium, Smith received a text that said Evans and Meadors were hurt and wouldn't play. I said I give us a 5 percent chance of winning without those two.

On the first several drives neither offense could move the ball much and there were a lot of punts. Thomas Hennigan was a true freshman from Greensboro who was starting in place of Meadors. He hadn't caught any passes yet, but I was impressed because he was the punt returner. I thought if the coaches had him returning punts in his first college game, at Sanford Stadium in front of 92,000 people, he must be a heck of a player (spoiler alert: he was). One of the App defensive linemen chased Eason out of bounds and tackled him late. He was flagged, but Eason was shaken up on the play. Everyone in the App section sitting around me was saying, "That's their quarterback! That's their quarterback!" I told them that may not be such a good thing for us. Sure enough, Fromm, the true freshman, who was a life-long Georgia fan and played in the Little League World Series as a youth, came in and led the Bulldogs to four straight touchdowns. The Bulldogs, ranked number 15, won the game 31-10. Fromm led the 'Dawgs to the national championship game. App State won their next two games to set up the showdown with Wake Forest.

Appalachian and Wake Forest had a nice rivalry at one time. In 1975 the schools met for the first time and the Mountaineers won. Starting in 1979 the schools met every year until 1996. They had played three times since then, and the Apps had won two. A lot of App people felt that's why they quit playing. All of the games in the series had been played in Winston-Salem. But now that Appalachian was an FBS program, the Demon Deacons were coming up the mountain. It was a great game because of the proximity between the campuses and so many App grads lived within an easy drive of Winston-

Salem. In 1985 and 1989, the App State game was the highest attended of all the Wake home games that season. Many App fans felt having the Deacs finally come to Boone was justification in the Appalachian program. The game was not televised but a record crowd of 35,126 was on hand. It was the largest crowd in the 23-game series.

Wake got the ball first and moved down the field. In only seven plays they had a first and goal. The defense stiffened and held the Deacs to a field goal. Appalachian responded with a touchdown pass, but the PAT was blocked. The Mountaineer defense came up huge and held Wake to five straight three and outs. The Rock was rocking. There were several "APP" "STATE" cheers that were deafening. I had goose bumps. But the offense could only register another field goal the rest of the half. After App State missed a 35-yard field goal at the end of the half, it was 9-3 Mountaineers.

On the first drive of the second half Lamb completed a pass to Jalen Virgil down to the Wake 32. But Virgil was penalized for unsportsmanlike conduct and the drive stalled. Wake went 97 yards for a touchdown to take a 10-9 lead. It only took Appalachian two plays to retake the lead. TJ Watkins took a jet sweep 84 yards and the Mountaineers were up 16-10. Wake retook the lead late in the third period, but Michael Rubino hit his second field goal and it was 19-17 with 10:35 to play. Could the Apps hold on? Sadly, no. Wake Forest drove down to the App seven and kicked a field goal to take a 20-19 lead. App punted back to Wake with 2:13 remaining and all three time outs. The defense held and Lamb had the ball at the App 42 with 1:42 remaining. The crowd was going crazy.

"The defense came up big in that game," said Smith.

Lamb moved the Mountaineers to the 27-yard line and on fourth and five with 10 seconds remaining they were lined up to kick a field goal to win. But Wake jumped offside, and the ball was moved up 5 yards and it was first down. Satterfield elected to go for the field goal, but Rubino's kick was blocked, and it was heartbreak again for the Mountaineers. That was a tough loss to take for me.

The team took it hard too. Smith was injured and didn't play but learned a lot watching that game.

"It taught me how much the little things matter," he said. "You could see the little mistakes that cost us; the level of discipline it takes. We wouldn't make them again."

The Apps reeled off three straight conference wins, but turnovers cost them in an overtime loss at a University of Massachusetts team that would finish the year 4-8. The next week, the Mountaineers lost a shoot out on the road to Louisiana-Monroe. But finishing the year strong earned them another Sun Belt conference championship. This one was shared with Troy, who the Mountaineers didn't play. The bowl game was a rematch against Toledo, but this year the game was in Mobile. Toledo wasn't thrilled with the rematch, and it showed. The Mountaineers won 34-0.

For the 2018 season Appalachian would continue its run of opening games at national powers. This year it was at number nine Penn State.

"I liked playing the big games early," said Smith. "No team knows what they are going to be in week one."

Smith's own team would be in that boat. The Mountaineers would have a new quarterback for the first time in four years. Zach Thomas was a redshirt sophomore from Trussville, Alabama, the Birmingham suburb that had produced Alabama's Jay Barker. It was a very strong program from when I covered high school football in Birmingham. He played four games in 2017, accumulating less than 80 yards of total offense. He was known for his strong arm. While I had a good feeling about the Georgia game the year before, at least until I learned Meadors and Evans were hurt, I had no idea what to expect with Thomas starting the game in front of one of the nation's most hostile environments.

    I was looking forward to going back to Happy Valley (See Chapter 6) and would be staying with my old friend from The Weather Channel, Jon Nese. I was with my wife, Terri, and we flew into Philadelphia Friday and had lunch in Lancaster at a famous Amish restaurant. Heading to State College, we ran into a torrential downpour that flooded the expressway and we were forced to detour on side roads. Several of them were flooded as well and it took us a while to get around them. I was trying to get updates from Nese about when the rain would end, but we eventually made it. Nese asked me about my expectations, and I told him I had no idea. That night we went over to see Mike the Mailman and visit with him. Saturday, we tailgated with several of Nese's friends and went into the stadium about 30 minutes before kickoff.

The game was being played at 3:30 on September 1 and was being televised by the Big Ten network. If that sounds familiar, App played Michigan on September 1 in a noon kick on the Big Ten Network (Chapter 7). Surely history wouldn't repeat itself. I sat in the App section in the upper deck in the corner of the stadium. More than 105,000 fans were on hand.

The Lions took the opening kickoff and gained nine yards on their first two plays. On third and 1, safety Desmond Franklin stopped PSU quarterback Trace McSorley for no gain and it appeared the Lions would have to punt. But, no, the Big Ten officials called Franklin for celebration, apparently for stepping over McSorley to get back on his side of the line of scrimmage. I couldn't believe an official would make that call on the third play of the season. Given new life, Penn State drove down the field and McSorley capped the drive with a 12-yard touchdown run.

However, just like against Michigan, the Mountaineers used a big play to respond after the Big Ten team took an early lead. Darrynton Evans took the kickoff at the goal line, found a seam, and went 100 yards and we were tied. When Penn State got the ball back, the Apps forced a three and out. Then Thomas led them on a 12-play, 60-yard drive that ended with a 38-yard field goal from Chandler Staton, which gave the Mountaineers a 10-7 lead. A Penn State field goal in the final seconds of the half tied the score at halftime. I was very pleased, but still wasn't sure what to expect in the second half.

App State got the ball, made one first down and had to punt. The Nittany Lions then went and scored. The Mountaineers were forced to punt again, and Penn State scored another touchdown. There was 2:41 to go in the third quarter and the Black and Gold was trailing by 14. Thomas showed his mettle on the next drive. On the second play of the fourth quarter, the Apps faced a third and 17. Thomas ran for 15 yards, but his helmet came off, so he had to sit out the next play: fourth and 2 at the Lion 24. Payton Derrick, a redshirt freshman who was getting his first snap as a college player came in for this huge play. Derrick hit Dominique Heath, a transfer wide receiver from Kansas State who ran down to the two. Thomas came back in, and the Mountaineers were called for their second 15-yard penalty of the drive and were backed up to the 17. No worries, Thomas hit Malik Williams for the touchdown and the Apps were within seven. The defense couldn't hold, and Penn State scored to go back up 14. But App responded again, going 80 yards in nine plays and Williams caught another touchdown pass from Thomas.

The Mountaineers retained possession when they recovered an onside kick. Thomas hit Corey Sutton on a pass to the one and Thomas scored on the next play. The defense did rise up on the next series and held the Lions to a three and out. However, they couldn't move the ball and Clayton Howell's 53-yard punt was downed at the four. The Black and Gold defense forced another three and out and took possession at their own 42. It was time for running back Jalin Moore to take over. On first down he caught a 10-yard pass from Thomas. On second down he gained 10 on a run. The next play was an eight-yard gain to the 16. Moore got it again and ran down the sideline into the end zone to give the Mountaineers the lead again 38-31 with 1:47 left to play. Rubino had touchbacks on all his kickoffs so far, but this one was fielded at the goal line by KJ Hamler and returned to midfield. This gave the momentum back to Penn State and their crowd was loud. The Lions faced a fourth and 2 with 1:06 to go on the App 40. McSorley converted a pass for a gain of 10 and the crowd was back into it. Three plays later McSorley hit Hamler from 15 yards out and after the PAT we were tied with 42 seconds on the clock. Appalachian had two timeouts left. On first down Thomas hit Sutton for 30 yards and the App fans had hope. But the drive bogged down and Staton missed from 56 yards as the game ended and we were headed to overtime.

Appalachian won the toss and chose to go on defense first. Penn State chose to play at the end of the stadium where their student section is. As I mentioned in Chapter 7, Penn State's student section is one of the largest and loudest in college football and covers much of the south end zone. I think I would have avoided that, but coaches like to have the ball last. Penn State scored a touchdown, so the Mountaineers would need to match that in front of the students. The first three plays netted 9 yards, and Evans gained a yard to convert the fourth down and keep the game going. However, on the next play Thomas was intercepted in the end zone by the Lions and the Mountaineers would fall short once again to a top 10, Power 5 school in heart-breaking fashion.

A picture of Penn State running back Miles Sanders in the end zone was on the cover of *Sports Illustrated* the next week. No Mountaineer defenders were in the picture, but you could see the Penn State students celebrating. The main title declared: "It's Lit! And the 2018 crazy is already off the charts." There was a caption that said: "Thanks to a Miles Sanders TD in OT the Nittany Lions barely escaped an upset bid by Appalachian State – 11 years to the day after the Mountaineers famously derailed Michigan's season."

Thomas was 25 of 38 for 270 yards and two touchdowns with only the overtime interception. It appeared the App State offense was in good hands once again. But I wasn't the only one surprised by his performance.

"Mid-week, Zach had thrown seven interceptions in practice," recalled Shawn Clark, at the time the offensive line coach. "We were going to let him start but have a quick hook and were going to replace him with [Jacob] Heusman. That has to be the best performance by a new QB ever. He made throws we had never seen him make."

In fact, the team's confidence in the close loss at Penn State sent them on a five-game winning streak that had them averaging 46 points per game while giving up less than 10 a game. The final game in the streak was a 27-17 win over Louisiana and the Apps earned their first ranking in the AP poll at number 25. Next up: arch-rival Georgia Southern on the road at Statesboro. The Mountaineers would be the first ranked team to ever play at Southern's Paulson Stadium. Nothing would make their fans happier than beating the hated Mountaineers and knocking them out of the rankings. Georgia Southern won the conference title their first year eligible, in part because App State beat Arkansas State and Louisiana, the preseason favorites, and the Eagles didn't have to play either one. But two losing seasons followed and Chad Lunsford, a former App State assistant coach, had been named head coach for the 2018 season. The Eagles were 6-1 coming into the game with the only loss coming at number two Clemson.

It rained on the Mountaineers' parade as a ranked team. Thomas was injured on a run during App State's first possession. Derrick replaced Thomas but couldn't duplicate the magic from Penn State. He was three of 12 for 73 yards and two interceptions. He was replaced in the second half by Huesman. All the blame can't be placed on Derrick. The team had five turnovers and committed 11 penalties. Georgia Southern only completed one pass in the game but it went for a 57-yard touchdown. The Eagles prevailed over App 34-14 for their program's first win over a ranked team.

But the Mountaineers didn't sulk. They had another road game the following Saturday at Coastal and it was doubtful Thomas would be able to play. He didn't. Huesman started and went nine for 19 with a touchdown and two interceptions. But the Apps went to their bread and butter; the running game and gained 278 yards on the ground. Evans had 159 and Marcus Williams had 103 with each getting a touchdown. The defense pitched a shutout and scored a safety as the Mountaineers prevailed 23-7. Coastal's only touchdown came on a pick six.

Thomas returned the following week at Texas State. App State won 38-7 as Thomas passed for 247 and the defense only gave up 218 yards. A return to Kidd Brewer Stadium was successful with a 45-17 win over Georgia State. That moved the Mountaineers record to 8-2 overall and 6-1 in the conference. It set up a showdown with Troy for the right to host the first ever Sun Belt Conference championship game. The Trojans were 9-2 and unbeaten in the conference. They had beaten unranked Nebraska earlier in the season but had lost at number 23 Boise State and at Liberty.

The Mountaineers scored three touchdowns in the first 19 minutes of the game and let their top ranked defense do their thing the rest of the way. App won 21-10, won the east division as a result of the head-to-head tiebreaker against Troy and their 7-1 conference record was better than western division champion Louisiana, who had a 5-3 conference record. The first-ever Sun Belt Conference football championship game would be played at Kidd Brewer Stadium.

The Mountaineers and Rajin' Cajuns had played every year since App State had joined the Sun Belt and the teams had developed quite a rivalry, although the Cajun' were yet to beat the Mountaineers. Their coach, Mark Hudspeth, had complained about the difficulty in getting to Boone. Also, he wasn't happy that he had to play in Boone in consecutive years. The addition of Coastal Carolina and the elimination of Idaho and New Mexico State forced the conference to redo the scheduling and created divisions. It was just chance they had to come to Boone again in 2017. It turned out to be the final game of the regular season and Appalachian dominated the Cajuns 63-14. After the game Hudspeth was fired as the Louisiana coach. He was replaced by Alabama assistant coach Billy Napier. Napier played his college football at Furman and was involved in one of the most famous plays in App State football history.

In 2002 the Mountaineers and Paladins were involved in one of their typical battles. Napier, the Furman quarterback, had thrown a touchdown pass to give Furman a 1-point lead with seven seconds remaining. Bobby Lamb, a former Furman quarterback and Taylor's dad, was in his first year as head coach of the Paladins. He called for a 2-point conversion, thinking (I guess?) that a 3-point lead would be better than 1, but not realizing it would be nearly impossible for the Mountaineers to return the kickoff into field goal range in less than seven seconds. I was watching on TV and remember screaming how stupid that was for him not to kick the point after touchdown when the offense was sent back on the field.

Anyway, Napier dropped back to pass. Appalachian's All-American defensive end, Josh Jeffries, read the play, dropped into coverage, and intercepted the pass at the 4-yard line. He took off down the sideline. Cornerback Derrick Black ran up next to Jeffries who lateraled the ball to Black. Black sidestepped an attempted tackle by Napier at the App 40 and made it to the end zone for 2 points for App State. Now the Mountaineers were back on top 16-15. App recovered the onside kick and ran out the clock. I hated not seeing that in person.

Napier made his return to The Rock earlier in the season and the Mountaineers prevailed 27-17. The

Mountaineers were 5-0 against the Cajuns heading into the championship game.

"Finally having [the championship] game was a huge deal for our program," said Smith. "Being able to host a game in December. It was cool seeing them dress up the stadium."

With only a week to prepare for the game, and wet weather, the crowd was only 14,963, but the fans who were there were loud. The Cajuns took the opening kickoff and drove down to the App State 25, but the Mountaineers defense made a stop on third down and forced a field goal. Evans, who had kickoff return for a touchdown against Penn State, took the kickoff and was inexplicitly tackled a yard short of the goal line. But the Mountaineers scored on the next play and had a 7-3 lead.

The next three possessions for each team resulted in punts. Louisiana finally was able to string together a few first downs, but the drive bogged down at the App 28 and had to settle for another field goal midway through the second quarter. The Mountaineers went to the ground game to drive down to the red zone. After a false start penalty, quarterback

Thomas kept the ball on a quarterback draw, got a great block from Evans and went up the middle of the field for a touchdown and that's how the half ended.

Late in the third quarter, the Cajuns got a short field goal to cut their deficit to 1 again, but on the last play of the quarter, Chandler Staton was good from 42 yards and the Apps were up 20-16.

The Mountaineer defense continued their good play. Defensive back Tae Hayes came up with an interception and returned it 32 yards to the Appalachian 44. Three plays gained nine yards and on fourth and 1, Thomas did it again with his legs, going 35 yards for the touchdown. The teams traded field goals and the final score was 30-19. The Mountaineers had their third consecutive conference championship and would play Middle Tennessee in the New Orleans Bowl.

The trophy celebration was held on the field and Satterfield accepted the conference championship trophy and Evans was presented a pro wrestling-style championship belt as the MVP of the championship game of "The Belt." The field was open to the fans and most of the people still in the stadium surrounded the stage and were getting showered in confetti.

Smith enjoyed the festive atmosphere.

"It was neat celebrating on the field with the team and the family later," he said.

However, a few days after the win over Louisiana it was announced that head coach Scott Satterfield was leaving the Mountaineer program to take over at Louisville. The move wasn't a shock since the rumors had been swirling. I was a little surprised. I knew he wouldn't stay at App forever, but I thought he would stay another season. The 2019 schedule included games at North Carolina and South Carolina, and there would be a lot of seniors on that team. Also, his son would be a senior in high school. But before the 2018 season, Satterfield hired Jimmy Sexton as his agent and Sexton is agent to the stars of coaches in college football, so I figured Sexton would encourage Satterfield to leave while his star was so bright. Mark Ivey was named the interim coach for the bowl game and Clark, the offensive line coach, would call the plays.

"It was one of those things, App meant so much to him, when he [Satterfield] wanted to leave, he deserved it," said Smith. "There were no bad feelings. We were wondering who else would go. The main task was winning the bowl game in New Orleans and there was a lot going on. It was a distraction."

"You have a lot of things running through your mind when hiring a coach," said Gillin. "There's a sense of urgency, but you have to make sure that everyone else's sense of urgency doesn't become your sense of urgency. There was a lot going on at that time."

I was disappointed I couldn't make that trip, because I love New Orleans and hadn't been down there in a while. A lot of my friends were going too. The team didn't let the loss of their coach slow them down at all. After falling behind 3-0, the Mountaineers scored 24 unanswered points in the second quarter en route to a 45-13 win.

Before the game it was announced that Eliah Drinkwitz would be hired as the head coach to replace Satterfield. Drinkwitz was largely unknown to Mountaineer fans. The 35-year-old had been offensive coordinator and quarterbacks coach at N.C. State the previous three seasons and the Wolfpack offense had set many records under his direction. There were a lot of App fans that wanted someone with App ties to get the job. Many people wanted Ivey to retain it. When he didn't get the job, Ivey joined the Louisville staff with Satterfield. Five other assistants went with Satterfield to Louisville, as well as several other staffers. Drinkwitz wasn't involved in the bowl game planning, but he watched the game from the coach's box.

"We knew Eli was strong on the offensive side," said Gillin. "He had played UNC and South Carolina. We wanted someone who had coached against the teams we were playing. We made that decision to go with him."

He assembled a good staff. There were four holdovers from the 2018 staff: Clark, who is an App grad; Justin Watts, who had been in Boone since 2015; DJ Smith, a freshman starter at linebacker in 2007, who spent three seasons in the NFL; and Greg Gasparto, who was in his second year coaching the defensive backs. Drinkwitz was just the fourth head football coach at the university since 1984 when Sparky Woods took over for Mack Brown. That lack of turnover at a school at the level of Appalachian is remarkable and a major reason the program had enjoyed the success it had. But Drinkwitz was not a member of "The Appalachian Family." I don't think that it is a bad thing to bring in outsiders every now and then because they will bring in new ideas and a fresh perspective on things. However, App State is a unique place, and the football program has a unique culture. I wasn't sure the program needed much from the outside.

"Eli kept me on," said Clark. "I could have gone to N.C. State, Maryland, a couple of other schools, but I bought into what Eli was trying to do. He knew the success we had had. He wants to do his thing, but not take the train off the tracks. I helped him with that."

"It was different," said Smith. "For our class we had an experienced group. During my time spent at App we knew it was a player run team. We had strong veteran leadership to deal with that adjustment. We had new strength coach, and things were different off the field day to day."

The roster had a lot of experience, and the schedule was favorable. Despite having two Power 5 games, North Carolina and South Carolina, those schools were considered beatable and weren't the powerhouse, highly ranked programs Appalachian had faced in the past several years.

The season got off to a good start with a 42-7 win against former Southern Conference rival East Tennessee State University. Week two was a closer than expected shootout against Charlotte, but the Mountaineers were unbeaten for the trip to Chapel Hill that App fans had been looking forward to since the game was announced two years earlier. The two schools had only played once before, with the Tar Heels picking up a 56-6 win in 1940. But this was a much different situation. App State was looking to show it could not only compete but win against the top teams in the state. In two games against less than stellar competition Drinkwitz showed his offensive chops. There was another wrinkle in the matchup because after the 2018 season North Carolina fired Larry Fedora as football coach and hired Mack Brown, the former Appalachian coach who coached the Tar Heels from 1988-97. Brown left UNC to coach Texas where he spent 16 years and won the 2005 National Championship. He had been inducted into the College Football Hall of Fame in 2018.

When the Tar Heels kicked off the 2019 season against South Carolina, Brown was 68 years old. It had been five years since he had been on the sidelines. He had been working at ESPN as a college football analyst, so had stayed in close touch with the game. Brown, who coached the Mountaineers in 1983 (see Chapter 1) had maintained a vacation home in the High Country, wasn't excited about the game.

"I thought it was a difficult thing because App State was so good," said Brown. "I feel like you have to win the state to be a national power. App State was one of the best teams in the state. We always like to play in state teams, to share the money with the in-state schools."

"In North Carolina it's up for grabs as to who is the best school," said Smith. "Mack had returned. We had a chip on our shoulder. They have better facilities and they're getting better fed."

Brown has always been a great recruiter. One of the first things he did after being named the Tar Heels coach was to convince Sam Howell, a high school quarterback from Indian Trail, North Carolina, to flip his commitment from Florida State (Brown's alma mater) to North Carolina. Howell was one of the nation's top quarterback recruits and during fall camp had earned the starting job for the Tar Heels.

Howell played well in the Tar Heels first three games. They had beaten South Carolina in Charlotte and Miami at home. The week before, in a game played on Friday night, they lost a close game at Wake Forest.

One young player who had developed into an important part of the Mountaineers offense in 2019 was true sophomore tight end Henry Pearson. The tight ends for App State frequently line up in the backfield and are used as a lead blocker for the running back or provide additional support for pass protection. They are used in the passing game as well and Pearson had played in every game as a true freshman. He caught 14 passes and scored two touchdowns. The New Jersey native's father had attended Appalachian but returned to New

Jersey before he graduated. The younger Pearson had spent time in North Carolina and was interested in coming south to play football.

"When I was in high school, I did a trip to the Carolinas," Pearson remembered. "I went to Duke, UNC, N.C. State, and none of them offered me a scholarship, so I went to other schools. App and Elon gave me an offer and I knew App would be the best place. I fell in love with coaches and the area."

I had driven up to Charlotte on Friday and spent the night with my brother, Hunter, who graduated from Appalachian four years after I did. He was excited about the matchup.

"It felt like we were getting respect and because we were FBS," he said. "It had always felt like the big time at App because of the success we had. Going to Chapel Hill was a big thing. Even though it wasn't one of their best teams, it was still nice to play there."

We rode up Saturday morning and found a good place to park and tailgate. There were a lot of App fans who parked there and there were a lot of tailgates with some people in black and gold and others in light blue. Several friends stopped by our spot, and it was fun.

"A lot of the tailgates had App and Carolina folks," said McMackin. "It was cool seeing so many App people there in Chapel Hill. I wasn't surprised because we always traveled well."

"I was impressed with the fans," said Witten, who had the vantage point of the radio booth in the press box. "I expected to see a lot of black and gold but to hear the chants break out it was amazing to see. Knowing we had the opportunity to play them after all these years."

Jeff Marcin was a freshman at Appalachian but had grown up in Chapel Hill and had been going to games at Kenan Stadium his whole life.

"That game was an awkward phase for me," said Marcin. "I wasn't fully into App then. I was still switching from a Carolina to an App fan. That game was awkward. I sat in my parents' seats in the first half, then went to the UNC student section in the second half. I was getting funny looks sitting there wearing my App stuff."

Kirk Sherrill and his wife Kim are both Appalachian grads, but their son Tyler was a freshman at UNC that fall. He was pledging a fraternity, so he didn't have a lot of time to spend with his parents.

"We got up there on Friday night and picked him up and took him out to dinner," said Kirk Sherrill. "He had to get back to the frat house, so we made plans to get together before the game. Saturday morning a big group of App fans had met at a place. The frat let Tyler come see us, but he had to ride a bike. We were busting his chops about the game. We got him something to eat. On our way to the stadium, we stopped by the frat house. We were the only people there in App gear and were getting it a little from everyone. He grew up being an App boy, we raised him as an App fan, but he was at Carolina now."

I didn't have a really strong feeling about the game. I knew we could win, and hoped the recent close calls would finally push them over the top against a Power 5 team.

Witten felt the same way.

"You have all this anticipation," he said. "Our program was coming off three conference championships. You knew the offense had potential, but there was so much talent on UNC side. It used to be 'I hope we don't get blown out,' now 'it's let's see how we do.'"

We had a nice walk across the campus to the stadium. I had been to Kenan Stadium several times growing up. My freshman year at App, I went to the Clemson-UNC game that was probably the biggest game ever involving teams from the Carolinas. Clemson, the eventual national champion, was ranked number two, and the Tar Heels with Lawrence Taylor were ranked number eight. Clemson won 10-8. I had been a few times when I was working in Florence and went to the Georgia Tech game there as part of my big tour in 2006. My friend Pete Weber was sitting with us. There was a great contingent of Mountaineers around the stadium. Several of them wore gold Appalachian stuff that stood out. I always try and wear the color of jerseys the team is wearing, and I was wearing a white polo shirt. It was a hot day, with temperatures in the mid-80s. But the Mountaineer fans were making themselves heard pregame.

"No one on the team will forget that," said Smith. "It felt like a home game. We could feel the fans. We had fans travel well. It was cool to have that environment."

Even though Pearson didn't grow up in North Carolina, he felt something personal playing against the Tar Heels.

"It did have a little more meaning to me," he said. "They had told me I wasn't good enough or tall enough to play there. It was a different staff, but I was playing against players they thought I wasn't as good as."

Carolina received the opening kickoff and stuck a dagger in the App fans with a return to the Mountaineer 21-yard line. Howell twisted the dagger when on the first play from scrimmage he hit Daz Newsome for a touchdown. But the App State offense responded well. Thomas faced a third and two from the UNC 4 but he was sacked for a 10-yard loss. Staton hit the field goal, but I knew we wouldn't win with field goals. The defense came up with a three and out and the offense got the ball and again moved into Tar Heel territory. But two incompletions sent Staton back out, this time from 43 yards.

The kick was good, and the deficit was just one. But I knew we would need touchdowns to win.

The Mountaineers got their touchdown, and it came from an unexpected source. The Heels had a third and 7 from their own 33. Howell dropped back to pass. Defensive end Demetrious Taylor was unblocked and hit Howell from behind just as he was beginning his passing motion. Howell fumbled the ball; Taylor picked it up and took off for the end zone. He made it and the Mountaineer fans across Kenan Stadium were going crazy, regardless of what color they were wearing. Staton's PAT made it 13-7. The play was on the opposite side of the field from us, so it was hard to follow, but what a play it was. Taylor was truly becoming a force off the edge. The week before against Charlotte he forced a fumble on a sack.

"That play Taylor made was incredible," said McMackin, my brother.

"I could see that one coming," said Witten. "Meech [Taylor's nickname] comes free, and Howell doesn't see him. I realize Meech will get a hit on him. It was just will he deliver the ball in time? That's the single most dominant defensive play by an individual I've ever seen. It shifted the momentum to us. I was thinking, we can win this game, especially if we are making plays like this."

The defense kept the momentum by forcing a Tar Heel punt after four plays. But the offense couldn't capitalize. Thomas was intercepted and Howell was back on the field. Again, he faced a third and 7, but this time the ball was at midfield. Carolina had a man on Taylor this time. The offensive tackle tried to take his legs out, but Taylor popped right up, deflected the ball in the air and caught it. He was headed to the end zone, but Howell wrapped him up and was dragged a few yards before finally getting Taylor to the ground.

"While playing you don't think about the magnitude of what he did in that game," said Pearson. "That is surprising for one player to do so much, in one game, but I was not surprised he made big plays. You expect the best players to make the best plays."

The App fans were loud again and this time the offense did their part. Thomas hit Sutton on three straight passes to get the ball to the 5. Evans took over from there and the

Mountaineers stretched the lead to 20-7 with 12:29 to go in the half.

Howell moved the Heels inside the App 10, but a second down pass was knocked down by Taylor at the line of scrimmage and a third down run was stopped short of the line to gain. This time it was UNC settling for the field goal and the App State lead was cut to 10.

The Mountaineers answered with a 10-play, 79-yard drive, mixing runs and passes. Evans went the last two yards on a run and the Apps were up 27-10 with less than three minutes in the half.

"We were making big plays on offense," said Witten. "Thomas was making big throws, Evans was scoring touchdowns, Hennigan making catches on 50/50 balls. We had to keep scoring to hope you could win that game."

Howell showed why he was such a sought-after recruit, moving the Heels down the field and hitting Michael Carter with a 11-yard touchdown pass with one second remaining in the half. That was tough, but the App fans felt good about where things stood and how well the defense was playing.

"We were in control of the game for the most part," said McMackin.

"Tyler came over to our seats at halftime and told us he thought the Heels would come back," said Kirk Sherrill. "We didn't see him the rest of the night but took him to breakfast Sunday before we went back to Charlotte."

"After building the lead we can't have three and outs and we can't have turnovers," said Witten. "We had to keep enough distance to keep the lead fend off a challenge."

The teams traded three and outs to start the third quarter. App State got one first down on their second possession but ended up punting. However, the Mountaineers downed the punt at the 2-yard line. Howell and the Tar Heels responded with a 15-play, 98-yard drive for a touchdown. The Tar Heels overcame another Taylor sack, converted a fourth down, and the Apps lead was down to three.

Appalachian responded to the challenge. Thomas hit deep balls to Thomas Hennigan for 31 yards and 43 yards to Malik Williams down to the three. Evans plunged in for his third touchdown to extend the lead back to 10 with just more than two minutes remaining in the quarter.

The Mountaineers continued to play inspired defense. The secondary in particular had been hard hit with attrition. Smith was one of several young defensive backs that had been forced into action.

"I had to wait my time. I was backup at safety and was on special teams," said Smith. "We had a lot of injuries. My number was called. I didn't think about that during the moment. You black out a little. It was a cool moment and a cool game."

"We had 19 guys out for camping," said Clark. "Two true freshmen playing corner. You leave Boone and it was 68 and it was close to 100 there. But guys stepped up and made plays."

Witten was getting a little concerned about attrition in the secondary.

"Really inexperienced guys were coming in," said Witten. "Howell has the ability to throw it around the yard, and we have inexperienced guys there. That underscores why

Taylor was so important in that game. His dominance was helping the young secondary. Davis-Gaither was having a big game too."

"That D was stacked," said Pearson. "Meech, [Akeem] Davis-Gaither, Sherm [Shamar Jean-Charles], Demarco [Jackson], [Jordan] Fehr. It was stacked. Everyone on that team could make a play."

Howell was intercepted by Davis-Gaither but the Mountaineers couldn't extend the lead. This time the punt bounded into the end zone and Carolina was 80 yards away. Howell covered the 80 yards in just eight plays and two and a half minutes. The Heels now trailed by three with 3:01 to play. Could the Mountaineers run out the clock? A Thomas scramble picked up one first down and forced the Tar Heels to use all their time outs. But another punt went to the end zone and the Heels were back on their 20 with 2:11 in the game. Howell moved them and connected with Newsome at the App 39 with five seconds left. Noah Ruggles was coming in to attempt a 56-yard field goal. He had hit his career long of 49 yards the week before against Wake Forest.

"Me and so many App fans were scarred by experience," said Witten when Ruggles was getting ready for the kick. "My first game doing play by play was the Tennessee game [in 2016]. At Penn Stare we scored and then they forced OT. Is this going to be another UT, PSU, etc.? When they line up for a long field goal, I think it's a long way, but it's going to happen."

The Mountaineers had one time out left and Drinkwitz called it, but as Smith explains, it wasn't to freeze Ruggles.

"We finally get the stop, and they are going to kick the field goal," said Smith. "The normal field goal block is the defense on the field. We have a special block on the end of game kicks. In that formation, the free safety comes out. Because of injuries, I was playing strong safety, so I felt I should be out there. We had 12 on the field, and I was the 12. Drink called time out, and I came out. Akeem blocks the kick. I like to think I had a little something to do with that."

Nick Hampton was the extra player who came in and he was the center of the defense and jumped up, but it was Davis-Gaither who found a seam and made the block.

"My analyst Sims [McElfresh] first said it was blocked," said Witten. "It wasn't an emphatic block like Corey's [at Michigan]. You couldn't even tell at first it was blocked. Then you saw the celebration."

The Mountaineers had finally done it; beaten a Power 5 team for the first time as an FBS program and for the first time since the Michigan win in 2007. A lot of comparisons were made between this game and Michigan with it ending with the Mountaineers blocking a kick, but there were several differences. First, Michigan's field goal attempt was 37 yards, certainly a makable distance. Carolina's attempt was a desperation try, 56-yard attempt, seven yards longer than his career long. Also, Michigan would have won the game with their kick and the UNC kick would have only forced overtime. But I didn't care. Appalachian had defeated the Tar Heels and could boast bragging rights.

"I think for App State it's never been about the moment getting too big," said Smith, who finished the game with five tackles. "We are the G5 [Group of Five] team they don't want to play. Internally the culture, since the Michigan game, you approach it as business. When we got that win in 2019. The monkey was off our backs. Before that it was cool heading into it, but we fell short. It breeds you for those moments and it's not too big for coaches or players."

"We never went into a game expecting to lose," said Pearson. "To the outside eyes it means more. We practiced that spring, the off season, preseason. We go into those games; you expect to win. It wasn't just for the instate guys, but it was big for me too. To be the number one team in the state that year felt good."

The celebration on the corner of field in front of the App fans lasted a while. There was a lot of pride going on. During the game, the Carolina students had been chanting, "Safety school!" while we were leading and the App fans responded with, "Football culture!" It was a lot of fun.

"The biggest thing I remember after the game and the players came out and celebrating in front of us," said McMackin. "That was really cool."

"After the game, I didn't want to leave the stadium," said Kirk Sherrill. "I went down to where the team buses are and hung around with some other fans and the players' families. We were all high fiving everyone."

Andy Ebert is an App grad but had to miss the game to be a good dad for his daughter Samantha, a student at N.C. State where it was Parents' Day.

"All the State fans had the game on and there was loud cheering when the game was finally over," said Ebert. "That was awesome, and the State fans were loving it."

The win didn't get Appalachian into the Top 25, but people were noticing. Taylor was selected by many publications as the national defensive player of the week after his day: two and a half sacks, two forced fumbles, one fumble recovery, one interception, and a fumble return for a touchdown. It was the first time an FBS player had that stat line since at least 2000.

It would have been easy to have a letdown after the emotional win over the Heels. But the team kept their focus, knowing the most important part of the season was just starting. Conference play would start against Coastal. The Chanticleers were still looking for their first win over App State.

"We always call conference games ring games because that will affect who is going to the conference champ game," said Smith.

The Apps won 56-37. Then, it was the anticipated championship game rematch in Lafayette against the Cajuns. The Mountaineers defense dominated and the Apps game away with a mid-week 17-7 win. The Apps made a return to the polls at number 24 in both the AP Writers' Poll and the Coaches' Poll. Two more blowouts had the Apps rising to number 20 in both polls. In 2019, college football was using the college football playoff system to determine the top four teams in the nation and those four schools would battle it out for the national championship. Teams were ranked one through 25 by the playoff selection committee, a group of 13 people who had been around college football for most of their lives. Not many people thought Appalachian would make it as one of the top four teams even if they went undefeated. But there was a legitimate possibility for them. The highest ranked "Group of Five" school (schools from the Sun Belt, Conference-USA, Mountain West, American Athletic Conference and the Mid-

American Conference) would play in one of the New Year's six bowls. Those bowls were the typical New Year's Day bowls. The committee didn't release their first poll until after games the first weekend in November, so a lot had to happen, but that didn't diminish the speculation.

Last year, the week the Apps were ranked in the poll they had to play Georgia Southern. This year, the Mountaineers had climbed to number 20 and the Eagles were next up on the schedule. Again, it was going to be a short week with the game on Thursday, but this year it would be in Boone. The Eagles hadn't won in Boone since the Apps' last national championship year of 2007. The forecast was not good for the game, to be played on October 31, Halloween.

The week of the App State-Georgia Southern football game is known as "Hate Week" in Boone. The two schools have played some classic games and knocked the other one off a lofty perch. From 2010-12 the loser in the game had been ranked number one in FCS coming in. The first time the schools met after Georgia Southern restored their football program in the early 80s was in the playoffs in 1986. The Mountaineers won 19-0, ending the Eagles run of two consecutive national championships and shutting them out for the first time since the program was restored. The Eagles were 4-3 coming into the 2019 game. Two of the wins came in overtime. However, in week two at Minnesota, the Gophers scored a touchdown with 13 seconds left to edge Southern 35-32. The Gophers finished the season 11-2. Georgia Southern was inconsistent and that had plagued the Eagles for the past several years. But they would always be fired up for the Black and Gold of App State.

"Lots of stuff went wrong that week," said Smith. "Coach Drink was trying to flip the script a little to get away from the Hate Week. It was the first time we stayed off campus the night before. [The team spent the night in a hotel in Hickory, about 45 miles away.] We didn't have the Mountaineer Walk [the pre-game walk of the team from the dining hall to the stadium, popular because fans line the path] because of the rain."

Georgia Southern had primarily run an option offense ever since they reinstated the program in the early 80s. Sometimes you would hear App fans complain about having to play Georgia Southern on a short week, but I never thought that was a problem. It wasn't like it was a surprise the Eagles were running the option and Smith agreed with me.

"It wasn't a problem getting ready for Georgia Southern that week," he said. "We were used to playing them on television on weekday games at that point and spent time prepping the triple option offense throughout the year."

The weather was not good. It was cold and wet and windy. Mountaineer weather, you would think. I didn't go, not because of the weather, but because of all the travel I had done, and it was a Thursday night. The Eagles got out to a quick start and led 10-0 early in the second quarter. The App State offense finally showed some signs of life with a 10-play, 92-yard drive in less than two minutes to cut the deficit to 3 with six seconds remaining in the half.

But the Eagles scored on two long touchdown runs early in the third quarter to extend their lead to 24-7. Thomas connected with Corey Sutton on two touchdown passes in the fourth quarter, but it wasn't enough as Southern ended the Mountaineers 13-game winning streak, the third longest in the country. The Eagles only completed one pass for four yards in the wind but gained 345 yards rushing with an average of six yards per carry. For the season, the App defense had only surrendered 129 yards rushing per game and less than four yards per carry. Surprisingly, given the conditions, there were no turnovers in the game, but the Mountaineers just weren't right all game.

"That was one of the toughest games of my career," said Smith. "For me, it was more than the weather. I didn't like getting outplayed on our field."

Being a Georgia native made the loss to the Eagles hurt a little more. Smith went to Mountain View High School in Gwinnett County in the suburbs northeast of downtown Atlanta. Some of the best high school football in the nation is played in Gwinnett County. Appalachian has had a lot of excellent football players from the county over the years. He got noticed by the Mountaineers when they were recruiting Kielan Whitner who was a year older than Smith. Whitner ended up going to Syracuse, but a year later Smith went to Boone for a visit.

"With the facilities and the people, Boone is a special place," said Smith. "I caught that when I was up there."

He was impressed with Scot Sloan who then was the defensive backs coach.

"He was the most honest in the process," said Smith. "Every school told me what I wanted to hear. He [Sloan] told me what I needed to do. He said if I did well at a camp, I would get an offer. I worked hard at the camp and got the offer and I accepted. App State used all the tricks. Even in 2016 the hype videos were great. I knew I wanted to be a part of that in the snow and in front of sold-out crowd."

Wide receiver Jalen Virgil was a high school classmate, and they made the trip together. Smith knew early on he wanted to get into sports journalism and was very involved in media while a student. He worked at the student newspaper and hosted the *135 Podcast* with Hennigan (Smith was number 13 and Hennigan number 5). He was Academic All-district with a GPA over 3.7 and virtually gave the December 2020 commencement speech for the Department of Fine and Applied Arts. After graduation, he worked for media outlet On3

Sports and co-hosts the *Frary and Smith Podcast* with Noah Frary. It focuses on sports in the Sun Belt Conference. In 2023 the athletic department started the *Mountaineer Insider Podcast* through their NIL collective to provide an NIL opportunity for App State student-athletes and he hosts that podcast as well.

"I knew him from afar as an assistant," said Clark. "I'm his third head coach. He had mentioned he wanted to be in the media. He's a perfect example of an App guy. He didn't start until his fourth and fifth year. He had the 'it' factor. Student of the game and he used football to make connections."

The second Power 5 game of the year was up next in Columbia, South Carolina, against the 4-5 Gamecocks. South Carolina had opened the season with a 24-20 loss in Charlotte against North Carolina, but their four wins included an overtime win in Athens against then-number three Georgia.

Appalachian was 1-8 all-time against the 'Cocks. The schools played every year from 1972 until 1977. South Carolina left the ACC after the 1970 football season and was an independent. In 1975 the Apps defeated the Gamecocks 39-34.

My favorite game was in 1985 when South Carolina escaped with a 20-13 win in the second game of the season. The week before they had beaten The Citadel 56-17. The 'Cocks were coming off their greatest season in history in 1984 and expectations were through the roof. I was living in Myrtle Beach, having just been hired at the Myrtle Beach bureau of WBTW-TV. I couldn't go to that game, because I was covering the annual Congressional Medal of Honor convention that was a very impressive program. John Settle ran for 193 yards, but the Apps had four turnovers. I'll never forget the AP reporter covering the game was a South Carolina grad and had the game on the radio in the press room. He kept getting so frustrated because they couldn't put the Apps away. I didn't say anything to him. The win took a lot of their confidence away and the Gamecocks finished 1985 5-6.

I went to several South Carolina games at Williams-Brice Stadium when I lived in South Carolina, and it was a nice stadium and there was a good environment. I have never been much of a South Carolina fan for some reason. Maybe it was because they left the ACC. I'm not sure.

I was looking forward to this game. I have a lot of friends from App who have kids that went to South Carolina. One of them, Karen Barnes, was a little sister in the fraternity and she parked near us for games in Boone. Her daughter had a roommate at USC whose family owned a chicken place about a mile from the stadium. Karen had arranged for us to park at a lot behind the restaurant. It worked out great because we had a place for food and a bathroom, and it was easy to get out after the game.

I went with Mike Ladd, and we got there early in the afternoon. Kickoff was at 7 p.m. and ESPN2 was showing the game. Hunter, and his wife, Susan, drove down from Charlotte and several of Karen's friends all parked with us. Some of the people there were folks I hadn't seen in years, so it was nice to catch up. The tailgate was fun. LSU and Alabama played that afternoon and there were some South Carolina fans parked near us who had the game on a TV, and I watched some of the game with them.

Ebert is another one of the App grads who tailgates with us for games at App. His youngest daughter Kristin would enroll at South Carolina in 2021, but they had no affiliation with the Gamecocks at that time. He did have a good customer who lived near Columbia and was a big fan of the 'Cocks.

"They have a building real close to the stadium and it was set up for tailgating," said Ebert. "I had been there before and asked if we could get a couple of parking spots for our game and we did. We got there and set up and were surrounded by garnet [South Carolina's colors are garnet and black]. It was fun. We had a good turnout, probably 10 to15 people there for App."

It was a pleasant afternoon, but once the sun went down, it got chilly. We walked up to the stadium and had decent seats in the App section. All the SEC schools have a decent area of seats in a corner of the lower level for the visiting fans and there was a good App contingent there and they were excited.

"It was cool being in there," said McMackin. "I had been there before, and it was cool to have so many more people than those games in the 90s when we played there."

"What were we [the team] thinking about?" wondered Witten coming into the game. "The game before that was

Georgia Southern, we were ranked, unbeaten, we are thinking New Year's six bowl game, etc. You lose to Georgia Southern on Thursday. Winning this is not as big a deal. We are playing for conference championships, and this won't help us with our season goals. But it's important. Would they be motivated after losing to Southern?"

"It's tough to do something twice, but we went in there with the same attitude," said Pearson. "As Shawn Clark always says, 'It's a nameless, faceless opponent. It doesn't matter how many stars he has. You are going to do what you can to beat him.'"

Jim Macholz is an App grad who has been a regular at games since he graduated. He was with Ebert's group for the tailgate but had the best spot to watch the game. He had won a silent auction bid for a sideline pass for the game.

"Having that perspective of being on the sideline was cool," said Macholz. "They were very athletic, and I thought our skill players matched up with them. At first their defensive line was manhandling us a little, but when we settled down, we did a great job against them."

The game started off slowly, at least as far as the offenses were concerned. The teams had exchanged field goals twice and it was 6-6 late in the second quarter when the Mountaineers faced a fourth and one at their own 45-yard line. Drink decided to punt and after Xavier Subotsch's punt was downed at the South Carolina 11, it looked like a good decision. The Gamecocks had lost 2 yards on two runs and Drink called timeout with 2:04 remaining and the 'Cocks facing a third and 12 on their own 9. Quarterback Ryan Hilinski dropped back to his end zone and his pass across the middle was tipped into the hands of freshman safety Nicholas Ross at the 20. Ross took off to the end zone and bulldozed his way in, right in front of the delirious bunch of App State fans.

"It sounded like it happened at Kidd Brewer Stadium," said Witten. "I'm yelling because I feel like I have to because of how loud that crowd was."

"[Ross] made an instant impact in the secondary as a freshman in our dime package for his aggressiveness and fearlessness," said Smith, who only played on special teams in this game. "Being at the right place at the right time as a safety is always important and he did that and capitalized in an iconic moment."

"We [Andy and his wife Robin] sat with Chris [his customer] and his wife," said Ebert. "We were opposite the App fans in the stadium, and we could see them. Off the bat it wasn't going well. His wife left at half time and didn't come back. She had had enough."

Ross's score gave App State the lead at 13-6 and that's how the half ended. The Mountaineer defense had held the Gamecocks to 29 yards rushing on 16 carries. Nine of the carries were one yard or less. It was definitely the App defense that was getting it done.

"That defense was special and definitely one of if not the best I've been a part of," said Smith. "Looking around at the talent you were surrounded with every time you played with that unit gave you a new level of confidence knowing everyone would likely win their individual matchup for a large majority of every game."

Appalachian received the second half kickoff, but Thomas threw an interception giving the Gamecocks the ball on the App 35, by far the 'Cocks best field position of the game. But the defense didn't give up a first down and South Carolina had to try a 50-yard field goal, that was good and cut the Apps lead to 4.

Jalen Virgil returned the ensuing kickoff 57 yards inside the Gamecocks 40 and the Mountaineers had the momentum again. Thomas led the team down to the 1 and he scored on a quarterback sneak. App State led 20-9 midway through the third quarter.

"We ran our game plan," said Pearson. "Number three [Javon Kinlaw, a first-round draft pick the next spring by the '49ers] was a big ass dude. We ran away from him."

South Carolina still couldn't sustain any offense, but neither could the Mountaineers. South Carolina took over late in the third quarter and had moved into App territory by the time the fourth quarter started. Facing a fourth and 10 on the App 35, Hilinski was sacked by Mountaineer linebacker Davis-Gaither. The Mountaineer fans were going crazy, and the Gamecock fans were heading to the exits. I couldn't believe their fans were giving up so easily. The upper decks in Williams-

Brice Stadium will sway when they are full and the fans sitting there are jumping around. Bumper stickers were popular with Gamecock fans saying: "If it ain't swayin', we ain't playin.' The only part of Williams-Brice that was swaying then was where the App fans were sitting.

"I mean, it was loud as hell," said Macholz. "By the third quarter, there were more App people there."

"At the UNC game I didn't look around but, in that game, I got to appreciate the fans," remembered Pearson. "That game, halfway through the third it was sea of black and yellow. They are blaring 'Sandstorm' at the beginning of the game and it's a great atmosphere. You get chills hearing that. You didn't hear 'Sandstorm' much late in the game. It shows how awesome our fans are as well."

South Carolina took possession with 5:01 remaining and Hilinski drove the team 78 yards on 12 plays, all passes, to score their only touchdown of the day. The failed extra point made the score 20-15 with slightly more than two minutes left.

The Mountaineers had a problem with the kickoff return and couldn't get a first down and punted the ball back to the 'Cocks with 1:50 remaining at their own 45.

By that time, the Appalachian fans were making a lot more noise than the Gamecock fans that remained. The pressure the Mountaineers were putting on Hilinski was beginning to take a toll. The Apps picked off a pass, but it was nullified because Davis-Gaither jumped offside. Linebacker Nick Hampton was causing all kinds of problems. He pressured Hilinski on Ross's interception and had a sack on this drive.

"He was huge for us," remembers Smith. "That sack on the last drive made it third and long. Rushing the quarterback Is what he does best, we saw a lot more of that in his last two seasons, but it was great to see him get one earlier in his career in his home state."

"We won it in the trenches," said Macholz. "I was impressed and proud how many fans we brought to that game. It seemed like we had a lot more people there than in a usual road game. There was a lot of black and gold in there."

In part because of the pressure the App defense was causing and the noise coming from the visiting section, the Gamecocks committed four false start penalties in the fourth quarter. Despite the pressure, Hilinski was hanging in there. He converted a fourth and 15 with a pass down to the App 9 with 19 seconds remaining. He spiked it on first down. On second down the Gamecocks were called for holding Hampton and pushed back 10 yards. Hilinski had Edwards open in the end zone but couldn't connect on the game's final play. Even if Edwards had made the catch, the Gamecocks had been called for holding Davis-Gaither. The penalty was declined, and the Mountaineers had done it again, beating a Power 5 school on the road. Hilinski had thrown for 325 yards on 57 attempts, but the offense had become one-dimensional. Even taking out the sacks (in college, sacks are considered rushing yards by the QB), South Carolina didn't gain 10 yards rushing in the second half and finished with 21 yards on 27 carries (including sacked yardage). The defense was credited with 11 pass break-ups. The Mountaineers only managed 202 yards of offense, but it was enough to get the job done, especially when the defense scored too.

The Appalachian fans were going crazy, and the players had gathered in front of the App section, joining in on the celebration, just like at Chapel Hill. Frequently after games like that on the road, the Mountaineer fans will start to cheer, "It's great ... to be ... a Mountaineer!" and you could hear that cheer ringing across Williams-Brice Stadium.

"The App fans were going crazy," said Ebert. "Walking out, we had our App stuff on and were getting the stink eye from some of the fans leaving the stadium. A lot of fans congratulated us but some of the students weren't happy."

Smith said the players had taken notice that the stadium had emptied out by the end.

"The game day environment was electric to start off the game but really fizzled out quickly throughout the contest," said Smith. "We were used to electric Power 5 crowds but South Carolina's that season was by far the worst I'd seen from a big-name opponent."

That was a very impressive win. The environment, especially at the beginning of the game, was raucous and it was the first time Appalachian had beaten a Southeastern Conference team. It was the first time a school had won non-conference road games against an ACC and SEC team in the same season since Houston did it in 1999. To have basically taken over the stadium by the end of the game was something I savored.

"It was a great game and a great win and watching the team celebrate was neat," said Ebert.

"It makes you real proud that we could go into a SEC stadium and beat those guys," said Ladd.

Not only did the Mountaineers impress pollsters with the road win over an SEC team, but they got some help in their bid to win the Eastern Division of the Sun Belt. Georgia State and Georgia Southern both lost that day and App State was back in control of their destiny in the division. The Apps would head to Atlanta to play Georgia State next.

When Charlie Cobb left Appalachian to take the AD position at Georgia State, Trent Miles was the head coach. After going 2-8 in 2016, Cobb fired Miles and went to his days at Appalachian to hire Shawn Elliott as the coach of the Panthers. Elliott had played on the defensive line for Jerry Moore on some of the great teams of the 1990s and was an assistant coach during the Mountaineers' run of national titles. A South Carolina native, he left the Mountaineers when Steve Spurrier hired him to be an assistant on his Gamecocks staff in 2010. When Spurrier abruptly retired from the Gamecocks in the middle of the 2015 season, one reason he did it when he did was because he wanted Elliott to be named interim coach and have a chance to show if he could handle the job. He won the first week against Vanderbilt but lost the last five games of the season. Will Muschamp was hired to take over the South Carolina program, but Elliott stayed in Columbia as an assistant for Muschamp until he was hired by Cobb to take over the Panthers.

Georgia State was 0-5 against Appalachian. It took them four years to score a touchdown. With Cobb and Elliott running things, you know they wanted to beat the Mountaineers. They were in the midst of an excellent season.

They had won at Tennessee in week one and were 6-2 before inexplicably losing the week before to Louisiana-Monroe, a team that finished 5-7.

The win over South Carolina had the Mountaineers back in the coaches' poll at number 24 and they were ranked number 25 in the all-important College Football Playoff rankings. The game was moved to an evening kickoff and was televised on ESPNU. I went to the game with Ladd and some other local guys, and we had a nice tailgate. I talked to Davis-Gaither's dad who had a tailgate set up near ours. He was a coach and had been on the Elon staff when Appalachian beat Elon to win the Southern Conference in 2009.

When Georgia State started their football program in 2010, they played in the Georgia Dome. When the Braves moved into their new stadium in the Atlanta suburbs in 2016, the Panthers took over Turner Field. They renamed it Georgia State Stadium and redesigned it with a capacity for football of 23,000. Before the Braves took over Turner Field, it was the Olympic Stadium for the 1996 games, hosting the Opening Ceremony with Muhammad Ali lighting the torch. It hosted track and field events too. Two of the greatest athletic feats I've seen in person happened in that building. I was there during the Olympics when Michael Johnson ran his 19.32 200 meters to set the world record. Dan O'Brien also won the decathlon that night too. In 1999, I was at Turner Field to see the Orioles and Braves face off on Sunday Night Baseball. Mike Mussina was pitching for the Orioles against John Smoltz and the Braves. I've been an Orioles fan since 1970, when I was 7 years old and, on this night, Cal Ripken went six for six with two homers, a double, and three singles and the Orioles won 22-1.

The visitors' sideline ran from the right field line across center field in the old, baseball configuration. There was a grandstand that was built along the sideline that had about 25 rows and that was the visitor's section. I was always surprised how many Appalachian fans were at the games in Atlanta.

The Panthers came out ready to play. The two teams traded touchdowns in the first quarter, but the Panthers took the lead again on a 67-yard run. When App State got the ball back, Thomas threw an interception that was returned for a touchdown and the Panthers were up 21-7 with 1:38 remaining in the quarter. I wondered to Ladd if Thomas should maybe take a series or two off, after throwing that pick six and an uninspiring performance against the Gamecocks.

Drinkwitz stuck with Thomas who promptly led a five-play, 75-yard touchdown drive in 1:29 that was capped with a 20-yard pass to Sutton. Any hopes the Panthers had of ending their streak against their coach's alma mater were quickly dashed. The Mountaineers scored three second quarter touchdowns to lead 35-21 at the half and added three more touchdowns in the second half before Georgia State got a garbage time touchdown. The final was 56-27 and impressed the voters in the polls. The Mountaineers were ranked the next week in the AP Poll as well as the other two. Two more conference blowouts gave the Apps another Eastern Division title, and they would be the host the conference championship game once again. And once again the Mountaineers would prevail with a big win over Louisiana. Evans scored three first quarter touchdowns as the Mountaineers cruised to a 35-17 halftime lead and would win by a 45-38 score. My brother Hunter brought his twin sons Sam, who would attend

Appalachian, and Max to the game and they sat with Ladd and me.

"The environment was really cool," said McMackin. "We were expecting to win. Having the twins there was cool and they enjoyed it. I remember having a hard time getting all the confetti off us before we got into the car. We got some real cool pictures with the players."

But just like last year, the joy of the conference championship was tempered by the coach leaving. Drinkwitz was hired away by Missouri. So, for the third straight year App State would have a new coach. This time Gillin didn't have to look far to make the hire. Shawn Clark was an offensive lineman for the Mountaineers in the 90s. He had been an assistant coach at several schools around the nation, including three years as the offensive line coach at Purdue. He returned to the Mountaineers staff in 2016.

"He bled black and gold and was going to stay," said Smith. "Internally he is a man of the people."

Since Clark was already on the staff, it was an easy transition for Clark to coach the team in the bowl game against

UAB. The Blazers lost the C-USA championship game but got off to a good start in the bowl game. They scored touchdowns on each of their first two drives. The Mountaineers still trailed 14-10 at the half but seemed to have gained control of the game. Twenty-one third quarter points did the trick, and the Mountaineers kept their perfect bowl record intact with a 31-17 win.

The team finished the season with a 13-1 record, the most wins ever for a FBS team in North Carolina as well as a team in the Sun Belt. Only one other "Group of Five" team had won more than 13 games in a season. The fifth-year seniors on that team went 54-12 over their careers. It was only the fifth time a school had won five bowl games and four conference championships in a five-year period. The fourth-year seniors went 43-10 and won a conference championship every year. The Mountaineers set Sun Belt records for points in a season with 543, as well as touchdowns with 73. They led the nation in road wins and was the only FBS team to go 6-0 on the road.

The Mountaineers finished the season ranked number 18 in the Coaches Poll and number 19 in the AP Poll. It was the first time a Sun Belt team had been ranked in the final poll of the season (The CFP doesn't release a poll after the bowl games are set). It was the second straight season Appalachian had finished the season as North Carolina's highest ranked team. Only Clemson, Alabama, Ohio State, and Oklahoma had a better record in the past five seasons than the Mountaineer's 54-12 mark. The defense was the strength of the team and nine players who played defense for App State in 2019 spent time on an NFL roster.

It was quite a season for App State. But another year of transition was looming. There were three head coaches of the App State football program from 1984 until 2018. Shawn Clark was the third in the past three years. Could the program survive another coaching change? The bar was set very high, and a first-time head coach was tasked with meeting those expectations. But the new coach, the entire sport and in fact the entire planet would be facing challenges no one could see coming in December of 2

Chapter 11: September to Remember

North Carolina at Appalachian State
September 3, 2022

Appalachian State at Texas A&M
September 10, 2022

Troy at Appalachian State
September 17, 2022

The 2022 football season for the Mountaineers would open with what I thought was the biggest event in Appalachian State history since the school dropped the TC (Teachers College) for the U (University). The University of North Carolina would come to Boone to play a football game. It was part of the three-game series that was agreed to in 2017. App State won the first game in 2019, 34-31, (Chapter 10).

There was a lot of excitement about the game. Temporary stands would be set up below the north end zone stands and attendance was expected to be more than 40,000. The capacity of Kidd Brewer Stadium, nicknamed The Rock, is listed as 30,000. Overflow seating is available on Miller Hill on the south side of the stadium. When season tickets went on sale, the athletic department warned folks that single game tickets for the Carolina game may not be available and the only way to guarantee a ticket for the game was to buy a season ticket. The contract called for 3,500 tickets to be available for Tar Heel fans, which is many more fans than a visitor would usually bring to The Rock. On July 19th, the App State ticket office announced that season tickets were sold out for the season. Although App State was one of the nation's leaders in attendance among Group of Five schools, it was the first time they had sold out of season tickets.

The game would have a record number of media requests too. Media attention, or the lack thereof was something that always bothered App State fans.

"We have always fought for publicity in our state," said Charles Haynes, a 2003 graduate and the co-host of the *Black and Gold Podcast* that focuses on App State athletics. "No one would listen to us, ever. You couldn't tell a Carolina fan that App State football was any good in 1985 or 2005 or whenever. Or a [North Carolina] State fan, or a Duke fan or a Wake [Forest] fan. We've always fought that. I think that is what is so unique about this battle that we have. I think we are jaded by having zero coverage. We had to absolutely earn it by going and beating them. I think that translates. We are there to be serious and to win because we've always been that way."

"We always like to play in state teams, to share the money with the in-state schools," said UNC Coach Mack Brown, the former App State coach who was not at North Carolina when the series was agreed to.

While tickets were being sold like never before, there were some questions about the product that would be taking the field against the in-state rivals on September 3.

The Mountaineers were on a two-game losing streak, their longest since 2017. The last game in that streak was in the

Boca Raton Bowl, a 59-38 loss to Western Kentucky. That was the first time in seven bowl games that the Mountaineers didn't finish the season with a win. A lot of players had graduated. The four leading wide receivers would need to be replaced and only four starters were returning on defense. The schedule had gotten decidedly more difficult in the off season too. In the fall of 2021, the Sun Belt Conference announced that four new schools would be joining the conference. Southern Mississippi, Marshall, and Old Dominion would be coming over from Conference USA and James Madison was making the move up from the FCS to the FBS. Marshall, JMU, and ODU would be joining the Mountaineers in the eastern division of the Sun Belt. Troy would move from the east to the west and that's where Southern Miss would play. When the moves were announced, it was stated that the new schools would join the SBC by the summer of 2024, but negotiations paved the way for the move to take effect in time for the 2022 season. Mountaineer fans were in favor of the moves. Marshall and Appalachian were in the Southern Conference together for many years and the Mountaineers and Dukes had played 16 times, including 12 times between 1980 to 1992. Not only were the Apps reunited with old rivals, but they were now geographically in the middle of the division, with road games being fairly easy trips. That was something Gillin said the conference was looking at when they discussed expansion.

"What we focused on collectively as a conference was brand names and passionate fan bases," said Gillin. "We didn't look at market size. That's a little different from what some of the others did. We feel like we can win at the gate. We don't have a big TV contract, yet. From a recruiting standpoint, from a competitive standpoint, these are guaranteed sellouts. That means more licensing sales, more concessions, more passion. They really fit what we are looking for. It helps recruiting in all sports. The states we are recruiting in, parents can drive to see their kids play home and away."

The new members were good at football too, especially Marshall and JMU. Georgia Southern (six), App State (three), Marshall (two), and James Madison (two) had won a combined 13 national championships in the FCS. What was already a difficult schedule for 2022 was made even tougher with the new teams in the division. Marshall was already on the schedule for the Mountaineers to visit in the third week of the season. The original schedule started with the UNC game, then App State was going to College Station to take on Texas A&M and then would go to Marshall. Already on a two-game losing streak, even the most optimistic App State fans knew a five-game skid wouldn't be out of the question. However, with the addition of the new schools, plus the Marshall game being a conference, instead of a non-conference game, the schedule was changed. The first two weeks wouldn't change, but in week three, Troy would be coming to Boone. That seemed like a breather for the Mountaineers. They had won four straight in the series and had blown out the Trojans in November 2021, 45-7. James Madison would come to Boone the week after that. Since they were making the move from FCS, they were ineligible for the conference title game. But they would have the full complement of 85 scholarship players at the FBS level. The Dukes and Mountaineers had played some classic games in the past. The improved schedule had also helped sell tickets.

In 2019 Eli Drinkwitz coached the Mountaineers to a 12-1 regular season that included the conference championship. After the championship game, Drinkwitz left to take the Missouri job. It was the second year in a row AD Doug Gillin had to hire a new coach.

Gillin had a bit of a decision to make. The Mountaineers had Sparky Woods, Jerry Moore, and Scott Satterfield as head coaches from 1984 until Satterfield left in 2018. The new coach would be the third coach in three years. Should Gillin hire someone who may leave after a year if he is successful, like Drinkwitz did, or should he hire someone with App State ties, who may be a little more likely to stay longer? This time Gillin stayed in-house and promoted former App State offensive lineman and current offensive line coach Shawn Clark.

"Recruiting at our level you must have consistency. Players want to know who will be there," said Gillin. "What I thought was Shawn was part of 2019, part of when Eli got here, he stayed and maybe he could have left. He did a great job in the bowl game. Shawn had come up through the ranks. He did a great job in the transition. He had proved himself as a leader."

Coming back to Appalachian was always part of the plan for Clark who started his coaching career at Louisville as a graduate assistant in 2001.

"In 2012, I was at Purdue, and I talked to Scott [Satterfield] and Charlie [Cobb]," said Clark. "I needed one more year at Purdue to get my retirement vesting so I decided that wasn't the best time. In 2015, [Dwayne] Ledford had left and I was on a plane coming back from a coach's clinic. I talked to Scott. I had interviews on a Friday, flew back to Kent [Clark left Purdue for Kent State when the Purdue coach was fired after the 2012 season], and got the offer. As soon as he told me, I took the job, I wasn't worried about money, what it paid, I just wanted to get back home to where it all started."

For three years he was the co-offensive coordinator and offensive line coach for Satterfield, the quarterback he protected as an offensive lineman at App State in the 90s. When Satterfield left for Louisville after the 2018 season, Clark stayed at his alma mater and was promoted to assistant head coach by Drinkwitz.

"It was his first year as head coach and we learned things together," said Clark of Drinkwitz. "We would talk about situations and had late night meetings. When he was hired at Missouri, I thought I was going to Mizzou. Gillin said I could be the interim coach for bowl game, so I stayed."

The Mountaineers won the bowl game over UAB, but the next day Clark was on the road recruiting. Gillin told him he would have an interview for the head coaching job.

"Tuesday night I get the call from Doug, 'You are interviewing with the chancellor on Wednesday morning,'" Clark recalled. "I only had one suit and I had taken it to the cleaners. I got up Wednesday morning and had forgotten it was at cleaners. I took the kids to school, went to the cleaners to get my suit, and met with Chancellor. We are having great discussions with Doug. Then they went into separate rooms, and I thought I had blown it. They came out and Doug said congrats, you can tell your wife, but don't tell anyone else. I finally got in touch with my wife, she is out shopping with some friends. I have to tell her not to make any facial expressions, I tell her I got the job, and she says, 'Great, have a nice day.' It wasn't until that night I had a chance to see her in person."

So, the dream had come true for the former FCS All-American. He got emotional at the news conference when he was introduced. He had thanked a lot of people who had helped him get to that point in his career, but he saved the most emphatic thanks for last.

"If it wasn't for you," he told his old coach, Jerry Moore, fighting back tears. "I wouldn't be here."

The relationship between Coach Moore and the football program had been tricky since Moore left the head coaching position after the 2012 season. He was at most of the home football games. In fact, for a time, his seats in the stadium were on the same row as mine. Even though AD Charlie Cobb had moved on, there were still some hard feelings. That was something Clark addressed right away.

"As long as I'm head coach, you are always welcome in this building," said Clark to his mentor, amid loud applause from the people at the news conference.

Clark realized being a head coach was something he wanted to do early on in his coaching career.

"It goes back to when I was a grad assistant at Louisville. I started getting involved with Jim McElwaine [the wide receivers and special teams coach then and later head coach at Florida] and I knew I wanted to be a head coach, but wanted to make sure I was ready for it. I started taking notes in my head coaching notebook. Danny Hope [the head coach at Purdue] helped me a lot. I told him I wanted to be a head coach."

So, in February 2020, the new coach started his first spring practice as head coach. In the spring, teams are allowed 15 practices in 35 days and have some other restrictions on contact and tackling. Appalachian has a tradition of practicing early in the spring semester, in part to get some bad weather practices in as well as to give anyone injured in spring practice extra time to recover before the fall. But this spring would be disrupted by something new: the outbreak of the global pandemic from COVID-19.

"We had completed our staff a week or two before that," said Clark. "I thought this would be a one- or two-week thing. I had a book for everything I wanted us to do. Day to day. Well, I threw it out the window. It changed from hour to hour. We are not playing; we're shutting down."

The Sun Belt decided to play football in the fall so fall camp started with the cloud of COVID.

"We got into camp, three practices in, and games started to be canceled so we were wondering are we going to even play?" remembered tight end Henry Pearson. "Some guys didn't want to practice, and Clark canceled some practices because you don't want to risk injuries if we aren't going to play games."

Eventually it was announced App State would play their opener a week later than originally scheduled, against Charlotte in Boone, on September 12. In North Carolina COVID restrictions mandated a maximum of 50 people could attend an outdoor event. Only a few parents of senior and junior players were able to watch the game in person.

"That's not how you want it for your first game," said Clark. "You go back to the Friday before game. We have to stay apart and wear a mask. [Charlotte Coach Will] Healy called me and said, 'I don't know if we can play. If we have guys test positive, we may not be able to play.' It was rainy and foggy in Boone. The director of operations calls me that morning and says, 'We have a problem. The scoreboard isn't working. There's no volume. Before we took the field Noah Hannon, our starting center, came up to me and said, 'What a game for your first game.' You laugh and run out. You could hear a parent or two yell, Go App!"

It was hard for the players to deal with the lack of atmosphere at The Rock.

"I had been waiting my turn to be an App State starting safety," remembers Kaiden Smith, who was entering his senior year. "Coming out of the tunnel all we hear is feet on the track. On my first third down in The Rock there was no noise. The lack of noise was disappointing. It felt like a high stakes scrimmage."

"You feed off the atmosphere, and you get so excited about that atmosphere," said Pearson. "Having no fans changed how you think about the game."

"No music, no fans, no communication with the officials. It was almost like a scrimmage," recalled Clark. "There were a few parents by fence in south end zone. This is unbelievable, my first game as App State head coach. You could hear what opposing D was calling!"

The Mountaineers won the game 35-20 and were ranked number 23 in the AP poll. Not to diminish the ranking, but many schools had not played games yet. It was nice to see App State had earned a little notoriety and a ranking. But they lost the next week at Marshall in a game televised nationally on CBS.

North Carolina relaxed its restrictions a little for football games but only about 7,000 tickets were available to fans. I was offered tickets to one game, but I couldn't go, so I gave the tickets to my brother. I couldn't believe I didn't get to see them play in person all year.

"Every minute was different," said Clark. "There is nothing you can throw at me now that I can't deal with. You could drop an elephant on Kidd Brewer Stadium, and I wouldn't be surprised. It is what is. Live life to the fullest."

Appalachian finished the regular season 8-3 but didn't make it to the conference championship game for the first time. Coastal was supposed to host Louisiana, but Coastal said they couldn't play the game because of a COVID outbreak. The Mountaineers did earn a bowl berth for the sixth straight year and behind a national record for rushing yards in a bowl game by Camerun Peoples, App State won its sixth straight bowl game, 56-28 over North Texas. Peoples finished the game with 317 yards on 22 carries and five touchdowns.

It just seemed to me a weird season, because I never got to go to Boone to see a game and that was very disappointing. But the best thing that came out of the 2020 season was the Mountaineers' statement that they were producing the best uniform reveal videos in the nation. It used to be that if your school was at home, you wore your dark jersey. If you were going to on the road, you wore the white jersey, except for LSU and Georgia Tech, who usually wore white at home. But now with uniform suppliers providing a wide range of uniforms and colors, you weren't sure what your team would wear. I'm one of the people that matters to, because I like to wear the color the team is wearing. In 2010, Nike started providing a gold jersey for App State to wear occasionally. In 2020 they had any combination of black, gold, and white. They had helmets, jerseys, and pants in all three colors and any combination was possible. This all started with Nike and Oregon providing unique uniform colors and combinations for the Ducks, then other schools wanted to get involved.

"It was awesome," said Smith. "I liked all white; I felt fastest in that. It's how you look and how you feel. But you know it's all about the black and gold at App."

Before the 2020 season opener against Charlotte, App State video team members Max Renfro, Hayden Chandler, and Wyeth Collins collaborated on the video. It opens with a mountain pool under a waterfall. There is a football floating in the pool. All of a sudden in slow motion, wide receiver Thomas

Hennigan rises from the water wearing his black helmet with a black face shield, his black jersey and you can see the top of his black pants. It was similar to the classic scene in "Apocalypse Now." The video team would post the video on Twitter at 5 p.m. on Thursday for a Saturday game. It immediately went viral. App fans were so pumped, and the video got a lot of likes from fans all over the country.

It became a big deal with the players and Smith had the chance to be involved.

"It was an honor to do them," said Smith. "I did my first one in the stadium. Max [Renfroe] had it inspired by the long shot in Goodfellas. He had me getting up from a nap and getting to the stadium. On Halloween I was in a corn maze. Those guys always did a great job with that. You knew who was doing reveal so people would ask them. Virgil had a cool reveal, and he didn't tell anyone."

"I think they are so fun, and the thing I always mention is that it's all student driven," said Joey Jones, Senior Associate Athletics Director for Strategic Communications, who handles media relations for football. "It's students with ideas and the student assistants pull it off. I have to say, we help with some guidance, but its student done, and we have great students doing that."

The video team gets the players pumped up in other ways than with the uniform reveals. This was something that had been handed down from students since Jake Stroot (Chapter 7) during the national championship era of the early 2000s.

"Our media department does such a great job," said Smith. "When you make a play and then see it on the hype video the next week and how it's used helps with morale of the team and they even make us look better than we are."

"We had the best video staff in the country," said Pearson. "To see how they can make a clip into a whole video, it was a special process. I have talked to guys at other schools about that and I'm convinced we have the best."

So even if most fans didn't have the chance to see the team in person, they were able to connect with them through the social media channels. But it was still a weird year.

"I don't want to say it was a wasted season, but it was the worst year I had," said Pearson. "I think that was good to get that year back, it benefited me."

Because of all of the abnormalities of the season, the NCAA announced that anyone who was on a team roster in 2020 would be granted an extra year of eligibility. Smith was a senior in 2020 and decided to take advantage of that extra year and return in 2021.

"In spring I tore my Achilles," said Smith. "Dr. Parker said he was going to get me ready to play. I worked hard to get back and in five and half months I was able to play again. But to start the season, I was working on the sidelines, as a signal caller to be involved and to be out there with my guys."

It was a newcomer to the program that had the biggest impact on the 2021 team. Zac Thomas had graduated, and Chase Brice had arrived in Boone and had assumed the role as starting quarterback. Brice was a highly recruited high school prospect from suburban Atlanta. He signed with Clemson in 2017 and was redshirted as a true freshman. The following year the Tigers had a quarterback battle between Kelly Bryant and true freshman Trevor Lawrence. After sharing time for most of the first four games, Lawrence was declared the starter. Bryant decided to enter the transfer portal and left the team to preserve his final year of eligibility. Brice was elevated to the backup. The following week against Syracuse, Lawrence was injured with Clemson trailing. Brice came in and led the Tigers on a 94-yard drive to score the winning touchdown. On the drive, he converted a fourth and 6 with a 20-yard pass, plus had a 17-yard run into the Syracuse red zone. Lawrence returned to the lineup the next week and led the Tigers to a 15-0 record and the national championship.

After another year as a backup the following season, Brice transferred to Duke. He threw for more than 2,100 yards and 10 touchdowns but had 15 interceptions. Not liking the way things went in Durham, he came to Boone and was named the starter for the season opener against East Carolina. The game was the Thursday before Labor Day in Charlotte at the Carolina Panthers' stadium.

It was a great day. I had come to Charlotte the night before. Early Thursday afternoon I picked up my brother and we headed Uptown to tailgate. Most of the guys from Charlotte had a tailgate place for Panthers' games and had secured parking for us there. It had been two years since I had seen most of those guys. Mike Ladd was staying at a hotel nearby, and we picked him up on our way to the tailgate. It was a great crowd there and many people were celebrating being out after being so cooped up with COVID. We all sat together at the game, and I ran into several other people at the game I hadn't seen in many years.

The game was considered an App home game. When the four-game contract was worked out between the schools, the Pirates would host two games in Greenville, one game would be played in Boone in 2023, and this game would be played in Charlotte. Duke's Mayonnaise sponsored the post-season bowl game played at the stadium and was also sponsoring this game as part of a weekend of college football that had highly ranked Clemson and Georgia playing on Saturday.

More than 36,000 fans were at the game. The Pirates scored a touchdown on their first possession but missed the

PAT. Appalachian responded when Brice hit Thomas Hennigan for a 34-yard touchdown. The Mountaineers stretched their lead to 33-9 before the Pirates got a garbage time touchdown. Brice made a good first impression on App fans, hitting 20 of 27 passes for 259 yards and two touchdowns. He made some incredible throws that I'm not sure any previous Mountaineer quarterback could have made.

Country music star and Appalachian alumnus Luke Combs attended the game and made an appearance in the Mountaineers' locker room after the game. It was a lot of fun for the players as they broke into a rendition of Combs' hit song, "Beer Never Broke My Heart."

"It was great being able to be in the locker room with him after the ECU game," said Jones. "It didn't matter to the players if they liked country music or knew who he was, it was cool to be there."

One reason Combs was at the game was that he was playing a concert at Kidd Brewer Stadium on Saturday night. It was the first major concert played at the stadium and was sold out. He put on a great show and regaled the crowd between songs with memories from when he was on campus. I didn't go, but my brother Hunter went as well as several of the folks I tailgate with. They all said it was the best concert environment they had ever seen because of the emotional link between Combs and the school, something that many in the crowd shared.

The following week the Mountaineers played in another NFL stadium. This time it was in the Dolphins' stadium against Miami in the return game from 2016. This was another Power 5 heartbreak for Appalachian as they fell to the Hurricanes 25-23. Brice had an interception inside his 5-yard line that led to a touchdown for the U. A bad snap on a punt gave Miami a safety and a fumbled snap on a 2-point conversion kept the Apps from taking a 3-point lead late in the game. The Hurricanes kicked a long field goal with two minutes remaining and kept the Mountaineers out of field goal range as the game ended.

Week three was the first game at Kidd Brewer Stadium without attendance restrictions in 651 days. Former Southern Conference rival Elon was the opponent. The Phoenix had moved to the Colonial Athletic Association but had remained FCS. The Mountaineers were honoring Coach Moore, a member of the College Football Hall of Fame, with a statue to be unveiled in the Jerry Moore Plaza outside the new North End Zone Complex. Moore was 11-0 against Elon as App State's coach.

The uniforms used in the reveal Virgil did were throwbacks the team wore to honor Coach Moore that day. On the reveal Virgil walked into a 50s style diner and sitting at the counter was Jerry Moore. Coach took away Virgil's helmet and said, "You've got the wrong helmet." He then pulled out another helmet that looked like the helmet Moore's first team in 1989 wore. "This is where it all started," said Moore. It was one of the many cleverly done videos Renfroe and his staff made.

Moore's former guard, Clark, now the head coach, won his first game with a full crowd as coach in Kidd Brewer Stadium 44-10. That set up the rematch with Marshall. The Mountaineers had a chance to get the bad taste out of their mouths from last year's loss. The game was on Thursday and

Ladd and I drove up for it. There was a great tailgate, and everyone was excited about the game. I felt like this was a big game for Clark. When he was hired, I felt he deserved the job and I have faith that Gillin knows better than anyone what is best for the program long term. Clark didn't really have any bad losses, but really hadn't pulled off a win that was unexpected. I knew if the Apps lost tonight, the heat on Clark would be turned up a few notches.

The environment was raucous at The Rock. Once the sun went down it was cool for September. A record 28,377 fans showed up for a mid-week game in Kidd Brewer Stadium.

"Those Marshall and Coastal games stand out with the crowd," said Smith. "The energy was different. We felt them a little more."

The Marshall game was special for Clark, a West Virginia native who had battled with the Herd for Southern Conference supremacy when he was a player.

"That game means a lot," said Clark. "Every year I played, either one of us won the conference. I'm familiar with the program. You could feel the energy. Players get a feel for that. It's going to be a 12-round battle between them. Do whatever it takes to win."

App State was ahead at the half 21-20. Marshall got 10 points in the third quarter, but the Mountaineers would not let their fans down. In the final minute of the third quarter, App State took over at their 9-yard line. In six plays and in only 1:41, the Black and Gold went 91 yards. Brice hit Corey Sutton with a 24-yard touchdown to cap the drive. The Mountaineers were now only down 2 with most of the fourth quarter to play. The defense stepped up and got the ball back for Appalachian. Brice drove the team into field goal range and Chandler Staton was good from 45 yards to put the Apps up by 1 with 5:45 to play. The Rock was rockin'. Marshall drove into App State territory, but the defense clamped down and forced the Herd to punt. Appalachian took over at their own 8-yard line with four minutes to play.

"All we have to do is run out the clock," said Clark. "They only had one time out. But we couldn't score. If we scored and then they scored and got a two-point conversion, we would be going to overtime."

Peoples had scored three touchdowns but was banged up and Nate Noel was in the game at running back. Four carries by Noel had the ball down to the Marshall 26 with 1:52 remaining and it was first and 10.

"We have a play, opossum, which is do not score. First down, get down," said Clark. "You could see they were going to let us score. Thirty-one smack, deuce right, opossum. He [Noel] breaks loose and goes down. Everyone in stadium was pissed off because they wanted him to score. We practice that a lot, situational football. It was checkers and chess, and we won that time."

Noel finished with 187 yards on 20 carries. The Mountaineers had perfect balance on offense with 283 yards rushing and passing. They won despite being minus two in the turnover battle and giving up a kickoff return touchdown.

"The crowd was incredible," said Smith. "The energy was different. We felt them a little more after missing them last year."

After the game we were standing around the parking lot waiting for the traffic to thin out a little and I heard a woman say we should have won by more. I couldn't believe that. Boy, are our fans getting spoiled. You take a win any way you can get it.

The next week kicked off the conference schedule with Georgia State in Atlanta. It's always nice for the Atlanta residents to have an easy travel day for the game. Ladd, Eric Race, Cam Spence, and I met with some other Atlanta alumni to tailgate. The family of one of the App players from Metro Atlanta had a tailgate set up next to ours. It was fun talking to them. The players know how important conference games are.

"It was not taken lightly. Every conference game we know we are going to get the best shot by everyone." said Smith.

Appalachian scored on their first possession as Noel ran it in from 23 yards. Georgia State had moved the visitors' fans from a section behind the visitors' bench to the end zone along what was the right field line at Turner Field. Ironically enough, Michael Tucker, who hit the first home run in Turner Field, was sitting in the section beside us. His son Milan is a cornerback and kick returner for App State. As Staton's PAT was coming through the uprights I said to myself, that's coming right to me. And it did. I decided to try and catch it. I made the catch. Everyone around me gave me an ovation and I held up the ball before throwing it back to the ball folks on the field. There were several other balls that were kicked through that goal post, but no one else was able to make the catch.

Brice had three long touchdown passes in the game and the Mountaineers pulled away in the second half to run their record against the Panthers to 8-0 all time with a 45-16 win.

Next up was another revenge game, this time at Louisiana on a Tuesday night. This result was not as good for App State as the Marshall game, with the Cajuns beating the Mountaineers in Lafayette for the first time 41-13.

"That game on Tuesday was a tough loss," said Smith. "That was my second game back, and I didn't play really well. We got outplayed and outcoached. They threw in some wrinkles, and we didn't adjust to them."

The next week was the third chance to get revenge from the previous season with Coastal Carolina coming to town in, again, a mid-week game. The Chanticleers were ranked number 14 in the nation, the highest ranked team to play in Kidd Brewer Stadium. The rowdy, packed house at The Rock was becoming routine, regardless of the day of the week the game was played. There were more than 30,000 folks in black and gold at Kidd Brewer Stadium on a Wednesday night. Since the Mountaineers made the jump to FBS, it was the largest Tuesday or Wednesday regular season crowd for any college football game in the nation. The fifth largest crowd in stadium history at 31,061 fans were in the house.

The enthusiasm was dampened some when the Chanticleers got out in front 14-0. App State scored a touchdown and pulled off an onside kick on the ensuing kickoff. With the crowd going crazy, the Mountaineers tied the game a few plays later. Clark described how the onside kick came about.

"The [pregame] plan was, we were going to win the toss, score, and do the onside kick go up 14," said Clark. "If you let them control the clock you are in trouble. Turns out we are down 14. Then we score and I say, we are going to do the onsides kick. I told [kicker] Michael Hughes, Demarco Jackson, and Milan [Tucker, who recovered it]."

Hughes kicked it toward the sideline, and it was about 15 yards downfield (it has to go at least 10 yards before the kicking team can touch it) and Tucker dove right on it. Coastal was totally caught off guard and the crowd loved it.

"It was executed to perfection," said Clark.

But Coastal was back in front 27-21, late in the third quarter when Appalachian scored a touchdown. But they couldn't take the lead because the holder fumbled the snap on the PAT.

The defense took over from there. After converting their first three third downs of the game, Coastal was 0-6 on third down the rest of the game. Appalachian had the ball at their own 38-yard line with 3:53 remaining. Two passes to Malik Williams got them into field goal range. Coastal had to use their timeouts. App State had a first down at their 11 and Peoples burst through a hole. Again, like Noel had done in the Marshall game, Peoples realized Coastal was letting him score and took a knee at the 6. There was 1:20 remaining so App would have to run another play. Noel centered the ball in the middle of the field for kicker Chandler Staton. Clark let the clock run down to three seconds and called time out to set up the field goal. Staton was 10 for 10 on the season and was lining up for the 24-yarder to win the game. There were no snap issues this time, the hold was good, and the kick was good. The Mountaineers had been 1-19 against ranked teams in their history but were now 2-19. The students stormed the field and order had been restored in the Sun Belt East, the Mountaineers controlled their destiny to win the division.

The win over Coastal kicked off a six-game winning streak and the Apps averaged 40 points per game while only giving up 14. The Mountaineers clinched the division title with a win at Troy Ladd and I attended. The defense really played well. Troy took a 7-0 lead on their opening possession, but over the last 51 minutes of the game, had one first down and 19 yards of offense.

After the win over Georgia Southern the following week for senior day, the seven sixth-year seniors, like Smith and Virgil, finished their careers with a 62-15 record. The fifth-year seniors, like Hennigan and Malik Williams, had a 28-3 record at Kidd Brewer Stadium.

Ladd and I made the decision to go to Lafayette for the championship game during the drive home from Troy. The Mountaineers' only loss in the conference was to the Cajuns so the game would be played there this year. I felt good about the team heading into the championship game. They had been in tough games this year and in the latter half of the season, they had come out on top. I felt like they had their mojo back. All those players who came back to win another championship wouldn't let it slip away. They had played poorly there earlier in the season and that wasn't the way they wanted to go out.

However, the Cajuns had a bit of mojo going for them. Their head coach Billy Napier had taken the Florida job earlier in the week under the condition he would coach the Cajuns in the Sun Belt title game. They would be trying to give their coach a send-off with a championship.

Ladd and I got a good price on a direct flight from Atlanta to Lafayette and we left early Friday afternoon. Staton's mom and girlfriend were on our flight, and we ran into them at a restaurant near the gate. We had a nice flight, but it took a while to get an Uber to the hotel. We made arrangements with the Uber driver to pick us up in the morning to take us to the stadium. Once we checked in and got settled at the hotel we went to supper. There was a seafood restaurant that looked good and that's where we were headed. It was packed and we would have about a 30-minute wait for a table. When we walked into the bar area to wait for the table, about every eye in the restaurant was following us. We were both wearing App shirts. There was a big table in the bar area that was filled with folks, and they invited us over and were so happy to see us. They were telling us everywhere we needed to go while we were in town as well as the best places to tailgate would be. It was like being in Montana again. It was great talking to everyone. They had so much respect for App State's football program. We finally got our table, and the food was excellent. We didn't stay out too late because we wanted to get to the stadium early.

At breakfast in the hotel, there were a lot of people wearing App Stuff. We realized many of them were parents of players. I sat with Hennigan's dad Joe and told him I surprised I was when Thomas was back returning punts at Georgia in his first college game as a true freshman in front of 92,000 fans. He told me Thomas had called him that week and told his dad he would be starting at wide receiver, plus returning punts. Hennigan had another son, Peter, who was a redshirt freshman on the team as well. I told him how much I had enjoyed watching his son play over his career.

We met up with our Uber to take us to the stadium. It's not on campus and there is a huge concrete parking lot around it. We went to where the folks last night said to go and there was a row of about 20 luxury motor homes that were lined up. Walking past one someone invited us over and gave us a beer. They had just started cooking. They were cooking Cajun meatballs in a huge cast iron pot and were stirring it with an oar. Ladd and I walked around the lot. Everyone was very friendly and welcoming. We met a few other App fans walking around. The baseball stadium shares the parking lot with the football stadium, and they were selling beer there, so we got one and walked into the ballpark. It was as impressive as any minor league ballpark I had been to. The Cajuns have an excellent baseball program and are proud of the stadium. While we were standing there a man came up and started talking to us. He seemed like he was well connected with the university. He told us to stop by a tailgate right outside the park. He said the university president would be there, as well as the play-by-play guy. We stopped by. There was a cook there and the food was wonderful, and everyone was very gracious to us.

We walked back over the RV area and ended up spending most of our time at one tailgate. It was Adam Hebert's motor home, and he was a great guy. He owns the Harley-Davidson dealership in Lafayette. In addition to the meatballs cooking in the pot, someone had made duck quesadillas, a result of the previous weekend's hunting trip.

The conversations with the Cajun fans were very interesting too. They were so impressed we had more than 30,000 people for the Coastal game on a Wednesday night. They were determined to get at least that many for this game. They had great respect for our program too. They don't like Coastal either, mostly because Coastal claimed they couldn't play the conference championship game last year because of a COVID outbreak. They don't like LSU just like Appalachian doesn't like North Carolina. There was a lot of talk about Napier leaving for Florida. Most were happy about what Napier had done to build the program back up and they felt he was leaving it in good hands. There were some rumors about Napier's replacement, but nothing official had been determined.

The University of Louisiana-Lafayette at the time was the only Sun Belt program that has never been in the FCS. Their stadium has a capacity of more than 41,000, but it had been a while since it had been close to being filled. The Cajuns hadn't been the Sun Belt leaders in attendance since 2011 when they drew an average of 29,171. That was the Sun Belt attendance record until App State broke it in 2021 with an average of 30,441. That was with three weekday games for Appalachian. The Cajuns had had big moments before but had not been able to sustain success. Alabama visited in 1990. Texas A&M was ranked 25th in the nation when they came to Lafayette in 1996. The Cajuns beat them that night 29-22. Brian Mitchell was a record setting quarterback for the Cajuns but made his mark as a kick returner in the NFL. He won a Super Bowl with the Redskins. Residents of North Carolina know that former Panthers quarterback Jake Delhomme was a former Cajun. We walked past his parking spot at the stadium when we were walking around.

The playing surface at Cajun Field sits two feet below sea level. You enter the stadium at the concourse level and walk down to your seats. I was a little surprised how many Mountaineers made the trip. Attendance was announced at 31,014.

The Cajuns started the season ranked number 23 in the nation and opened at number 21 Texas. The Longhorns won 38-18. That was the Cajuns' only loss of the year. They had come back into the rankings for this game at number 24.

Smith said the team was ready.

"It's a championship game. The year before we didn't get to play for the ring. Everyone was up for the game, and we didn't need motivation. We had never played a championship game on the road. It was different."

It was the first Sun Belt game played between teams with double digit wins. The Cajuns jumped out to a 14-0 lead and went on to a 24-16 win. It was a weird game. App State just seemed a little out of it. They never stopped playing hard, but they just couldn't get much done. Hennigan caught a touchdown pass with 5:06 remaining. That capped the Mountaineers best drive of the game: 12 plays for 83 yards in 3:10. After the touchdown Clark elected to go for two, but Brice's pass was incomplete. In the App State section, we were a little puzzled about the decision to go for two then, and not when that would have given us the lead after another touchdown (Apparently that is what the analytics folks say you should do now. No one in the group of people sitting with us had seen that happen). It wouldn't have mattered. The Cajuns got the ball to the App 35 and the clock was down to 29 seconds when they turned the ball over on downs. Brice was sacked and fumbled, the Cajuns recovered, and they started celebrating.

"We knew what we were going to get, but they were still able to make it happen," lamented Smith, who led the defense with 12 tackles. "They used the run to set up play action. We had a chance to get back in it. That was the best roster they had. They were one of the two or three best teams we played while I was at App. It was a game I won't forget. It was tough being on that stage and not being successful."

I felt bad for Smith and the rest of the seniors. It was a group of guys that had provided me with a lot of enjoyment over the years. It was truly a special group. There were only a few guys from the 2016 class of true freshmen class left in Boone, but it was one of the best recruiting classes the Mountaineers ever had. Darrynton Evans, Clifton Duck, Shermar Jean-Charles, Jordan Fehr, Zac Thomas, Virgil, Baer Hunter, and Smith were in that class.

"That core group mostly got redshirted," said Smith. "We didn't know what we were doing. It was the hardest time. I came from out of state. I was going through the wringer. But that's how we bonded through those workouts. It made a man out of you ... tougher physically and mentally. We would have dinner together. It wasn't our time, but we were working. You see more members getting playing time. I have been in and will be in weddings. I'm an only child, these are my brothers. I've run up Howard Knob with this guy, I've seen him do things on the field. Duck, Fehr, Evans. The next year Williams and Hennigan. We had a level of trust that goes beyond football. That's what App State is always going to have; good people and keeping the culture going."

It was the third game App State had played against a ranked team that season, the most ranked teams they had ever played in one season. Ladd and I walked back to Hebert's tailgate area and congratulated them on the win. We had a couple more beers while we talked about the result. We decided to walk to the place where we were going to eat supper. It was less than a mile away and we figured an Uber would be hard to get. Besides, the exercise would do us good. We had walked past a motor home and a woman wearing a Cajun uniform top saw us and asked us if we wanted something to eat. I told her no thanks; we were on our way to supper. I was holding a beer that was about empty and she asked me if I needed a beer. I kind of wanted one but wanted to wait until we got to the restaurant. She said, "You hesitated; come on in here."

So, Ladd and I went into their area. They had another nice motor home. She was wearing the jersey of ULL's best wide receiver, Peter LeBlanc, and I asked her if she was his mother. She said yes, and this was the family. He was the Cajuns' leading receiver in the championship game. As a true freshman he had a big game against Appalachian with 118 receiving yards and two touchdowns. He had always played well against the Mountaineers. Mrs. LaBlanc was impressed I had remembered her son. She talked about how much fun they had in Boone and how nice everyone was. I told her we had a great time today. We ended up spending about an hour and a half with them and it could have been longer, but I told her we had to get to the restaurant. It wasn't a bad walk to the barbecue place. As soon as we went in and sat down the waitress took our drink order and came back with a plate of burnt ends. She said they were the restaurant's signature appetizer, and these were on the house, from the owner. When she brought the drinks, she said the guy at the corner of the bar picked up that round. We thanked him and congratulated him on the win. After we finished eating, we went to the bar and sat with about six folks, the bartender and the owner had come over too. We were just talking about football, and it was really nice.

The next day, we found out App State would be making their first trip to Florida for the bowl game. Western Kentucky would be the opponent for the game in Boca Raton at Florida Atlantic's stadium on December 18, just two weeks after the SBC Championship game. Ladd and I flew into Ft. Lauderdale on Friday afternoon and drove to Boca. The game was at noon on Saturday. The tailgate group had gotten our tickets together and there were about 20 or so people in our group. It was 81 degrees and humid, I was dressed for it, but the sun was hot.

The Hilltoppers had lost in the Conference USA championship game and were 8-5 coming into the Boca Raton Bowl. They had won seven in a row before the loss to UTSA in their title game. They were led on offense by Bradley Zappe who had transferred from Houston Baptist before the season and had thrown for 5,545 yards and 56 touchdowns and could set the NCAA record in both categories during the bowl game. Friday night before the game, word got out that Sean Jolly, the

Mountaineers' best cover cornerback and first team all-Sun Belt, would not be eligible to play.

The offenses were as hot as the weather. Both teams were putting up the points and scoring on big plays. Zappe had his fourth touchdown pass of the half 29 seconds before halftime to give WKU a 31-24 lead. On the opening drive of the second half App State was moving deep into Hilltopper territory. When he was being tackled, Peoples was flipped and fumbled as he hit the ground. The officials ruled on the field he was down by contact, but upon review the call on the field was reversed and the Hilltoppers got the ball. It was a very close play and the kind you don't often see overturned. But Western Kentucky had the ball at the App 14. The play took the air out of the Mountaineer crowd and the defense seemed to let down too. On the next play a Hilltopper running back went 86 yards for a touchdown and the game was pretty much over. Zappe threw for 422 yards and six touchdowns and ended up with the records for yards and touchdowns in a season. The final was 59-38 and the App State historic bowl streak was over. They were now 6-1 in bowl games. Brice completed 15 of 23 passes for 351 yards and four touchdowns. Two receivers who would be counted on a lot next year, Dashaun Davis and Christian Wells each caught long touchdowns. Despite the loss, the Mountaineers kept their string of nine-win seasons alive. Only three other FBS programs had won at least nine games every season since 2015. The Mountaineers were one of eight programs with at least 10 wins in five of the last seven years. But there was a lot of uncertainty around the program. They didn't win the conference championship for the second year in a row. For the first time they had lost a bowl game.

I really enjoyed watching the 2021 football team play. The East Carolina, Marshall, and Coastal games were some of the most enjoyable games I'd experienced. The routs on the road at Georgia State and Troy were fun. Despite the loss to Louisiana, that was a fun trip. But the end of the season was disappointing.

Things got a little better three days after the bowl game when Brice announced that he would return to Appalachian for his sixth year. That was good news. I knew the four receivers, Sutton, Hennigan, Virgil, and Williams would be gone, but I liked what we had returning. Wells, Davis, and Christian Horn had played a pretty good bit over the past two years when the veterans had missed time for injuries. There was a 6'4", 200-pound redshirt freshman receiver, Dalton Stroman, who I couldn't wait to see play. I had watched him in warmups and loved his size. He got to play in the bowl game and caught a pass. After the bowl game Ladd and I were in a restaurant and ran into a couple wearing App stuff and I talked to him about the game. He and his wife were graduates and had a son who would be a freshman football player in the fall. I mentioned Stroman to him, and he laughed and said, "That guy is an athletic freak and could be as good as we've ever had." Peoples announced he would return too.

While the players were working to put the end of 2021 behind them, work was well under way in Boone to prepare for the Heels coming to town.

"The logistics were such a big thing," said Jones. "All the summer, administratively we met weekly, just talking about UNC prep. We usually meet monthly, but to make sure it would be the best experience that all of our visitors ever had, we met weekly."

In late May it was announced that ESPNU would televise the game and it would kick off at noon. I wasn't happy about that for a couple of reasons. One, N.C. State was playing East Carolina at the same time on ESPN. I was surprised that those games were scheduled head-to-head. It would hurt the ratings for both games because so many fans would be interested in both games.

The other reason I didn't like the early start was because I was afraid there would be a lot of congestion at the gates as the game was about to kickoff. I'm not usually pessimistic, but there would be so many people who had never been to a game in Boone, or who hadn't been to one in a long time and that could create problems. The athletic department was going to use electronic tickets for the first time for football games. That was something else that had me worried. As a live TV producer and even as a dog walker now, I try to eliminate the potential for things to go wrong as best as I can.

Gillin was confident they could pull it off. At the Luke Combs concert the year before, electronic tickets were used without a problem for that crowd that exceeded 34,000.

"We had had bigger and bigger events," said Gillin. "We've kind of done it before. This was a different level for UNC, but we had the model in place. We had temporary bleachers. We made sure we had the amenities, getting people in and out of the gates. We opened the gates earlier to get people in."

"When the game was announced. I was more excited about going to Chapel Hill," said Kirk Sherrill, a 1990 graduate of App State. "Winning that one [in 2019, Chapter 10] was icing on the cake. I was looking forward to seeing the Tar Heels coming to Boone. I don't think you would have ever imagined that 20, even 10 years ago. I was afraid they would cancel."

Sherrill shared that feeling with other App fans. I never thought it would be cancelled because it was an in-state school and there would be pressure from the legislature to play it. I was worried about a tropical weather system forcing it to be postponed. The University of Miami was supposed to go to

Arkansas State in 2017, but with Hurricane Irma threatening South Florida, Miami decided not to go and never rescheduled the game.

I didn't think Coach Brown would let the game get canceled and in August of 2022, it was announced that UNC had scheduled a week zero game (schools can petition the NCAA for a waiver to get a game the weekend before Labor Day) against FCS Florida A&M. That showed me they were serious about coming to Boone. Going into the 2022 season, Sam Howell, who was a freshman in 2019, was the starting quarterback since his first game and was the quarterback against App in the 2019 game. Howell had played well in his first two years and was being touted as a high NFL draft pick if he had a good junior year. I figured it meant Howell was as good as gone, and Carolina scheduled the game so their new quarterback wouldn't have his first college experience at Kidd Brewer Stadium, against our defense. I didn't like it, but I understood it. You could look at it as a little cheap or smart depending on your perspective. It would give the new quarterback a chance to get some experience, but it would also give the App coaches to see what UNC had. Although against an FCS team, Carolina wouldn't need to show a lot of its offense. But all the players would be exposed to an injury.

The Friday before the scheduled game, reports were coming out of Tallahassee that the Rattlers wouldn't be able to play the game because of eligibility issues with several players. It wasn't until late Friday A&M arrived in Chapel Hill, and while several players didn't make the trip, the Rattlers had enough players to play the game. I was secretly hoping the game wouldn't get played, and it would be justice being served. The Tar Heels won 56-24. Redshirt freshman Drake Maye was the starting quarterback, and he had a great day. He was 29 of 37 for 294 yards and five touchdowns. Maye's father, Mark, was star quarterback for Carolina in the late 80s. My brother, Hunter, had played against Mark in high school. Drake's brother Luke was a basketball standout at UNC, so you knew he had the bloodlines to be a good player.

"The excitement of having them finally come up here to play was incredible," said Mike Wolfe, a 1992 graduate of Appalachian. "I knew they would give us a good game. They wouldn't forget we had beaten them. I know the Maye family and I was hoping it would play in our favor, but it didn't play out that way. I knew we would get their best shot."

Maye did lose a key offensive weapon against the Rattlers. Wide receiver Josh Downs was hurt and was questionable for the App State game. Even with the game under his belt, UNC coach Mack Brown, who coached the Mountaineers in 1983 (Chapter 1) knew what he was getting into.

"I thought it was a difficult thing because App State was so good," recalled Brown. "I feel like you have to win the state to be a national power. App State was one of the best teams in the state. It will be tough going to their place. They have done an amazing job of evaluating and developing. They play with so much confidence."

Meanwhile the Appalachian players and coaches were trying their best to stay focused.

"That was my senior year," said Pearson. "This is weird, I had guys who had been here my whole time Virgil, Malik, Corey, Hennigan in one year all gone. It could go one way or the other. From such a veteran receiving corps to so young, and I was the old guy, and I could talk to them. It was the course of life. I had a new role to have to play."

"As far as a coach, you have to keep things grounded. It's just a game," said Clark. "But as it got closer, you could feel it. The biggest game in school history. You could feel it building up. They are adding bleachers. But we had a lot of experience, especially on offense. I knew how we played in fall camp is how we would play in that game."

The students were beginning to feel the excitement as well. Paige Sherrill was starting her sophomore year. The daughter of Kirk and Kim, who met when they were students at Appalachian, Paige had been coming to games in Boone for as long as she can remember.

"I was little, little when I first went to an App game," recalled Paige Sherrill. "I was 7 or so and dressed up like a cheerleader. I had a book, and cheerleaders and players would sign it. We were all so pumped up two weeks before the Carolina game."

Another child of one of our tailgate crew was just starting his first year as a student at Appalachian. Jackson Wolfe, the son of Mike and Ashley. He had been coming to games with his dad as much as he could.

"That was definitely a big factor," said Jackson Wolfe, who like Paige Sherrill had joined the student Yosef Club. "I had been there so much, it just felt right for me to come here. Everyone was kind of worried because the first three games were so tough, people were worried we would be 0-3. I was excited, but a little bit worried about it."

Not only would there be a record crowd in the stands, but the press box would also be over capacity.

"For the first time in my six years at App we had to deny a few requests," said Jones. "We just didn't have the space. We issued nearly 150 credentials for people in the press box and on the sideline."

I was so excited. The first game of the season is always exciting. It's great to see the guys again, plus it's just great to be in Boone and to get a look at the team. I left Atlanta Friday morning and stopped at Bridges Barbeque in Shelby, North

Carolina (It's my favorite barbecue place in the world. My parents took me there as a baby before I was eating solid food). Most of the guy in our tailgate group who were in Boone already were meeting at one of the breweries in town that I hadn't been to yet. I called the hotel to see if the room was ready and it was, so I stopped by there and dropped off my stuff and went over to the brewery, Booneshine.

It was a nice afternoon and there was a crowd there already. Hunter was on his way up from Charlotte and would meet us there. We hung out at Booneshine for several hours and many of the folks were heading to Blowing Rock for the evening. There was a hotel there that had live music and a big crowd and Hunter and I went there. I ran into many people I hadn't seen in a long time. It was a fun night. We didn't stay out too late because of the early start we were getting.

Ladd had gotten season tickets for the year, so he and his wife could go to the UNC game. His brother was a UNC grad and was going to the game with his wife. The four of them were all staying at the same hotel as us. Like many new season ticket holders for this season, parking wasn't available with their season ticket. Ladd's car was pretty big, so we decided that we would all pile in the car and park in my spot. Then the Ladds and their wives could tour the town and campus, while Hunter and I were hanging out at the tailgate. The school had announced the lots would open at 7 a.m. and I declared that I would be leaving the hotel at 6:50 and anyone who wanted to ride with me would need to be downstairs then. On Friday, I suggested to Ladd that he drop off Hunter and I at the lot at 7 a.m. and then he could drive back with the parking pass so the women wouldn't have to get ready so early.

The crowd of women staying with Paige Sherrill weren't worried about sleeping in.

"The day of the game 12 people stayed at our apartment across from campus," she said. "We were up at 5 a.m. and got to the tailgate at 7:00. We got to Peacock around 8."

I was surprised how many people in our group had said they were interested in mimosas to start the tailgate. I love mimosas and I love bubbly, but most in our group are beer and liquor guys. I brought a bottle of bubbly and some orange juice and had several mimosas. It was a nice way to kick off the season, especially as early as we were tailgating. Earlier that summer I had learned how to use a saber to open a bottle of bubbly and I thought what a cool way that would be to kick off the tailgate and football season. I knew there wouldn't be too many people there that early, but there isn't any grass around that lot. I'm not sure where the top goes when I saber it, but in that lot, it would land on the asphalt, and I was afraid it would send glass shards all over the place. I said I like to eliminate the chances of problems, so I decided to leave the saber at home.

The lots filled quickly, and you could tell the vibe was different. The first weekend is always special, but there was something different about this game. Emily Pegues and her husband were there as always with her father, Mike Nauman, both graduates of Appalachian.

"It means so much to my dad," said Pegues. "App Football season is the highlight of his life every year. It's important to be a part of that."

"Forty thousand at Boone?" exclaimed Kirk Sherrill. "Incredible. Incredible showing. It was a great tailgate. I didn't like the 12:00 kick, but you do what you have to do."

"The environment was amazing," said Jim Macholz, a graduate in 1991. "There wasn't as much blue as I thought there would be. It was a great atmosphere and I think UNC fans would admit that too."

Ted Cabot is a 2004 graduate of App. He works for Macholz's company selling medical equipment. He was a regular at our tailgates until he moved to Northern Italy in 2018. He wasn't going to miss seeing North Carolina come to Boone.

"My wife and I's flights were cancelled on Thursday, two days before the game and the day before we were due to fly," said Cabot. "It was due to a Lufthansa strike, and they had no other flights on Friday. Being the game was the following day I took the small credit from them and proceeded to spend about four grand on two roundtrip tickets booked for the next day with British Airways!"

Cabot was there at the tailgate with us. There were several old friends I had heard were in town and wanted to see before the game started. A few stopped by our tailgate, and I would stop by a few tailgates to meet them. It was great catching up. Jeff Horne is a fraternity brother and a former roommate. He has a parking spot on the deck very close to the stadium. I always stop by his tailgate, because there are always a lot of guys I was in school with that stop by there. Horne's seats are a few rows in front of me at the stadium. Mike McKay lives in the Boone area and is always hanging out at Horne's spot. McKay introduced me to a guy who was wearing a Clemson shirt and an App hat. He was tall and when I heard his name, I asked if he used to play for Clemson and he said yes. His name was John Phillips and was an all-American guard for the Tigers when I was working in Florence (see Chapter 2). He was surprised I remembered him, and we talked about how good those teams were and how much I loved Death Valley. It was a great morning, one fitting for what was about to come in the stadium.

"To me it was validation. We are going toe-to-toe. We are not scared of you," said Alex Johnson, a 2011 graduate who has hosted the *Black and Gold Podcast* with Haynes since 2015.

"We showed you in 2019 we were better than you on the field and we are going to do it again. We checked all the boxes. To me, the only bad thing about that day was the final score. But ultimately, that's all that matters. I think App State showed up extremely well; the crowd showed up."

One of the people guaranteed to have a media credential and a great seat in the radio booth is Adam Witten, the play-by-play voice of the Mountaineers on the Appalachian Sports Network. He had been aware of all the preparation by so many people to get to this point.

"It was the biggest event in Boone history, in stadium history," said Witten. "This is a monumental moment because of all the people involved. From my perspective, you try not to get too caught up in it, I have a job to do, but talking to people involved in facilities and all the things they were having to do. This was a big day for the community."

Jeff Marcin, now a senior, was the sports director at WASU, and he was getting ready to do play-by-play for a college football game for the first time. He comes from a family of UNC season ticket holders. His family was in Boone for the game, and he spent some time with them before the game.

"The mixing of the fan bases was fun for me," said Marcin. "My parents had only been to a few games at App. A lot of families had the mix of two fan bases. This game had a lot of anticipation and the family affairs added to that."

I wanted to get to the stadium early as I usually do. I wanted to make sure I got in before things got too crazy. There was a band playing outside the stadium in the Jerry Moore Plaza, something very smart the administration had set up to get people to the stadium earlier than usual. I didn't have any problem getting in. Hunter was sitting with me, and we walked around the stadium some to soak up the atmosphere. Walking through the concourse, I ran into a guy decked out in Georgia Bulldogs stuff and I got Hunter to take a picture of us so I could send to my 'Dawgs fans in Georgia. Hunter and I got some people to take pictures of us from the top of the hill end of the stadium and the student section was already jammed and going crazy.

"There was a whole panic, people worried about getting a student ticket," said Paige Sherrill. "You had to be a member of the Student Yosef Club to get a ticket to that game. Then they did a raffle. A friend paid $150 for a student ticket, but they didn't scan them. People were lined up before 8 a.m. to get in the student section. Totally general admission."

"I got to the stadium about 11:30. We walked in right before everything was kicking off," said Jackson Wolfe. "I sat on the Hill. That was my first time on the Hill. I usually sat with my dad. It seemed like it was more interactive and there were more people to be involved with. I sat on the Hill for every game."

There were a lot of people paying big bucks for tickets to the game. The athletic department didn't raise the cost of a season ticket from 2021 to 2022. But individual game ticket prices were raised significantly. The face value for the ticket for the UNC game was $150. A few single game tickets were available to Yosef Club members, but they sold out quickly. On the secondary market it was the third highest priced ticket nationally for the weekend, selling for as much as $283. Only the Notre Dame at Ohio State and the Georgia-Oregon game in Atlanta were selling for more.

Eventually Hunter and I settled into our seats. Most of the folks around me have been there for several years and it's good to see everyone again for the first game. The seats to my right aren't usually taken by the same folks and there was a guy who was a Carolina grad sitting there today. He was from Las Vegas and had never been to Boone before.

I felt like Appalachian had the edge in the game, primarily because of the quarterback position. I felt like Maye was going to be a good player, but Chase Brice had five years on him, and was a good quarterback in his own right. I was worried about our defense but didn't think Carolina had a very good defense either.

It was a surreal moment for me, sitting in that stadium jammed packed with more than 40,000 people, ready to scream like crazy for their team. I never thought the University of North Carolina would play a football game at Kidd Brewer Stadium. I thought it was so great when the series was announced and now that we were seconds from the game kicking off, I was having a hard time believing it. It was very emotional for me, soaking in the atmosphere and the pride I felt as an Appalachian graduate. It's amazing just how far our athletic program, as well as the university, has come in the 41 years since I was a naïve freshman. There were fewer than 9,000 students on campus, then, in the fall of 1981, and now there are more than 20,000 students. Talking about that experience later to other App graduates, I realized I wasn't the only one who felt that way.

"North Carolina coming to Boone is another one of those things I couldn't even dream of happening," said Brian Hoagland, a 1985 graduate and former sports editor of *The Appalachian*. "Luxury boxes, the beauty of the stadium, going to bowl games, setting NCAA records for going to seven bowl games and winning. It makes you extra proud of your alma mater. Forty thousand for a game? Hell no!"

"I've been to games there when there weren't 5,000 people there," reflected Mike Wolfe. "Looking across to the stadium itself that's changed, the teams we play, the crowds we draw. You couldn't fathom that when I was a student. It's awesome for someone like me who has been going the entire time. It's such a sense of pride for me. We're on the map now."

"It was crazy, just like every game there is now," said Hunter McMackin, my brother, who graduated in 1990. "The 'App' – 'State' back and forth. All the extra seating and the portable seats were amazing to see."

"I did not think they would ever come to Boone," said Cabot. "I, like most of us, have a bunch of friends that went there, and they always talk about it being a lose/lose for them to play us, blah, blah, blah. I am glad their administration came to Boone, and I think it should happen often."

"It was exciting being my first game as student," said Jackson Wolfe. "I didn't know what to expect and what would be different to what I had experienced in the past."

"The school spirit was unmatched. Everyone had one mindset, hate Carolina," said Paige Sherrill. Her older brother, Tyler was a student at Carolina (Chapter 10). "I was trash-talking him every day. Even during the game, we were texting."

The game finally kicked off and the Mountaineers went down the field and scored a touchdown. Carolina answered with a touchdown of their own with Maye converting a fourth and three with a run. He looked very poised.

App State responded with another touchdown. Brice hit Stroman for 41 yards, then hit Pearson for 22 yards and the touchdown.

When Carolina got the ball back, they were facing third and long and got a false start penalty. That really got the crowd going and after the pass was incomplete and the Heels were forced to punt.

The Mountaineers took the ball down the field and scored another touchdown on a short pass. The drive lasted 10 plays and covered 65 yards in about five and a half minutes. The Mountaineers led 21-7 and the record crowd of 40,168 squeezed into Kidd Brewer Stadium was being loud.

When the Tar Heels got the ball back, Nick Hampton sacked Maye. Undaunted, he completed a pass on the next play for a gain of 18. After a short run, Maye was sacked again, and the Tar Heels faced a third and 11 at the App 47-yard line. I think the next play was the pivotal play of the game. Maye hit running back Caleb Hood in the flat and two Appalachian defenders converged on him short of the line to gain. The two defenders collided with each other, and Hood spun away and gained 22 yards. Carolina would go on to score a touchdown and that seemed to energize the Heels. The Mountaineers responded with three runs and a face mask penalty gave them a first down in Carolina territory. To this point Brice was eight for eleven and 114 yards and two touchdowns. The Mountaineers had converted all five of their third downs. They hadn't really even been slowed down. But Brice threw two incomplete passes and on third and 10, he tried a quarterback draw and was tackled for no gain. Sophomore Michael Hughes was called on to try his first field goal attempt as a collegian. Hughes was the Apps kickoff specialist as a freshman but had yet to try a place kick. This attempt was 51 yards, and it missed.

It only took the Tar Heels 3:05 to go down the field and tie the game. On the play before the Heels' touchdown the Mountaineers suffered a significant loss that would be a theme for the season. Linebacker Brendan Harrington was injured. He wouldn't play again the rest of the season. Coming into the season, while the defense had some question marks on the line and in the secondary, the linebacking corps was unquestionably the strength of the defense.

Outside linebacker Hampton, who already had a sack in this game, was back for his fifth year. He had added about 25 pounds in the off-season and was the team's best pro prospect. Inside linebacker Trey Cobb was the leader, and the team's leading returning tackler. Cobb, a captain, was the only FBS player in 2021 to have at least 75 tackles, five and a half tackles for loss, three interceptions, and seven passes defended. The other inside linebacker was newcomer Andrew Parker, a four-year transfer from Arkansas, who at 240 pounds was much bigger than a typical App State inside linebacker. Harrington was similar to Hampton and although smaller; he was a nice bookend opposite Hampton. Jalen McLeod and KeSean Brown provided quality depth at the edge positions and fifth-year players Tyler Bird and Logan Doublin provided experience at the inside positions. It didn't appear that Harrington's injury would hurt the team too much.

When Appalachian got the ball back, Brice completed a pass for a first down on the first play, but on the next play,

Pearson was called for a personal foul, and it was first and 25. Despite the long distance for the first down, the Mountaineers called two running plays, I guess to run down the clock which was under three minutes. After a pass on third down was way short of the first down, Brown called time out. After the punt, Carolina took over at the App 28 with 1:44 left in the half. It took Maye 1:43 to cover the 72 yards and Bryson Nesbit caught a 10-yard pass to give the Heels the lead for the first time in the game.

"I went in thinking we would beat them," said Hunter McMackin. "Maye coming in like that, I wasn't expecting him to go off like that."

"I have a friend who went to Carolina and married an App girl, and he bought season tickets so he would get a ticket for this game," said Johnson. "I saw him on the concourse at half time and he said, 'I can't describe to you what a blast this is. This is so much fun. This game should be played all the time!'"

Carolina got the ball to start the third quarter and kept on scoring. Maye capped the first drive of the half with a 10-

yard run, and they led 35-21. The Mountaineers moved the ball down into Carolina territory but on fourth and 7 on the UNC 32, Brice was sacked. The Rock was uncharacteristically quiet.

"We knew were facing a challenge," said Witten. "They had a good QB and had played the week before. I was breaking in a new analyst, and we were going over things, how to shorten info and were having baptism by fire. It was challenging, but a lot of fun. It was frustrating; we could not fluster him [Maye] and get him off the field. He rarely made mistakes. A phenomenal player at QB. I thought we could get him to make a mistake, but he never did."

When Maye and the offense came on the field, they quickly drove into App territory again. However, on a third and seven at the App 22, App State blitzed and forced Maye to throw an incompletion. The 41-yard field goal was good and UNC was up 38-21. The defense had slowed down the Tar Heels, but on the next drive, Brice was intercepted, and Carolina took over at the App 28. The defense rose up to the challenge and held them to another field goal. However, the lead was now 41-

21 and Carolina had scored 34 points in a row. Eleven seconds were left to play in the quarter.

"I was in the stands," said Paige Sherrill. "No one was speaking, we were just so disappointed. I know more about football than my friends and I didn't give up hope, but it wasn't a good look."

When the Mountaineers got the ball back, Daetrich Harrington, the third string running back on the depth chart, but an energetic, sixth-year senior, gained 35 yards on the first four plays of the drive to move the ball into Carolina territory. Then Brice hit Dashaun Davis for 21 down to the 15-yard line and The Rock was coming back to life. Nate Noel had replaced Harrington at tailback and covered the final 15 yards on three runs and it was 41-28 with 12:10 remaining.

On the Mountaineer sideline Shawn Clark hadn't given up on his team.

"We were positive as coaches," he said. "I had confidence in our offense. As coaches we've got to believe, and when we scored the first TD, you could see the players begin to believe and the fans were back into it."

After a touchback on the kickoff, Maye was hit by Hampton and fumbled. Tyler Bird recovered it at the 28 for the Mountaineers and the stadium sounded like it did in the first quarter. Brice hit another touchdown pass three plays later and after the PAT, the Apps were somehow within a touchdown at 41-35. I was convinced we would win.

"At first I was having a hard time getting into the flow of the game," said Marcin. "In the second quarter I got in the flow and could focus on the game and being comfortable. In my opener to the fourth quarter I sound defeated. I can't believe we are getting walked on our home field. Then we get the Noel TD, hold them and get another TD, you feel it start to build up and chaos ensues."

The Tar Heels quickly quieted the crowd. Hood took a handoff and broke past the line of scrimmage and there were no defenders in sight. Safety Nick Ross ran down Hood at the four to temporarily save the touchdown. Two plays later, UNC scored, Maye ran in the two-point conversion and the lead was back to 14.

"We felt at the half, both teams gave out on defense," said Brown. "It was hot for an App State game. Neither team stopped anyone in the fourth quarter. It was so crazy."

But App State didn't get to this point as a football program by giving up. Most of the fans were still there and trying to pump up the offense. One good thing was that since Carolina scored so quickly, there was still more than nine minutes left to play. Brice led a nice drive with some help from the Tar Heel defense. Two third and longs were converted by App when Carolina was guilty of pass interference. The drive ended with Brice's fourth touchdown pass of the day. Christian Horn hauled in the pass, and it stood up on review. The deficit was back to 7, but there were still more than seven minutes left to play.

Jackson Wolfe couldn't believe what he was seeing on the Hill, which had thinned out a little during the third quarter. He had gone to the same high school as Maye for two years before Maye transferred.

"We were thinking this game was over, we have no shot," said Jackson Wolfe. "It was surreal. I wasn't sure what was going on. I couldn't believe that we had come back and had a chance at it."

Maye faced a third and 8 as well as a loud crowd after the Heels got the ball back. He converted it with a 16-yard completion. After a short run on first down, UNC had a false start penalty that energized the crowd. Hampton pressured Maye to throw early and it was incomplete. Steven Jones, Jr. broke up the third down pass and the defense had forced the punt for only the second time in the game.

"That was the most into a game I have ever seen my wife," said Cabot. "She barely remembers it. It was one of the most raucous crowds I have ever seen at Kidd Brewer."

Appalachian got a face mask penalty and a run by Brice to have a second and 1 at the Carolina 38. Peoples ran through a huge hole, made a move on a defensive back and took it to the house. App State kicked the extra point and with four minutes left, we were tied at 49. What a game! Hunter and I as well as the Tar Heel fan sitting beside me couldn't believe what we had seen. That guy said he was amazed with the environment at The Rock. He was the only Carolina fan sitting around us and except for one brief instance, when the App fans behind us exchanged some words with the Carolina fan, everyone was well behaved.

So how could the last four minutes of the quarter live up to the previous 11? The App State defense couldn't continue the momentum of the punt from the last series. Maye quickly moved the Heels into Appalachian territory and capped off another touchdown drive with a 42-yard touchdown pass. The five-play drive covered 75 yards and only took 1:10 off the clock.

Brice quickly moved the Apps into Tar Heel territory. But a long Noel run was called back for a holding penalty. The Mountaineers hadn't done very well when faced with long yardage situations. Brice threw two incompletions and scrambled for 10 on third down. App State was facing a do or die fourth and 10 from the Carolina 42. The Heels' defense bailed out the Mountaineers again, by committing a holding penalty. Two plays later, Brice hit Davis for a touchdown with 31 seconds remaining. The score was 56-55 and there was no hesitation from Clark to keep the offense on the field.

"We score, we're down one, and we're going for two," said Clark. "There was never a question in my mind. We are going to go for two to win the game."

I thought that was the right decision. I have never heard from a coach or anyone who has studied this, but I think it's a no-brainer. Unless you have an obvious personnel advantage, I think you should go for two to win. I think it's easier to make three yards to win the game than it is to go 25 yards in overtime, and even more importantly, stopping the other team from getting 25 yards.

The people in the stadium were wondering what play would be called. Some of the people who had tickets weren't in the stadium any longer.

"Carolina was up when I left my seat," said Kirk Sherrill.

"We left early in the UNC game," said Hoagland.

"I thought it was over and I left the north end zone [seating section]," said Nauman. "I was out those doors and fireworks started going off. We went running back in."

"Hell no, I didn't leave," said Macholz. "I was down at that end."

"I thought about leaving," said Jackson Wolfe. "I just wanted to see how it played out. It's not the craziest thing to come back. Forty points was crazy, but we had come back before."

At the line of scrimmage, the Mountaineers put the ball on the left hashmark. Pearson was lined up as a wingback on the right side and Davis was off the line, but outside the split receiver on the left side. Davis came in motion just before the ball was snapped and it appeared Brice could have flipped him the ball on a jet sweep. But Brice held the ball. Davis ran past the UNC defensive end and was suddenly in the clear in the end zone. Brice threw the ball in his direction, but Davis turns to face Brice and starts backpedaling as the ball sailed over his head and Davis fell backwards in the end zone. He would lie there face down until teammates came to pick him up. The App fans were hanging their heads in frustration. The Carolina fans, most of whom were in that end of the stadium, were cheering in delight.

"It was just a matter of inches a couple of ways," said Clark.

"When we missed the two-pointer, I couldn't believe it," said Macholz.

In the press box, Witten was trying to put aside his disappointment.

"You have the huge rush of emotion to climb within one," he said. "You are nervous. They drew up the right play, it was a miscommunication. It wasn't one thing, it wasn't a bad pass, wasn't a bad route, but it just didn't work out. You can see up high [from the press box] it's there, and we can do this! Then it's missed and it's such a letdown. That's certainly not where the game was lost. You have to stay professional. We knew we still had a chance with the onside kick."

"As coaches you have to believe in the situation," said Clark. "As it goes on, your players have to believe, too. We did a great job of that in the fourth quarter.

App State had converted an onside kick the previous year to switch the momentum against Coastal. However, that was a surprise move, based on how Coastal deployed their coverage teams. This time UNC was looking for it. Hughes hit it pretty good; it bounced high in the air. However, the Carolina players did what they were supposed to do, and took out all the App State players, so they couldn't get to the ball. Nesbit grabbed it and if Carolina had the "opossum" play, he would have fallen down, and the game would have been over. But of course, that didn't happen. Nesbit ran down the sideline and did the only thing that kept the Mountaineers in the game. He scored a touchdown. I was delighted. I couldn't believe he did that. The PAT gave the Heels an 8-point lead, but the Apps were getting the ball back. The fact that there were only 25 seconds remaining didn't matter.

Carolina was penalized 15 yards for excessive celebration after the touchdown and that was enforced on the kickoff. Tucker had a great return, and the Mountaineers had the ball in UNC territory with 19 seconds remaining. Brice hit Caden Robinson on the sideline for 22 yards to the 26. Could the Mountaineers pull this off? There were 14 seconds left. With Carolina's defense playing the sidelines, Robinson ran a post pattern and Brice hit him in stride just across the goal line and the Mountaineers were within two with nine seconds on the clock. The crowd was roaring in cautious optimism. Did offensive coordinator Kevin Barbay have another two-point play up his sleeve?

App came out in a different formation from the previous two-point attempt. The ball was on the right side of the field, but about halfway between the center of the field and the hashmarks. Three receivers were split out to the left side of the field. Pearson was the tight end on the right. Peoples was lined up about three yards behind Brice, who was in the shotgun. Brown called a timeout.

The Mountaineers didn't change the formation after the timeout. Davis came in motion again just like the last one. This time, the corner stayed with him, and Brice didn't have anywhere to go. He tucked the ball, but a defender was on him. Brice is a big guy and carried him to the 1-yard line where several other Tar Heel defenders converged and stopped him short of the goal line. This time it looked like the Mountaineers were done for sure.

"Man, those two two-point conversions," lamented McMackin. "Basically, the same play twice. They shouldn't have run that same play."

Nesbit recovered the onside kick again but was tackled and the game was finally over. UNC prevailed 63-61. It was the most points Appalachian had ever scored in a loss.

"Those two-point conversions were so close," said Marcin. "Just one little thing happens, and we could have won."

Hunter and I sat there in shock. I wished the Carolina fan sitting beside me well. Our section was slow to clear after what they had just endured. I was listening to Witten and the post-game show as we eventually made our way out of the stadium. I don't remember if I realized it by figuring up the score, or I heard it mentioned by the radio crew that App State had scored 40 points in the fourth quarter. The first FBS team to do that in 15 years.

"I had no idea," said Witten. I had no clue until the game was over. I was so locked in. I didn't look at stat monitor much in the fourth quarter."

I do remember the radio crew also mentioning the two schools had played in basketball the previous season and "only" scored 120 points in that game. The 62 total points in the fourth quarter was 1 shy of the FBS record. It was the highest scoring game either program had played. Brice ended up passing for a career-high 361 yards on 25 for 36 and a school record six touchdown passes. Six different players caught the touchdowns. Maye was 24 of 36 for 352 yards and four touchdowns and no interceptions. He also had a net of 76 rushing yards and the touchdown.

"I thought that would be the craziest finish we would see all year," said Marcin.

Coach Brown was gracious in victory.

"In 2019 we had a chance to come back," he said. "This year they came back. You have to be proud of the coaches and the culture in place."

"That was one of the best games in the state of North Carolina and we are appreciative of Coach Brown coming to Boone to play us," said Clark.

I wouldn't say it was any tougher loss than another," said Pearson, who caught four passes for 46 yards and the touchdown. "It's a tough pill to swallow, you score 61 points, but it's one of those games. We gave our all, there was no such thing as quit in our team, but we didn't win."

"It was the most fun I ever had at a loss!" said Cabot. "Seriously, I have never felt so good about losing a game. I was not happy, but I felt like I played in that game and left it all out on the field. I was done afterwards, nap time."

"Everyone was pretty upset," said Jackson Wolfe. "We had a chance to tie it. We were impressed that we had hung in there and fought our way back into it."

"When we lost there was devastation all around campus," said Paige Sherrill. "No one out, no parties. Even though we lost the game, I don't think anyone lost pride."

"It gave me a weird feeling we could be 0-2 looking to next week," said Marcin. "I was proud. The offense was question mark after losing so many players. Look at the UNC offense and it's just that they are good. I was encouraged they could compete and keep it competitive."

"For me I'm not going to elevate that game," said Haynes. "It was great to see that an ACC school would come to Boone and maybe others would follow suit. If we weren't good, they wouldn't have considered it. But because we are good, they had to. Because I think they were getting the pressure.

Good for Bubba Cunningham and Doug Gillin for making it happen. Showing it could happen is really cool."

"If you told me my freshman year, UNC would play here in 15 years I would have laughed at you," said Pat Mills, who was an offensive lineman from 2006-10. "To see it go on and going toe-to-toe with them. I'm proud of the small part I played in elevating the program where it is."

Back at our parking lot, there were a few people there and we rehashed what we had just seen. Eventually the Ladds made it back and the six of us packed into Mike's car to go back to the hotel. I was driving to Charlotte to spend the rest of the weekend with my mom.

"We had plans that night that we just canceled because no one could move," said Johnson. "Everyone was just so exhausted from the day. We're just going home."

Driving home I realized what a big deal that was today. We had already proven we could beat North Carolina and any of the teams in the state. But today it was not just the football team that was on display. The athletic department and the whole university proved they could handle a big situation with ease.

"The school did a great job, and everything went smoothly," said Macholz. "I thought we showed really well what we can do. Showing big teams we can handle a big crowd. They won't get as many tickets allotted as they are used to, but it will be a good time."

"I thought everyone had a great experience," said Witten. "We talked about that in fourth quarter of the game. Doug [Gillin] said we are like, 'It's kind of like hosting a Super Bowl party. You are trying to create a great experience for everyone else and you may not get to watch much of the game.'"

"I think it's really important that things went as well as they did," said Gillin. "We've shown we can be a really good host. This is a good place to come and play, it's unique. The UNC folks, we took care of them. They tell folks, 'It's a great place to play!' We want people to come here. In the new situation in college football, playing App State home and away is a really good game."

"I thought operations-wise it went as good as could be expected," said Witten. "When people talk about their experience in Boone, I think it's a great experience for fan bases to visit in the fall. What a chance for fans of other schools to come to the mountains for the weekend. That sounds amazing for a fan."

Gillin has set up the schedule and worked hard to get the state and regional teams to come to Boone. In the fall of 2022 N.C. State was scheduled to come in 2025. The South Carolina game has been pushed back a few years, but Gillin says it's still on the schedule. Wake Forest owes App a game in Boone, but it hasn't been given a date yet. Several games have been scheduled against Charlotte and the ECU series has two more games in Greenville to be played.

Before this book went to print, N.C. State announced they would play Virginia in a non-conference game on the same date in 2025 they were supposed to come to Boone. That announcement came just days after the ACC commissioner said ACC schools should not play road games against non-autonomy schools. The commissioner was trying to boost his conference's image after Florida State was not selected for the College Football Playoff in 2023 in part because their schedule wasn't considered difficult enough.

Having games like UNC and consistently drawing big crowds to The Rock means the program doesn't need to play "money games," a one-time trip to play a big school in their stadium for a $1 million+ payout.

Ironically, the last of these games on the schedule was up next: College Station, Texas, and the Aggies of Texas A&M. The Mountaineers would receive $1.5 million for making the trip. The Aggies were ranked number six and had just signed the nation's top recruiting class. While some of the fans were looking forward to the trip, the coaches and players had work to do to get ready.

"Having Texas A&M next helped," said Pearson. "You watch film and forget it. We're not using that game plan anymore, go on to next game. Fix the mistakes you made."

"We have a 24-hour rule after a big win or tough loss, put it to bed," said Coach Clark. "I have to have a positive attitude. I had watched a lot of A&M from the previous season.

They had a lot of draft picks. After watching their first game this year, it wasn't the same team. I convinced myself we would win."

One of the things I love about college football is the traditions. No school embraces traditions like Texas A&M. The Aggies stadium, 102,733 seat Kyle Field, had been near the top of my bucket list to visit for years. I saw A&M play Duke in the 2013 Peach Bowl, when Johnny Manziel played for the Aggies. I was captivated by their band and the precision and the different ways people in the band dressed. I asked an Aggie fan sitting nearby and they explained it was because of their classes. I thought it was so neat. When they joined the SEC in 2012, I told my Georgia friends, I wanted to go with them when the 'Dawgs played there. Amazingly, Georgia has never been to College Station, and I was getting to go to see App State play there. Ladd and I had planned the trip in the spring.

I first met John Myers at the game at Troy in 2021. He was sitting near Ladd and I and told me he appreciated my enthusiasm. He grew up in Fayetteville, North Carolina, and graduated from Appalachian in 1994. He moved from Florida to the Charlotte area in 2020 and has been going to games frequently since then. He was excited about the trip to Aggieland.

"I love going to road games," said Myers. "I am a college football fan. I love the tradition and pageantry. I'm there for traditions and experiencing the different environments. Going to these big SEC stadiums is fun."

The football team was trying to prepare for the sixth-ranked Aggies and was in a situation it wasn't used to. With the North Carolina loss coming after the two losses to close the 2021 season, the Mountaineers were on their first three-game losing streak since they lost four in a row in 2014, their first season in FBS.

"We had a third straight loss, and that doesn't happen very much at App," said Clark.

He turned to his secret weapon, his old coach, Jerry Moore. Moore was a native Texan who played against the Aggies in the old Southwest Conference while a player at Baylor. He had also been the head coach at Texas Tech.

"I met with Coach Moore, and he talked about playing A&M," Clark said. "He said, 'If you hit 'em in the mouth you have a chance to win in the fourth quarter.' I told the team, 'You have to win your battle every play, and you will break their will. It may not be in the second quarter or the third quarter, but you will break them down. Take the logo off the helmets and look at them differently. Win the battle every play. Win your play.'"

Would they be able to put the loss behind them?" wondered Witten. "You knew the schedule was going to be very tough. You are thinking after UNC, you could easily be 0-2. Are we going to be able to get off the mat? Mindset wise, App doesn't go into a situation wondering if it can win."

Bryan Luhn was a former co-worker at The Weather Channel. His in-laws are Tennessee season ticket holders and he had given me their tickets for the App State-Tennessee game in 2017. Luhn is a Texas native and University of Texas alum. He had recently moved to Houston. I asked him for a good Texas barbecue place to try for lunch on Friday. He knew of a good one very close to Hobby airport, where we were flying into. It was Killen's BBQ in Pearland. He met us there. The food was good. I got a mixed plate with brisket, sausage, and a couple of ribs. I'll always prefer Bridges and the North Carolina style but enjoyed my first taste of barbecue in Texas.

I usually don't put window flags on my car when driving to games, because I like to drive with the windows down and I'll forget I have the flags on and lower a window and the flag flies off. I do have a couple window flags I keep in my trunk. I decided to take them and put them on the rental car. Luhn took a picture of Ladd and I standing beside the car at the restaurant. Luhn's wife Carly works at an accounting firm in Houston with a big A&M booster. She had told him that Ladd and I were coming to the game, and he invited us to their tailgate. We had about a two-hour drive to College Station, and it was expressway the whole way. It was an easy drive to the hotel. We checked in and were ready for happy hour.

Our hotel was a couple of miles from campus on the main drag, University Drive. We headed toward campus and stopped at a sports bar that looked interesting, but there wasn't much going on. After a beer, we went closer to campus. We found a bar with a wonderful rooftop with a great view overlooking the campus, but there wasn't anyone there. We had a beer and admired the view of campus. A couple of App fans came up there and we were wondering where everyone was on a football Friday afternoon with beautiful weather. There were nearly 75,000 students at Texas A&M in the fall of 2022 and I couldn't believe a few hundred weren't at this bar. We went downstairs and hung out there for another hour or so. We met a guy, Murphy Swansy, who was from Charlotte and was a walk-on during the later years of Coach Moore's tenure. He lives in Chicago and doesn't get many chances to see the Mountaineers play. I enjoyed talking to him.

There was an App Alumni event at an A&M building across the street from the stadium. We ate supper there. There was a good crowd. We didn't know many people, but I ran into Myers. We talked about last week's game and what he was expecting to happen tomorrow. He's very analytical and I enjoyed getting his perspective. He was really looking forward to seeing the Midnight Yell later that night.

At 11:30 Ladd and I headed over to the stadium to see the Midnight Yell. That is perhaps A&M's most famous tradition. A&M doesn't have cheerleaders, they have Yell Leaders. That's because Aggies don't cheer, they yell. On Friday nights before home games, at midnight, the Yell Leaders get the crowd ready for the game by practicing the yells that will be done during the game. As many as 25,000 people routinely attend the Midnight Yell. It wasn't that long ago that App State would be tickled to get 25,000 people at the game on Saturday afternoon. When we found some seats, there were two Yell Leaders walking from the end zones to midfield where they would slap hands and do it again. There was a woman sitting in front of us who I could tell was an A&M fan and asked her to explain everything to us. Her dad had gone to A&M before it was co-ed and explained what was happening. The Yell team is composed of three seniors and two juniors. The juniors had to keep moving. At midnight, the band enters the stadium and leads the group in several songs. The junior Yell Leaders do push-ups during the songs. Someone told me they have to do the number of push-ups for their class year! The Yell leaders signal to the crowd what yell they are going to do and then it's done. One of the leaders is on a mic and encouraging the crowd.

He will also tell fables about the team they are playing and it's not complimentary. I was laughing at the stuff they were saying about App. It sounded like they had spent about 15 minutes on Google trying to find something about us. He was pronouncing it App-uh-LAY-chin, which I thought was funny. It was typical pep rally stuff. Near the end of the event, which lasts about 25 minutes, the lights on the stadium are turned off so people can kiss their dates. This tradition extends to the games when everyone kisses their dates after the Aggies score. The tradition is, "When one Aggie scores, all Aggies score."

"My best friend growing up went there," said Myers. "I saw him, and we went to yell practice, which was frickin' awesome. The coolest thing I've been to."

We had parked in the Gene Stallings Deck across the street. I thought it was nice that he was honored like that. We went straight back to the hotel.

Saturday morning, we got up and stopped on the way to buy a Styrofoam cooler and some Lone Star beer. Luhn had emailed me a map of where Carly's boss's tailgate was. Apparently, there was an area with a lot of fancy tailgates, kind of a smaller version of the Grove at Ole Miss. I had bought a parking pass several months ago but it was on the other side of the stadium from where we were going. We ended up walking at least two miles from the parking spot to where we were going to tailgate, but at least we got to see a good bit of the campus. When we finally got to the area we were looking for, it was really nice. It was divided up into spaces with tents. Everything was catered with fancy carving stations and bar areas with lots of liquor bottles. Most of the areas didn't have many people there yet. It was about 10 a.m. and kickoff was at 2:30. I walked to the spot where Carly's boss's tailgate was supposed to be. I asked if this was that firm, but no one seemed to know anything about it.

Ladd and I walked around and found an App family that had one of the tents and we stopped there to hang out. It was the family of defensive back Jackson Greene, who was from Boone. The Greenes had a company set up a tailgate for them for the UNC game and the company asked them if they wanted them to do any other games. The company said they do A&M games, so the Greenes said yes. One of the people at the tailgate was Tommy Sofield, who was the donor who gave the money for App State's indoor practice facility. He said he went with some athletic department officials Friday on a tour of Kyle Field. He said the A&M officials told them they had remodeled the stadium to build more boxes and premium seating. I noticed last night at the Yell how many boxes and levels of club seating they had for such an old stadium. Kyle Field has been the home of Aggie football games since 1905. After the 2013 season, the west stands were torn down and rebuilt before the next season started. After the 2014 season, they did the same thing with the east side. It's an impressive facility. This game would be the fifth trip for the Mountaineers to a stadium that holds more than 100,000. The Mountaineers played well in the spacious venues. There were the two trips to Michigan (a win and loss) as well as the overtime losses at Tennessee and Penn State.

One of the things you get when you pay these companies to set up your tailgates is satellite TV. We watched the end of ESPN's *College GameDay*, then the Alabama at Texas game, which was surprisingly close. Ladd and I walked back over to where the tailgate we were invited to was supposed to be, but no one there knew anything about it. There were several of the fancy set ups with just the people there serving the food and booze standing around and there was no one else there. I was amazed there weren't more people there.

Another Aggie tradition is to greet other Aggies and visitors with a "Howdy!" Everywhere we went, we got a "Howdy!" They were very hospitable. We started talking to the folks at the tailgate next to where the Greenes were, and they were a family from San Antonio. They told us this area was new and how it was developed. They were making brisket sandwiches, and I couldn't turn it down when offered. It was grilled brisket with cheddar cheese on Texas toast. Very good. They had a son who had gone to Texas State. He proclaimed that App would win today, but they would lose in San Marcos later in the season. I told him I thought he was going to be off on at least one of those.

We finally made our way to the stadium, which was just across the street from where we were tailgating. Our seats were good, in the end zone on the southeast corner. There was a good App contingent there. We could tell it was going to be hot already. Ladd and I had finished our beers at the tailgate and were drinking water in the stadium. There was beginning to be a little buzz in the App section because Notre Dame was losing to new Sun Belt member Marshall. The Irish were ranked number eight, despite losing the week before at Ohio State.

Back in Boone, Jackson Wolfe was watching the game at a fraternity house.

"I didn't really think it would be a close game," he said. "I knew they were ranked high, so I didn't think we would have much of a chance."

As the team ran out on the field, I was disappointed to see Noel was at the back of the group and just jogging out there. It was obvious he had been injured against North Carolina and wouldn't play. Brendan Harrington, as expected, wasn't even dressed after his injury against the Tar Heels.

The Mountaineers got the kickoff. Brice converted a third and 9 by hitting Christian Wells for 27 yards to get into Aggie territory, but they would have to punt a few plays later. A&M got one first down too but had to punt as well. On the second drive for the Mountaineers, we began to see the game plan Barbay had come up with. Mixing runs with short passes, the Mountaineers were taking it to the young defensive line of the Aggies. Sitting in the end zone, you could see the motions App State was using. The Mountaineers converted two fourth and ones. Once, A&M jumped offside. Another time, Peoples powered his way to the first down. After getting to the A&M 25, Brice missed on three straight passes and Hughes was on to try from the 42. He missed, but on the drive the Apps ran 15 plays, moved the ball 55 yards and took more than eight minutes off the clock.

"At first we had some different pulls and some different motions," said Pearson. "The gameplan was run it down their throats. Those stars [recruiting rankings] don't mean a damn thing, and we did it well."

Sophomore Haynes King was the starting quarterback for the Aggies. The week before, in a storm-delayed, 31-0 win over Sam Houston State, King had thrown for 364 and three touchdowns, but also two interceptions. He was one of the top recruits in the country in 2020. Facing a third and six, Jalen

McLeod, a replacement for Harrington at linebacker, sacked King and forced a fumble. DeAndre Dingle-Prince made the recovery for the Apps, and they had a first down at the A&M 29. The game turned sloppy as the Aggies gave the Mountaineers three first downs as a result of penalties. App State committed an unsportsmanlike conduct penalty and faced a second and 25, but one of the A&M penalties gave App an automatic first down at the Aggie 13-yard line. A short run and another penalty gave the Mountaineers a first and goal from the four when the quarter ended.

App State had 11:29 time of possession in the quarter. They were doing what they wanted, except for scoring. But on the first play of the quarter, reserve running back Ahmani Marshall took it in for the touchdown. We were feeling good in the App State section. On the ESPN2 broadcast, the cutaway shot of the App fans showed Ladd and I exchanging a high five.

We were both surprised by the way we were moving the ball. In the radio booth, Witten wasn't surprised, based on the conversation he had with the coaches the night before.

"They had a really good feeling about moving the ball," he said. "I'm going to be surprised if that didn't happen. Early on, we didn't score, but were moving the ball. There were enough signs; we are getting push from the O-line, we are moving the ball without tricks and gimmicks. As the first half wore on, we knew we knew we could move the ball."

The Aggies' most consistent offensive weapon was running back Devon Achane. The speedster took the kickoff from the goal line and Appalachian did a good job to keep him from getting past the 25-yard line. King completed a pass for a first down, then later in drive showed his speed and moves on a 31-yard gain to the App 32. After a six-yard pass, Achane took it up the middle for 26 yards to tie the game. Was it here we go again for the defense?

They had plenty of time to talk about what happened on the scoring drive, because the offense put on another long drive. Peoples converted a third and five with a six-yard run. Marshall gained two on fourth and one. They were down inside the Aggie 40. On fourth and six, Brice was hurried into an incompletion. However, the drive took 13 plays, gained 38 yards, and took six minutes off the clock. It was a hot day and that time on the field had to be taking a toll on the Aggie defense.

Whatever the defense talked about on the sideline worked. McLeod had another sack on first down and the Mountaineers got a three and out. The Mountaineer offense couldn't get a first down and punted back to the Aggies. But the defense responded with another three and out and the Apps ran two plays to run out the half. I was so impressed with the defense and was happy with the way the offense was moving the ball, but they would have to score.

"At the half Kevin Barbay said we are going to keep running it down their throat," recalled Pearson. "They kept taking it so we kept doing it. Keep it away from them and run up the time of possession."

Usually at halftime, I don't pay a lot of attention to the band. I love their music and think bands are one of the things that sets college football apart from professional football. I usually walk around a little to stretch my legs. I don't like to wait in line for anything, so I usually seek out some friends to discuss the first half. But today, I was going to watch the A&M band. I was so impressed with them when I saw them at the Peach Bowl. As it seems with everything involving Aggies, there are different uniforms based on class. They march with such precision and in tight formations. It is so neat to watch. You can see the school's military heritage on display.

"The way that band moves in and out of each other is incredible," said Myers. "My buddy was in the band, and he said, 'You get hit, that's just how it works.'"

The schools traded punts after the half. On the Aggies second drive Achane picked up 15 yards on three carries. On the third run, Cobb was injured and came out of the game. On the next play King hit Evan Stewart near the sideline. He made a move on a Mountaineer defender near the first down mark. While he was dancing around, the defense was able to converge on him and Dexter Lawson, Jr. knocked the ball loose. Hampton pounced on it and the App State defense had made another huge play.

The Apps ran the ball for one yard, six yards, and six yards for a first down. Brice caught the Aggie defense looking for the run and completed a pass to Davis for 21 yards and to Horn for three more. Then it was runs for five, one, six, one, and three yards, and the Mountaineers are suddenly inside the Aggie 10 facing a third and six from the 9. Pearson was lined up as the wingback on the left of the formation. After the ball was snapped, he ran across the line of scrimmage and was uncovered in the right flat. Brice dumped it off to him and he tip toed down the sideline and stepped behind the pylon and the Mountaineers were back in front.

"We were going to win up front and we did it," said Witten. "We looked like the most conditioned team at the end. That's what we want. To line up with big boys and take it to them. We played them straight up for the most part."

There was 2:34 remaining in the third quarter. The Mountaineer defense would have to hold on for about 17 and a half minutes to pull off the upset. They couldn't hold it for 14 seconds. Achane took the kickoff at the 5 and ran straight up the field. He broke a tackle at the 30 and two App players ran by him and he exploded into the clear and scored. The PAT made it 14-14. Last year in A&M's big upset win against

Alabama, Achane went 96 yards with a kickoff return. The 12th Man, the Aggies' name for their crowd, was back in the game. And I had that same feeling that I had at Tennessee, Auburn, Penn State, and last Saturday: we would play so well, but it may be just a little short.

The Mountaineers quickly ran off the final minutes of the third quarter and had the ball at their own 40 when the fourth quarter started. Through the first 45 minutes played, the Mountaineers time of possession was at 30 minutes, 51 seconds. App State had run 61 plays to the Aggies' 30. The Apps had 113 yards rushing and 229 total yards through three quarters. A&M only had 128 yards of total offense.

"App had way more snaps and time of possession," said Witten. "That was the stat we kept going back to. Time of possession and number of plays run. We were still playing at a high level. It was amazing to see that continuing to happen."

It took App State two plays in the fourth quarter to get into Aggie territory. On this drive they would convert four third downs and move the ball inside the Aggie 15. But on the fifth third down, Brice had Wells open at the 2, but the pass was a little behind him and as Wells spun to try and catch it, the ball hit his hands, but he couldn't hold on. So, Hughes, who still hadn't made a field goal as a collegian, would be on to attempt one from 29 yards out. The crowd of more than 92,000 were screaming, but he drilled it, and the Mountaineers were back out front. They didn't get a touchdown, but the drive lasted 18 plays, gained 63 yards and ran more than nine minutes off the clock. Because of the time-consuming App State drives and the Achane kickoff return, King hadn't been on the field since there were nearly nine minutes remaining in the third quarter. Now there was 8:05 left in the fourth quarter.

The Aggies got the ball and were backed up near the area where the App fans were sitting. It was third and 15 on their 20. We were making a lot of noise. Just like at South Carolina, the home team, in front of the App fan section, committed a false start penalty late in the game in a crucial situation. I don't know why that happens. Is it the crowd noise? Is it the jumping around our defense was doing? Is it nerves because they were about to lose a game to a team they thought they should beat? Who knows, but it kept happening. It was now third and 20 from the 15 and we were making even more noise. The pressure came and King was forced out of the pocket and threw incomplete, back across his body. However, after he released the ball, McLeod pushed him, he fell down and drew the flag for roughing the passer, 15 yards and automatic first down. We were stunned in the App section. It wasn't much of a push, but McLeod should have known not to have done that.

"I just remember everyone was on their feet, about three feet from TV, for the last five minutes waiting to see what would happen," said Jackson Wolfe, who was still at the fraternity house.

King then hit Stewart with two passes and A&M was in Mountaineer territory. Achane gained 12 and set up a first and 10 at the 34. Doublin, who was in for Cobb, stopped Achane for a loss of one. On third and 11, King completed a pass, but it was short of the first down. The Aggies tried a 47-yard field goal. The Apps didn't block it, but it wasn't even close to being good. The Mountaineers had the lead, the ball and there was 3:43 left for App State to run out. Peoples had been strong all game and everyone figured he would be getting again. He did. On first down he carried the pile for four yards. On second down, he ran over two A&M defenders at the yard to gain and it was ruled he had picked up the first down. However, after a lengthy review, it was determined that he was short, and it was third and one. During the review, the "APP" "STATE" cheer was ringing out.

"We were talking about how impressed we were with the offensive line," said Witten. "To see App State linemen winning battles against four and five stars. It was a lot of pride. We've always had speed and skill, but where it's tough to make up ground is up front. We won the line of scrimmage."

Peoples picked up the first down, barely. The Aggies called their second time out.

"I had COVID that weekend and I did not go watch with friends and stayed in isolation," said Kirk Sherrill. "It was nice weather. I watched with the garage door open, and I got progressively louder as the game went on. I had to shut door I was making so much noise. I couldn't believe it."

On first down, App State mixed it up a bit, and Peoples went outside. He gave a stiff arm to a defender and broke into the clear down the sideline running toward the App section. He was pushed out of bounds at the 12. The App section was loud. The 12th Man was down to about 11.213 as Aggie fans were heading to the exits.

"We ran the same plays, outside zone and inside zone 40 times," said Pearson. "When you double the time of possession it's hard to lose."

The Mountaineers were now in position to run out the clock.

"I watched the A&M game at my house," said Mike Wolfe. "I wanted to be able to pay attention and focus. At halftime, a couple of buddies asked to come over. I said, 'You can come over, but I can't guarantee my mood.' They ended up watching the second half with me. They are getting into it. Even casual fans understood the magnitude."

"In Europe they have an app called "ESPNplayer" that allows you to pay 14 Euros a month and get most every App game and all the ESPN+ stuff," said Cabot. "I have stayed up till the middle of the night to watch many a game. A&M was just amazing, my wife and I could not sit down. I was just pacing."

It took all four downs, but the Apps ran out the clock and for the first time since 2007, they had defeated a top 10 team. The Aggies had been 33-1 against non-conference opposition at Kyle Field since 2010. The only other loss was to number two Clemson in 2018.

"I've experienced some big moments and that was the next big moment," said Gillin. "Going to a storied program, ranked in top six, they had great recruiting class. One of my best friends is the A&M AD. It was a unique opportunity, that program is one of the best and for us to go in there and win like we did, coming off the shootout, only allow them to score 14 points. It was an amazing game I'll never forget."

"We had the ball 40 minutes," said Clark. "Our D only had a few plays. It was very lopsided. Our kids won that game."

"Their QB wasn't very good," said Myers. "P5 defenses don't go exotic against us. They were just base, base, base, and we gutted it out. I left A&M thinking no one in the Sun Belt can hold us under 40 except for Troy. They had a great D."

Most of the App fans had moved down to the edge of the stands by the field and Ladd and I had moved over to the stands toward the bench area to congratulate the players and coaches as they slowly made their way towards the locker room. They were all soaking up the adulation. It was a great scene. I felt there was a sense of relief, especially among the coaches.

"It was very satisfying, but I was happy for the players," said Clark. "I knew it had been said Shawn Clark can't win the big game, although we had beaten a ranked Coastal team. It was gratifying that what we do is right, but I wanted to make sure the attention wasn't on me."

"It was a scary time for App State football," said Pearson. "Honestly, that was the first losing streak I had had. I didn't say anything out loud, but I was worried. We are throwing away what teams before us had accomplished and letting other's legacy down. For us to keep a losing streak, that falls on our shoulder. It meant more than just beating number six, it was keeping the App State legacy going."

Media outlets were reaching out to Jones. For the second week in a row, the Mountaineers were involved in the game of the day.

"My phone was dinging and ringing at that point," recalled Jones. "From the end of game, getting stuff from friends, news outlets, 'Can we talk to Clark, Chase, Cam?' I gathered our staff, get high priority interviews done, then doing the post-game newser [news conference], and working with the creative team to get stuff out on social media and take care of the external requests."

Once the players finally made their way to the locker room Ladd and I headed to the bar where we were the night before. Walking up the stadium steps it was hilarious that there was about an eight to one ratio of water bottles to beer bottles under the seats. I couldn't wait for a shower but needed to drink some beer and celebrate for a while first. The bar was on the way to where the car was parked. App fans were regaling each other with "APP" "STATE" chants on the walk across campus. The A&M fans were gracious and congratulated us on the win. They were frustrated with Fisher and the quarterback situation. Ladd and I ran into Swanzy and his girlfriend at the bar. They had gotten their tickets from a resell site and they weren't in the App section. There was a decent crowd at the bar now. Many people were watching the games that had just kicked off. We were checking the scores from earlier in the day and Marshall did end up beating Notre Dame. The Aggies were ranked higher than the Irish, so App State had the highest ranked win over a ranked team by a Sun Belt team. The day for the conference would get even better later than night as Georgia Southern beat unranked Nebraska. Three Sun Belt wins over three schools in the top 21 of FBS wins all time was quite an achievement.

Another reason I wanted to get to the bar was to recharge and turn on my phone. It would always lose power at the stadium so I kept it off, except to take pictures. And I took a lot of pictures, especially at the end of the game. In a lot of modern stadium layouts, the big scoreboard has become a thing of the past because of video boards and the ribbon boards that line the front of the concourses. I found a board near us that had the score, and I got a picture before the clock had reached :00, but quickly after the game was officially over, the scoreboards were turned off.

Another reason I keep the phone off is that I get frustrated getting texts from people who don't bother coming to App games and complain to me, the eternal optimist, about why the defense allows 55 yards on the opening drive, or why we run the ball on third down. I am on a text thread with all the guys I tailgate with, and they had sent out an SOS to me. Some were concerned I had done too much celebrating, but all were happy for me for making the trip and getting to see the win. I let them know I was good; the phone was charging, and I was ready to start celebrating!

Our celebration in College Station was minor compared to what was transpiring in Boone.

"After the game, we ran out to King Street [the main street through downtown]," said Jackson Wolfe. "It was crazy, you would see a crowd on one end running down to your end. It was just a pretty big party on King Street until they shut it down."

There wasn't social media when the Mountaineers beat Michigan in 2007, but this time the word of the crowds was spreading quickly. Later, video was posted to social media about what Jackson was talking about on King Street. It was viral quickly and mainstream news outlets, as well as the college football games that were ongoing were showing the video. Paige Sherrill wasn't able to watch the game because she was involved in sorority rush.

"We were in a little room with no TV and I was checking the score," she said. "Someone says, 'They are rushing King!' So, we wonder what's going on. We got out at 9 p.m., so I couldn't go to King Street. It was crazy, pop-up parties everywhere."

"I was watching the game in my apartment," said Marcin. "I jumped on the next bus and went to campus and met up with friends. I was at the Duck Pond. I jumped in. It was dreary and cold, and everyone had a party there. It was super fun! The water's not as bad as you think."

"Everyone headed to the stadium to take the goal posts down, but there was security there already," said Jackson Wolf. "Then we headed to the Duck Pond. There were already thousands there. You couldn't see how far back it went. Watching everyone else do it [jump in the Duck Pond], and I thought I may not have another chance to do it again, so I did it."

"Everyone was jumping in the Duck Pond, but I didn't do that," declared Paige Sherrill.

"It was the craziest I had seen campus to that point," said Marcin, a senior. "Winning Sun Belt was just another year of winning the Sun Belt, but when you get that opportunity to beat number six, you go crazy. Being a road game and everyone coming out of their apartment or dorm and coming together to have a party was so much fun."

You would think nothing could happen to dampen the spirit of the team. But there was bad news when they got to the airport.

"We are trying to get on the plane, and I'm told we have a flat tire," said Clark. "I say, 'Change it or pump it up, let's go.' It doesn't work that way on a plane."

"We were still so excited, even not being able to take off," said Gillin. "Control what you can control – don't worry about little things."

Jones was still setting up a lot of interviews with media outlets from around the country.

"It was fun, a rush, a fun reason to be overwhelmed," said Jones. "What I wasn't expecting was a call from Connecticut, from the producer of *College GameDay*, telling me they are thinking about coming to Boone!"

"We have a lot of collaboration on the site," said Rece Davis, the *College GameDay* host. "I'll get a text on Saturday night, what do you think? Sometimes it's obvious. Sometimes there are differences of opinion. Kirk [co-host Herbstreit] and I were in alignment. Management may overrule occasionally, but they are good about listening but providing counterpoint."

"We're on the tarmac and Joey had heard from ESPN," recalled Gillin. "We were one of a couple they were considering. I called my boss, Chancellor [Shari] Everts, and said we were in the mix. They would let us know in about 30 minutes. Thirty minutes later we found out they were coming. We had to let everyone know. We wanted the team to know first, so we got some videos ready and had video of the players reacting that we were going to host."

"We were sitting around on the tarmac, and coach calls us all together," said Pearson. "We think we are getting ready to be leaving, but he tells us we are going to be on *College GameDay*. It made sitting there a little bit better."

"We don't have a lot of firsts at App, but never had we had *College GameDay* at Boone," said Clark. "Players and coaches were excited. Great day for us."

"It was apparent what App State had done the first two weeks of the season," said Davis. "The game everyone was talking about at the end of each Saturday was App State, so why don't we go there?"

Paige Sherrill said, "Everyone was excited when they heard about *GameDay*. All the girls, we will wear this outfit and make this sign!"

"After the announcement came out, I said, 'wait a minute; am I dreaming here?'" said Mike Wolfe. "We just throttled A&M and in seven days *College GameDay* will be in Boone? I would have never dreamed that."

Brian Metcalf, a 1985 graduate who lives in Raleigh and is frustrated with the lack of coverage the program gets, was shocked.

"I never thought that would happen. I was very pleased and proud of it."

"We sit for another 30 minutes or so, but we can't use that plane, another one has to come down from Minnesota," said Jones. "So, we go back to the hotel. It was sitting around until 3:00. Players, coaches, support staff all laying down, asleep in the hallway in the hotel. At the middle of the night, when you were so excited after the win and the *College GameDay* and this, and you don't know what to think."

"It was the most painful thing," said Pearson. "They put us in a room, four dudes in a room. We slept for an hour and a half, then they said, let's go. It was miserable. Greatest time in your life and to go through that made it rough."

"I do know I had the best pizza I've ever eaten at 2 a.m.!" said Jones, laughing. "We were all starving! I had to communicate with the folks in Boone about when we will return. We got back about 10 or 11 a.m. on Sunday. Still a good crowd to welcome us back home."

The work was just getting started for Jones and his staff. The problems with the airplane just added a layer to the story of the Mountaineers. Plus, it was released that *College GameDay* had planned on being College Station that week because the Aggies were going to host Miami. But not only did App State beat the Aggies on the field, but they also took their $1.5 million and took *College GameDay* away from them. Also, videos of the Yell Practice before the Appalachian game had gone viral. People had posted clips of them making fun of App State and remarking App State had won the game. Those people didn't realize the Aggies have been doing that for about 90 years and making fun of your opponent is something that has been going on at pep rallies around the country at all levels of schools for years.

Video of the crowds on King Street and everyone jumping in the Duck Pond had gone viral. App State was trending like never before and that increased the interest in media outlets to talk to the Mountaineers. Jones and Clark devised a strategy similar to what Jerry Moore and Mike Flynn had done after the Michigan game.

"We pow-wowed and said, 'We have to take advantage of this,'" said Jones. "People want to talk about App State, we have to take advantage of that."

In a normal week, I do three or four interviews on camera," said Clark. "We weren't going to say no to anyone. We counted them up, and I did 42. College football Final, The Jim Rome Show, other national shows."

"I had 185 interview requests for players and coaches," recalled Jones. "We had to spread the love around. It may not have been Clark or Chase or Cam for all of them, because they just couldn't do that many, but we gave them someone."

"For a lot of people it was a little different with the attention," said Pearson. "Chase, Coach, Cam were kind of used to that. No one cares about the FB and TE, but local news in Charlotte interviewed me after A&M."

"I have to get my mind on the game," said Clark. "I told my assistants, 'I need your help. We can't let distractions affect the team.' Boone is electric. The team is excited. We are the media darlings that week. We knew we were playing a tough team."

"Hosting a show like *College GameDay*, it's not just an athletics event, it's the whole university," said Jones. "We had meetings at the chancellor's house, which is not normal."

"The leadership was great from [Chancellor] Dr. Everts," said Gillin. "She brought together everyone and explained what a big deal this was for the whole campus. She understood the impact it would have. All the campus folks worked together, like they always do. It was great because everyone came together for one cause. To do it in six days was amazing!"

"I had worked on a staff at Ole Miss that hosted *College GameDay* in 2014 so I had some familiarity with that," said Jones. "But I was just one of a large staff. Here, there's just a handful of us, and I'm one of the primary point people for that. It was a large, full plate that week. Our staff had to breakdown who was going to do what. I had to delegate more because I was on Shawn Clark and ESPN duty that week."

"I live in Winston-Salem. A normal week for me is to be up there for Tuesday," said Witten. "I leave around lunch, go to practice, visit with folks, have our coaches show. Pretty routine day. I'm not a full-time athletic department employee. The people I normally meet with, their availability was limited. Just the media requests that came in. You had beaten a top 10 team and are hosting *College GameDay*; the media requests were insane. I was getting them too, as people not involved in game preparation, we say yes to maximize this opportunity."

Marty Smith is a reporter for *College GameDay* who gets to town early and as Davis said, "Captures the flavor of an area." Since *College GameDay* had never been to Boone, they did a tour of the town. Smith grew up in Southwestern Virginia, not too far from Boone. He had covered App State games before and was familiar with the program and the town.

"I was Marty Smith's assistant," said Jones. "We went to Dan'l Boone Inn and ate biscuits with Clark and Brice. When he jumped in the Duck Pond, I had to quickly walk him back up the hill [to the locker room] to get a shower. He didn't say much on the walk up the hill. He didn't want to get sick from what he had just jumped into. I have never walked that fast and I don't think he got sick."

"Marty Smith went and had a beer [at Booneshine] with a guy who sponsors our podcast," said Haynes. "Are you kidding me? Marty Smith went and had biscuits at a table I've sat at. I've seen Marty Smith before; he's done games for us. That's our Marty. I've jumped in the Duck Pond, I've been in that nasty water, we've done all those things and to have someone give the nation a synopsis of what life in Boone is all about was great."

It was determined that Sanford Mall, in the center of campus, would be where the set would be constructed. It's a wide-open area next to the student union and could accommodate the expected crowd. When I was a student, the library and dining halls surrounded two of the sides of the mall, but the dining hall had been torn down and a new one built nearby. There's a new library, but the old building remains and has been repurposed. There would be nice shots of campus as the backdrop too.

"I got a little of that it was different," said Pearson. "Even in class people and even teachers were asking you about that. The years prior and all the adversity will prepare you for things, whether it's good or bad. You have pat answers for the questions you were going to be asked on campus."

"It was something in the communication building," said Marcin. "People knew it was a big deal. I grew up watching that show and being a huge fan, it meant a lot to have them here. Everyone wanted to cover it. We have our three main student media outlets: paper, TV, and radio. I threw my name out for media coverage to hang around the set. Of the three outlets, we were the only one that didn't get a credential. I got some good stuff outside the student union, but I was outside the set area."

"There was a hangover during the week," said Pearson. "Practice Tuesday was shitty. Wednesday, we picked it up, trying to get everyone focused. Guys were getting interviewed, and we were trying to get people focused on football."

"It was so fun to see that set walking to class," said Paige Sherrill. "This is going to be such an awesome weekend.

It was so big because something like that hadn't happened before. It made us feel like we were good and recognized."

"It was a huge stage you never thought you would see at Apps's campus," said Jackson Wolfe. "Getting ready to host one of the biggest things they would ever host there. Everybody was so excited."

It's rare for me to make it up to Boone from my home in suburban Atlanta for all the home games. When the schedule originally came out, I wasn't going to go to Troy. After the A&M trip it would be a good week to take a knee. Also, I was really looking forward to the James Madison game. That was the rivalry I was most excited about with the new schools for the Sun Belt.

After the schedule is released by the conference in early spring, the athletic department assigns a promotion for each home game. It may be Homecoming, Family Weekend, Black Saturday, etc. The Troy game was going to be Hall of Fame weekend. The Appalachian Sports Hall of Fame induction ceremony would be the morning before the Troy game. My former classmate from high school, Ed Boyd (Chapter 1), was getting inducted in this year's class and even though we weren't especially close and hadn't seen each other in years, I wanted to be there for his induction. Macholz has a place in Blowing Rock and said I could spend the weekend there. Ladd wasn't going to be able to come, so Ladd's friend Mike Smith was going to use my other ticket. Smith is a board member of the Appalachian Former Athletes Association, the group that puts on the Hall of Fame breakfast.

"*College GameDay* coming?" said Smith "I thought, really? I was ecstatic and I hoped it wouldn't jinx us. With the Hall of Fame breakfast that morning it made things easier because all the distractions were at the Mall, and we could honor these guys at the stadium appropriately."

Thursday afternoon, the *College GameDay* bus arrived on campus and hundreds of people were outside the stadium to greet it. It was quickly trending on social media. It also kind of symbolized the beginning of the party that would engulf the whole town for three days.

"Living in Boone I was able to see that unfold slowly," said Haynes. "It was a big deal the bus coming here. All week long, that setup, it starts early. They just don't pop that up on Saturday. I was able to walk on campus and see David Pollack doing live shots."

"The Thursday when the bus got here there were four or five people in a class," said Marcin.

"Campus was even more geeked than UNC," said Paige Sherrill. "Bigger than I had ever seen it. Friday class was canceled before *College GameDay*. They knew no one was showing up."

"I didn't have any classes called off!" said Jackson Wolfe.

"It was a three-day tailgate!" said Paige's friend Sarah McCully.

Davis and most of the rest of the on-set hosts arrived in town that afternoon. Most of them were staying at the Horton Hotel, a new boutique hotel on King Street. At the time, it was the only hotel of its kind in Boone. It doesn't have many rooms and is run kind of like a bed and breakfast. The front desk isn't staffed 24 hours. David Pollack didn't arrive in Boone on Thursday before the desk closed, and the front doors were locked. He ended up spending the night in his truck in front of the hotel.

"I asked him in the morning, 'Why didn't you text me?'" said Davis. "I could have gone down and let you in!"

Davis enjoyed his time on campus and getting a first-hand look at campus and the football facilities.

"It's a beautiful, hidden gem," he said. "They've done a good job with the stadium and football facility. An elite, next tier type program. Could they be a Boise? Maybe, something like that, below the Power 5. It's a good program but with a ceiling. They are prideful; they feel they can beat anyone, just give them a shot. They relish that opportunity."

Pat McAfee, who was in his first season on the *College GameDay* team, hosted his radio show from the set on Friday and was frequently tweeting things from the set and was getting a lot of attention.

"Normally on Friday, I go to work in Winston-Salem, then go up [to Boone] at lunch," said Witten. "I have three kids, two are old enough to enjoy App football. I pulled them out of school Friday, so they could come with us. This was a once in a lifetime chance to see that and experience *College GameDay*."

Davis spends a lot of time trying to get the local color of an area. For the major schools where he has done plenty of shows and seen plenty of games and is familiar with the history, it's easy. But when he goes to a place he's not familiar with, it could take some time.

"I may get some things to use the right vernacular of the area," he said. "I do my own research. I do it myself, may ask the SID a few things. I use fight songs, the battle cry and try to get an understanding of the area and how they say things."

"People started sitting out in Sanford like 6 p.m. the night before, waiting," said Jackson Wolfe. "I didn't go until the next morning. I thought it would be better for me to get some sleep and enjoy it, instead of being there so close."

"The night before the game I went to Sanford Mall and as far as you could see were students sleeping there," said Pearson. "I hadn't seen that before. It was, 'holy crap, this the most insane, in a good way, I've ever seen.' That was when I saw first-hand what it meant. As a player you don't get to see the tailgating. You get to see folks on the Mountaineer Walk, but this was a whole different thing."

Witten had gotten up earlier than usual on a game day, so he could get a few things ready in the radio booth, then have some time to hang out with his family at *College GameDay*.

"I saw the mass of humanity there," he said. "I got there about 8:15, hung out, saw some folks. I haven't been around so many people except for a game. I savored the moment about how special that was. Met my wife, dropped off kids with her, then went to stadium and it was normal for me."

The lots opened early, and I got there first in our group and walked over to Sanford Mall to see what was going on. It was impressive all the people there, more than an hour before the show would start. There were a lot of sleeping bags out there. Mike Smith parked not far from the Mall, and we had arranged to meet there and walk up to the stadium together for the Hall of Fame breakfast. It was great to see Boyd and catch up with him. The center who played with Boyd was Jay Wilson and we had had several classes together and talked a while. It was neat seeing some of the other older players, most of whom I had never met. Former Georgia Tech basketball coach Bobby Cremins and his long-time assistant Kevin Cantwell were there too. When Cremins was the Appalachian coach, the person who was the manager was getting inducted that day. It was nice they were there. Cremins left App State for Atlanta the spring before my freshman year and Cantwell took over as the head coach for the Mountaineers.

It was a nice ceremony and I'm glad I was there. However, I was ready to get involved with the *College GameDay* party. I wore slacks to breakfast and went to the lot and changed into shorts. There were several guys there then and they were working to get the TV set up. Some had already been to the Mall to watch the show, which was already underway. The crowd was much bigger now than when I had stopped by earlier. Everyone was going crazy, something that helps the hosts.

The show came on the air with a drone shot of the sun rising over a mountain top. Davis said, "In Boone, North Carolina, Pioneers are respected; but Mountaineers are revered!" Boone's high school, Watauga High School, is nicknamed the Pioneers. I asked Davis if he knew that or if it was a coincidence, and he laughed and said it was a coincidence. Out of the taped open, there was a mix of live camera shots wide and tight, of the crowds and the signs. It looked very impressive. On the set you could see the mountains behind them and some of the other buildings on campus. After Davis introduced everyone on the set, Desmond Howard, a former Michigan player, said he had a bone to pick with the App fans. The crowd got quiet, thinking he would say something about 2007.

He said, "I've forgiven you for that, but beating Texas A&M last week. That was my pick to win the national championship!"

Herbstreit acknowledged being there for the first time. Lee Corso was wearing a black suit with a gold tie and said, "My first prediction, Troy, No Chance." Davis, ever the journalist, made sure to mention that Troy had some big wins of their own, winning at Lincoln and Baton Rouge. McAfee played it up with the crowd.

"They don't really come out there to see us," said Davis. "They do a little, but they come to show the rest of the country how great their fandom is. They can use us as their vehicle. The secret sauce of the show, it's about the sport and their fandom and they show that through us."

"I left Charlotte around 5:30 and got to the lot about 7:30," said Kirk Sherrill. "That's one of the things you never thought you would see, *College GameDay* at Boone. I tried to get a good standing area, but we kept getting moved back. That's a top five moment for me. Maybe number one at home."

"Oh my gosh, that was so much fun," said Hoagland. "[My friend] Mack and I were up there. We got pretty close, and It was fun. An electric atmosphere in the air. You could feel it."

"We deserved this before," said Johnson. "There's a competitiveness to that. There's no doubt, every Appalachian fan will say, 'Is Boone worthy of *College GameDay* and everyone would say, absolutely.' And just being a part of the process to prove it was a ton of fun."

"Oh man, I couldn't believe they were coming to Boone," said Macholz. "I got some backstage passes from a friend who works on the show. It's one of the most beautiful sights on our campus. It's just continuing on what we've done."

"I spent about an hour there at the show," said Mike Wolfe. "I went up there, took it in. We set up the TV and you could watch it better on the TV. The environment was just crazy. You couldn't follow the broadcast there. Ashley [his wife] came back and she took those passes and spent more time up there than I did."

"It's not a pregame show for App and Troy," said Davis. "And when we are in Columbus it's not a pregame show for Ohio State and Michigan either. We have to balance the national perspective with the location of the game."

There weren't a lot of big national games that week, except for the Miami and A&M game. It's a little early in the season for important conference games, so the show took a lot of time to talk about App State. Clark was on the set with Herbstreit, and they talked about Coach Moore. There was a clip from Bill Murray talking about how much he liked Boone. They pitched to the Marty Smith feature and there was a huge roar from the crowd when they had a feature about some of the big games App State had won.

"You get there for breakfast, and the TVs are on," said Pearson. "*College GameDay* comes on and it's right there. This is really happening. It's another game, but there's pressure. We can't lose this game. You definitely have pressure on your shoulders; if you lose it would erase what we did last week."

Part of the charm of the show is the signs that students make. There are plenty of cameras to show close ups of the signs and the people in the crowd. A long-time tradition of the show is that there is a Washington State flag in the crowd. The guy holding it was near me. I talked to him and there was a group of people to take care of the WSU flag. There is an App State faculty member who's a Wazzu grad, so he was sent the flag to have on the show. It's a neat thing they've done. On a lot of shows the student who makes the best sign gets free tuition for the school year. Appalachian had decided to take that a step farther.

"The chancellor made the decision that we would award a whole year of tuition to the winner," said Jones. But behind the scenes, she had worked it out to give the three finalists the free tuition and the moment that made on TV was great."

"I think the crowd helps ratings, but a good crowd is not necessary for a great show," said Davis. "If people are channel surfing and they see a good crowd, they may stop to watch. It's way more fun if you have that. It's not a studio show, it's live. If conversation is sparked about a sign, that's a great thing. I think what our guys do well is capture that. We don't have scripts and a teleprompter; I do write stuff to organize my thoughts. The spontaneity is there when you have that crowd and McAfee is brilliant with that."

"I didn't get there that early on Saturday morning," said Paige Sherrill. "We walked over there, and you lost all your friends because it was so crazy. People wouldn't move. A wall of people. I was there about 30 minutes. I went to the stadium early that day. I was in the front row on the Hill."

"I got there around 9:30 or so and stayed about an hour," said Jackson Wolfe. "I thought that was insane to see all those people there. A whole new level to see all those people there and everyone was so amped up!"

"It was a nice reward for the school and the fan base," said Jeff Owen, who graduated Appalachian in 1983. "I thought we blew them away as we do everyone that comes up here. Genuine football fans that we are, with participation and enthusiasm."

"It's not nerves, it's adrenaline," said Davis, about the feeling on the set. "If you don't feel that you need to be doing something else. We all love this sport. It's changed [the former players'] lives. There's a great appreciation of the sport: the culture and the impact on people. People like me who didn't play but have an affection for it. I'm tied to it and understand the significance of how important that Saturday is. You have to have a sense of responsibility that we represent the show and want people to feel it. If it's a rare or first-time appearance and there's a nice little boost there that's fun."

Each week the show's final segment is the picks for the weekend's big games. *College GameDay* has a celebrity flown in to make the picks with the rest of the show's hosts.

Sometimes, but not always, the celebrity has a tie to the host school. Early in the week, there was a lot of speculation about who it would be. The logical choice was Luke Combs, but he was scheduled for concerts in Green Bay, Wisconsin, on Friday and Saturday. Fortunately, the celebrity picker segment is sponsored by a private jet aircraft company and that makes it easy to get people anywhere, even Boone. Combs would be there to make the picks.

"He had wanted to be the guest picker before," said Davis. "We had asked him one week and he politely declined. He had a show that night and wanted his voice to be great for the show."

But there was nothing that was going to keep him away from Boone. As he made his way from the RV where he had been waiting, he fired Yosef's musket. The crowd was going crazy. Many signs made reference to his hit song, "Beer Never Broke My Heart."

"Luke Combs, that was awesome," said Macholz. "It was exactly who should have done it. I think he is tremendous. He speaks from the heart. I think he is great ambassador for us."

"It's hard to explain his impact," said Owens. "He's a real live Yosef. He's a normal guy who hit it big and he loves App State, he's just like everyone else. His story is pretty incredible. He's hit it big and keeps reaching new levels. He has true App State qualities."

"That's so cool he would be able to do that," said Jackson Wolfe. "It shows how much he loves App and what a great place to go to school because it's so much fun."

When Jake Stroot was the football video coordinator, one of his student assistants, Tyler Adams, wanted to use the editing equipment to edit a video he had shot for a fellow student.

"This guy comes in and looks like a bum," said Stroot. "Tyler says, 'This guy will be the next big thing.' It was Luke Combs!"

Combs still uses Adams for his video stuff. He was on the set wearing a black App State cap. The crowd was chanting, "APP!" "STATE!" You could tell he was having a lot of fun up there and he had done some research too.

When they finally got around to making the pick for App State or Troy, Howard went first and said what I had been worrying about all week, that the Mountaineers had been hearing all week they were the greatest thing since sliced bread. But he said he loved the culture of App State and thought it would propel them to victory. When it came to McAfee's pick, he raved about the atmosphere surrounding the set and said the only thing he was 'more sure' about than this pick was, "A long neck, cold beer ain't never broke my heart!" Combs, sitting beside him, started singing along, as did the thousands on Sanford Mall. It was great stuff. Howard said, "That must be a lyric."

When it was time for Combs to pick, he was serenaded with the song by the fans around the stage. He was listing all the App State big wins and close calls before proclaiming, "App State by a million!" to the delight of the crowd. The final pick is always made by Corso. He gives a brief analysis of how he thinks the game will play out and pulls out the head gear worn by the mascot of the team he is picking to win. It's become great TV over the years and is a great way to close out the show, which was running over into the noon time slot. Corso was having some trouble pronouncing Yosef, but said he echoed his pick from earlier and said into the camera, "Troy, no shot." He then put on the Yosef head gear as Herbstreit helped him with the hat. Combs, sitting on the other side of Corso, was clapping in approval. It was a great way to cap off a three-hour celebration of Appalachian State University.

"I think the ambassador he's [Combs] been for App, we can't thank him enough," says Gillin. "His passion is awesome and that helps us. The fact he would make the time to come over early in the morning from Wisconsin, what it means, not just to me and the university but the fan base. It comes naturally. Obviously, he has a connection to App and he's passionate about that. None of this happens without him. No one is pushing him to do anything, and he just does it."

"The dude loves App State," says Johnson. "He represents App State proudly and he talks about App State with enthusiasm. And he has given App State a lot of free press. He wanted his first stadium concert to be in Kidd Brewer Stadium."

"That's when it hit me was when I saw it on TV," said Haynes. "That is our music, that is our people, those are our signs and our cheerleaders and our band, etc. and on and on and on. They say all those buzzwords, Pat McAfee, long neck cold beer, and all those things about Boone/App state culture. I stood on Sanford Mall, and it was almost like you couldn't believe what you saw, it was so surreal. I was trying to take it all in."

"It will never be as special at Georgia and Alabama as it was for us," declared Johnson.

But in three and a half hours, there was a football game to be played. I'm sure the Troy players had been watching the three-hour App State infomercial and they couldn't have been happy about being told in front of a national television audience that they had no chance. By this time, most people were at their tailgate but there were some folks who actually have to work during the game.

"It was tough to balance the excitement about *College GameDay*, then get ready for the game," said Marcin. "I went straight from *College GameDay* to get radio stuff to Kidd Brewer

Stadium to do game prep there. We had a 30-minute pregame show."

Witten had already been at the stadium for more than 30 minutes when *College GameDay* signed off. He had been at the airport with the team in College Station when they realized the flight would be delayed and that had him concerned.

"The thing that I go back to is how we would be from an energy standpoint," he said. "I thought our coaches did a good job of the hype. It's important to embrace those moments, but there were things they couldn't control. We had a nightmare of traveling coming back from A&M. Arriving back on campus it was broad daylight, 10 or 11 a.m. and Sunday is typically a practice day."

I did my usual tailgate hopping and got to the stadium about 3 for the 3:30 kickoff. There was a good crowd and a good energy to the crowd already. Smith joined me and he was confident.

"After the way we played against A&M, I wasn't worried about Troy," he said.

The Trojans had a new coach, Jon Sumrall, who had been defensive coordinator at his alma mater, Kentucky. This was his first head coaching job. They had lost at Ole Miss in week one and had defeated FCS Alabama A&M in week two. I had seen the Mountaineers destroy Troy last season, and I felt we had better personnel than they did, but I too, was worried about the A&M and *College GameDay* hangover. Something Witten and his analyst Brandon Turner were talking about in the pregame.

"You are coming off an emotional win, a physical win," he said. "You have no sleep, flying back on the plane, on the bus, they are only a few hours away from practice. You basically lose a whole day of recovery. Took normal Monday off day but you have classes and there were all the interviews."

Some of the worries went away on the first play from scrimmage, when Lawson intercepted Gunnar Watson at the 38-yard line. The Rock erupted. On first down, Brice hit tight end Miller Gibbs for 11. The next play Peoples went for 10 and another first down. Barbay went deep in the playbook for the next call. Dashaun Davis came in motion from left to right and

Brice handed him the ball. Davis dropped back slightly and lofted a pass to the end zone and Wells caught it and the Mountaineers had a 7-0 lead. All the worries about the hangover and overconfidence seemed to be for naught.

"We get the pick, then then the touchdown and the players and coaches relaxed a little," said Clark.

"We were big favorites," said Marcin from the WASU booth. "We figured it would be a typical Sun Belt game, we will rollover the opponent."

Troy showed they had changed under Sumrall when they went 75 yards in seven minutes to tie the game. The Mountaineer offense that had first downs on their first four plays, was suddenly struggling with the adjustments the Trojans had made. They punted twice, sandwiched around a Troy punt.

With 12:34 remaining in the half, Troy took over at their 19-yard line and covered the 81 yards in only eight plays. The Mountaineers were suddenly trailing and the mood at The Rock had changed.

"Once we got behind, no one really knew what Troy had," said Witten. "We knew they had a good coach, but at same time, it's his first year, early in season. Even when we got behind, we made some mistakes and gave up a long drive."

Brice helped get the crowd back in the game with a nice drive, mixing passes and Peoples runs. Facing third and 10 from the Troy 18, Brice hit Anderson Castle out of the backfield, and it was tied again with 1:22 remaining. I was feeling better about things, because App State would have the ball to start the third quarter and we could establish ourselves again. Watson had other ideas. Three completions had the Trojans in Mountaineer territory. On third and 10 Watson completed a pass for 36 yards. A few plays later, after a pass interference penalty on Lawson, it was first and goal at the 1. A run for no gain and an incomplete pass gave the Trojans a third down with only three seconds remaining. Watson snuck the ball and after some delay, it was determined he crossed the goal line as time expired. It was a deflating way to end the half.

"The first half went by quick," said Pearson. "In the locker room I was thinking, we are going to lose; we will throw it away. We started having a man to man talk among all of us to get going. It was one of those things."

It seemed to work. The Mountaineers took the kickoff to open the second half and ran off a nine-play, 75-yard drive to tie the game. Harrington capped the drive with a 19-yard run. The defense picked up on the offensive momentum by forcing the Trojans into a three and out. Appalachian had to punt when they got the ball back and Troy was able to move the ball into App State territory. The Trojans got down to the 15, but the Mountaineers got a good pass rush and forced Watson to three straight incompletions. The field goal was no good.

App State took advantage. Starting at their 20, Brice hit Pearson for 11 on the first play. After picking up a first down mixing the run and pass, Brice found Robinson for 42 yards down to the Trojan 14 and that got the crowd back in the game. The drive bogged down there, but Hughes was good from 23 yards and the Mountaineers had their first lead since it was 7-0 and the crowd was alive. The Mountaineers were 29 seconds from the fourth quarter, the quarter they had dominated all year. I finally felt good about things and the guys had finally shaken off the hangover from A&M and *College GameDay*. App State was leading 24-21, had the ball for nearly 10 minutes in the quarter, outscored the Trojans 10-0, outgained them 158 to 73, and kept Troy from converting a third down in three tries.

"We played great in third, hold Troy, and now you are ahead going to the fourth," said Witten. "We saw the fourth quarter where we have done things, and the team would put this away."

The Trojans had a nice kickoff return and despite heavy pressure and tight coverage, converted a third and nine for their first third down conversion of the half. Watson hit passes of 11 and 14 yards and Troy was down to the App 13. The defense forced a third and three, but Watson completed a pass to running back Kimani Vidal to the one and it was it was first and goal. On the next play Vidal gave the Trojans the lead again when he bounced around the end and into the end zone. Suddenly the Mountaineers were behind again, and they would need a touchdown to win. The good thing was that there were more than 10 minutes remaining in the game.

"I'm really embarrassed," said Paige Sherrill. "I have never left a game early, but I did that day. My friends left; I was mad the whole entire game. Everyone is watching this, and this is the one day we are going to lose when the most eyes are on us."

"Are we going to embarrass ourselves after we had the college football world looking at us?" wondered Marcin from the WASU booth.

After a touchback, two runs by Peoples left the Apps facing a third and five. Brice hit Pearson in the seam. He bounced off two Troy defenders and gained 15 more yards and into Troy territory. Peoples was stopped for no gain and then Brice was incomplete, setting up a third and 10. The Mountaineers decided to run it and Harrington gained seven. Clark called timeout. The Mountaineers had converted four of seven fourth downs on the season. Clark had gained a bit of a reputation as a gambler who would go for it on fourth down. There was 7:03 remaining and App State still had two time outs. So, if he decided to punt, there would be time to get the ball back, as long as the defense could come up with a stop. I felt like he would go for it, and he did. Brice hit Gibbs for seven at the sideline and Pearson blocked the corner to allow Gibbs to get the first down. The ball was at the 27. Brice hit Horn for six, then Clark didn't forgo the run, giving it to Harrington for five and a first down at the 16. Then Peoples went for 3. The clock showed five minutes remaining.

We were thinking that Clark was going to try and score with as little time as possible and that's why he was still running it so much. Brice missed Robinson in the back of the end zone to set up a third and seven. It was another run, but Peoples could only pick up four and it was fourth and three with 4:18 remaining. After the play, Peoples limped to the sideline. Marshall, the biggest healthy running back, replaced Peoples. On the fourth down play, Brice hit Marshall at the 5. Robinson had taken the corner to the back of the end zone and there was a clear path for Marshall to get into the end zone, but as he turned his body up field, he fell down. His gain was enough for the first down, but would it be costly that he didn't get into the end zone. The crowd was roaring, as much as they do when the offense has the ball. Marshall gained a yard on a handoff on first down. Brice rolled out on second down, but Troy had good coverage and Brice was sacked at the 7. The clock was down to 2:20 when Brice took the shotgun snap on third and goal from the 7. He found Robinson, but the receiver was brought down immediately at the 2. It was another fourth down. This time, Brice couldn't convert. His pass to tight end Eli Wilson was incomplete in the back of the end zone. It looked like Wilson would have been out of the end zone even if he could have made the catch. The Mountaineers appeared to have come up short. The drive was 17 plays and 73 yards, but two yards short. Would there be time for the defense to get the ball back? There was 1:13 remaining and the Mountaineers had two time outs. They should be able to get the ball back. But a lot of fans started to leave.

"We were out of the game the whole day. We just weren't playing well," said Kirk Sherrill, who had left the stadium. "If I had a hotel I would have stayed."

"I thought that was the game right there," said Jackson Wolfe. "I didn't think there was any way we would get the ball back."

"We had the long drive and didn't score," said Marcin. "There is no way we can win this game."

"From my perspective, is Troy really going to do that to this team that has been such a story?" thought Witten. "Credit to Troy, they didn't allow App to get the knockout punch and they were in position to win at the end."

The Trojans took over at the 2, up 4 points. Watson gained three on a keeper and App State called their second time out. Vidal got a yard on second down and the Apps quickly called time out. Vidal gained five on third down but was a yard short. It was fourth down on the 11-yard line.

"I was down there in the end zone," said Gillin. "I always meet the team on the way to locker room. We all thought barring a miracle we weren't going to win. I wasn't feeling woe is me at that time. I was still very proud to be a Mountaineer."

Troy called time out to set up what they were going to do. Sumrall sent Watson and the offense back on the field. It looked like they were going to take a safety. That's what they did. Watson ran around in the end zone for five seconds before he was pushed out of bounds for the safety. The Mountaineers were now down two points, but only 20 seconds were left in the game.

"The safety is the interesting thing. Do you punt or take a safety?" wondered Witten. "When we got the ball back, absolutely I thought we had a chance. I saw what we did against North Carolina, after the returned kick for a touchdown, the way we moved the ball, that is what I thought we would do. Hit a quick pass, get out of bounds, maybe you have 30 yards for a field goal."

"I still don't know why they did that [take the safety]," said Marcin. "That's one of the dumber coaching decisions I've seen. Then they squib it, and we get a good return. It sets in maybe we can win. All we need is a field goal."

Marshall took the squibbed kick to the App 47. He was trying to move the pile and get as many yards as he could, but the clock was running down. Finally, he was tackled, and 15 seconds were on the clock. Hughes hadn't shown much range so far in his career, his career long was only 29 yards. The Mountaineers would need to move the ball to at least the Troy

25 for a 42-yard field goal attempt. That would be 28 yards. I was hopeful they could do it.

On first down, Brice couldn't connect with Davis on the sideline. Troy was really covering the sideline. Second down Brice went for Robinson downfield at the hashmarks, but he couldn't make the catch.

"As long as you have time to run two plays, you have a chance," said Witten. The second down play you thought, 'Oh no!' Robinson was open, didn't make play. Third down, seven seconds left. Do you have enough time? You had to run a long enough pattern."

On third down Stroman looked like he had his hands on ball, but even if he caught it would be about the Troy 41, so a field goal attempt of nearly 60 yards. There were two seconds on the clock.

"We were right at the cut-off line to how far we could throw the football," said Clark. "If you had two yards farther back, we would have run razzle dazzle. We practice that every Thursday from different spots on the field. I told Kevin [Barbay] to throw it."

"I remember talking with Brandon; we saw the Miracle on the Mountain [the 2002 win over Furman]" said Witten. "He played and I was on the sideline. I don't know if we'll see anything like that again."

"I was on the bench with Tyler Bird and Jackson Greene," said Pearson. "They were down and saying this isn't going to happen. I was saying, 'You gotta believe; crazier shit has happened. This could happen.' I was trying to make a joke, just to keep them up."

"You can hear it, the disappointment and dejection in my voice," said Marcin. "Of course, we get *College GameDay*, and we lose with the entire college football world watching. To lose a game as a two-touchdown favorite. It's not a good look; we would be 1-2."

"It's the longest, best day of my professional life," said Jones. "I've been up since 4:45. It's been fun. We had all the great content. A big day of publicity for App State, and we are going to lose this game. We can't lose this game!"

"What I said before the play, is what is Troy going to do defensively?" said Witten. "He's [Brice] not great at buying time, where he can extend the play to give the receivers time to get down there."

"I was looking at the formation to see what the plan was going to be," said Myers. "Here we go, it's the last play. I wasn't nervous. Who's out there? Where was it going? I was surprised Hertzel was out there. Stroman, I expected because he could jump."

Horn was split wide to the right, the wide side of the field. Craig Hetzel was closest to the Troy sideline but was off the line of scrimmage. Stroman was next to Hetzel, on the line. Originally, Robinson was lined up on the right, but he looked confused. I wasn't sure if that was to throw Troy off or not. He went in motion and came set right behind the tackle. There were three seconds on the play clock.

"I'm on the sideline at the end of the game. I was in the end zone at the App side," recalled Jones. "We were pretty dejected. Everyone knows it's a prayer. Ninety-five percent chance it's not going to work."

"Will Troy rush three or four? That's what I was watching for initially," said Witten. "They rushed three initially, then another one came. It gave him too much time."

The ball was snapped with two on the play clock. Brice took the snap and dropped a couple of steps back. The Trojans got good pressure from Brice's left side, and he was forced to step up. Guard Bucky Williams almost got in his way, but he slid to his left, took a hop and let it go.

Marcin, in an almost monotone voice, described it like this: "Brice rolls left. Going to heave it deep. ... It's not going to get there."

"I turned around and saw the ball wobbling in the air," said Pearson.

"When I've seen that play practiced, it's been thrown to the end zone," said Witten. "When the ball looked short, I immediately thought, what a crushing day after all that's happened. You always think you have a chance, but Chase had to throw it so high to give guys a chance to set up the way it's designed. You see it short; it's not meant to be. When I saw the ball was short, I thought, that was it."

Witten's call went like this: "Chase going to step up in the pocket ... sets, throws ... high into the air ... up for grabs."

Horn, from the left side of the formation was sprinting down the field. The corner covering him, was watching the ball and let Horn get up near where Stroman was.

Jackson Wolfe was still a few rows back on the Hill, at the opposite end of the field where the play was heading.

"I saw the ball go up," he said. "I didn't think it would come down far enough."

Stroman, who's 6'4", was at the 5-yard line, behind Troy linebacker KJ Robertson.

"Stroman could go up and he would catch it or tip it," said Clark. "He tipped it to Horn. It was just how we planned it."

Horn caught it at the 8 and headed for the sideline. Robinson turned around at the 6 and sealed the edge with a great block on Craig Slocum, who had made 13 tackles in the game. Jones and his staff said Horn took 12 steps after he caught the ball and crossed the goal line. He raised both arms in the air triumphantly, flipped the ball away, and ran into the arms of an athletic department worker behind the end zone.

Robinson and the other receivers on the play quickly piled on and all the players sprinted from the sideline to the pile.

On the broadcast, you can hear Witten say, "It's juggled." Then Turner yells and you hear Witten say, "It's caught!" You can't tell what else he was saying because Turner is yelling. I could make out, "An App State touchdown! Miracle part two. They did it!"

Marcin's call went like this, "It's caught by Christian Horn!" His voice went up an octave from monotone to screaming, "He scores! He scores! App State wins! Holy Mother Meatballs! It's a touchdown for App State!"

"It was caught, and we all ran over to the corner," recalled Pearson. "That's the only time I've ever won on a Hail Mary so it's best experience without a doubt."

"I watched the play develop and everyone is going nuts," said Mike Smith. "When I saw it develop, I thought that is one of the best coaching moves I've seen in a long time. Practiced tipping and that was a great move. People talk about the catch, but if he doesn't seal that edge, it doesn't work. If I was a coach somewhere, I'd show it to our team."

"We are up so high [in the radio booth] I use binoculars for every play," said Witten. "I don't believe I used my binoculars on that play. I see the ball thrown in a collection of players. I see Horn running with the ball. I don't think I realized what happened until I saw him running and people chasing him. Seeing the replay, collecting our thoughts, exactly in that moment I could not see the details of what had happened, until I saw him running. That was how I experienced it in real time."

"I'll never forget the elation," said Gillin. "It was really cool."

"It happened right in front of me," said Myers. "They are fun to watch in general, the mass of bodies. There's not going to be a penalty."

"I'm a professional, but I went crazy then," said Jones. "I was high fiving players and boosters. It could not have been a more crazy and magical game than it ended up being."

Smith and I were still in our seats. I was listening to Witten on the radio with my earphones but wasn't paying much attention to him once the play started. I couldn't hear anything once the ball was caught because of all the yelling around me. I did hear him say, "Miracle part two!" I had no intention of leaving. I had been there that long. We erupted and exchanged high fives with each other and everyone around us. I started taking pictures of the bedlam on the field, where students were storming the field.

"At first a few people jumped over and then everyone went there," said Jackson Wolfe. "You had to jump over the fence. I ran down to the end [of the field]. I lost my friends. Everyone was jumping around and going crazy. I hadn't experienced anything like that before. Once it settled down, I looked up and saw my dad and Jim [Macholz in the north end zone' and I jumped over the barricade to get up there. They all looked at me and said, 'Where did you come from?'"

Most of the players were in the pile around Horn in the corner of the end zone. Brice, however, had gone to the sideline. The App student section is the lower levels of the stadium on the west side behind the Mountaineers bench. There is a wall about six feet high, and students were jumping off of it to get to the field. Brice started helping students get down from the wall onto the field. Like so much of the aftermath and celebration, it quickly went viral on social media.

"It was mayhem; people were everywhere," said Pearson. "I don't remember much of the celebration; I don't know if that was because I didn't celebrate or I celebrated really well!"

"They were the better team that day and we got lucky," said Macholz. "You could tell we practiced that. Troy played well, but they didn't play for 60 minutes. I was upset that we let them hang around with us. You are upset, but then they were a pretty damn good team."

Owens sits a few rows in front of me.

"I couldn't watch that Troy play," he said. "I didn't think it would turn out the way it did."

"I was walking down Rivers Street and I hear everyone go crazy and I think, 'Oh my God, we did it!" said Paige Sherrill. "I ran home. The guys who were there said this is insane!"

"We were listening to Adam [Witten] and when we won it, we were in Granite Falls [38 miles from Kidd Brewer

Stadium]," admitted Kirk Sherrill. "I had a buddy with me who was at his first App game and wasn't happy with me."

"For that game to end the way it did, we didn't see it," said Hoagland. "We were in the elevator coming down. We went out the gate. As soon as we stepped out of the gate the fireworks went off. Crazy, crazy."

"I was prepared to feel like I did at Penn State," said Jones. "It was nice it went the other way."

"I think it was lady luck, but we practice that," said Pearson. "Being down, being down 3, four-minute, two-minute, we go through every single scenario. We have to set the ball on this side. Nate Noel taking a knee against Marshall. You have to run a 15-yard out to get out of bounds. We had practiced them; the question was would they work? My grandfather said, 'The harder you work, the luckier you get,' and it all came together for us."

"It was a crazy day and a crazy week," recalled Clark. "Cap that with the Hail Mary to win. I have four more interviews after the game. I didn't have a chance to take a shower at the stadium before I left. I fell asleep on the couch about 10 p.m. in my game clothes."

"Broadcasters don't practice those moments," said Witten. "We are broadcasters. We are App fans, we broadcast for App, you can say we are homers. We celebrate the wins and suffer the losses. We had seen something historical. You just react, you are not prepared for what your mind and body will say. The ball got thrown, Christian Horn caught it, and it was a TD, that was the only thing I was sure about. Brandon's going crazy. There's a lot of noise, I'm trying to make sure to get across, we won! I had never called a moment like that. We knew we were going to win the A&M game. The closest I had come to that was in 2019 in the UNC game. I'm just trying to convey the emotion."

"I was in as much shock as I've ever been," recalled Marcin. "When you can't think of something to say you go to expletives, and I wasn't going to say a four-letter word. You can't say that. It [Holy Mother Meatballs!] was the first thing I could think of. A kid on social media says it all the time. I didn't realize I said it. You kind of black out a little and say what the heck just happened?"

Smith and I stayed standing in our seats and watched the celebration on the field. I thought about going down there but decided not to. I had a better view from there. For the third Saturday in a row, App State was the talk of college football.

It was such a relief for me. We were able to pull it out. App State rose to the occasion. So many of us were wrong to doubt the heart of the team. They had practiced, they had prepared, they had run up Howard Knob, they had done all the lifting and workouts in the off-season. Today, all of them had truly given their all for Appalachian State. And the fans who stayed were rewarded with a game they will never forget and a day they will always remember. Appalachian fans have so much to be proud of and we have a lot of great moments to savor. Sure, there have been heartbreaks and tough losses, but we are Mountaineers. We'll still be back next week to have fun at the tailgate and watch our team play a game in the place that is so special to all of us.

Epilogue

Eventually I made it back to the parking lot and we were all trying to understand what we had just seen. Of course, we were ranking it as far as the greatest App State football moments, especially at home. I had been listening to Adam and it was indeed similar to the "Miracle on the Mountain" in 2002 against Furman. The thing about the Miracle that I like so much is that it is a rare play, intercepting a two-point conversion, and was unexpected. Of course, it's unexpected to score on a Hail Mary, but it's attempted a lot.

I spent the night at Jim Macholz's house, and we watched the night games from around the country and talked about things. It didn't get old, seeing the ESPN ticker say, "The lead – App State wins on Hail Mary." It was great watching the play over and over again on all the highlight shows. It was truly a great day. I told Macholz, how crazy would it be for the freshman at App this fall? They have these three games and *College GameDay*. Unless we are in the College Football Playoffs, you can't top this. There is nowhere else to go but down. Jackson Wolfe, a freshman in the fall of 2022, wondered the same thing.

"I thought about how crazy it was," Wolfe said. "I was talking to my dad about that, and I realized how wild this football season started off."

Jeff Marcin's radio call with the "Holy Mother Meatballs" on WASU had earned him some notoriety.

"I didn't think it would get as big as it did," he said. "That was kind of the thing when we posted it to Twitter. The reaction was 99 percent positive, it made you feel good. People wanted T-shirts. I went on a few radio shows as well. They used the clip on the Andy Staples show. My assistant director Lucas listens to that show every weekend. He heard it and posted it [on social media]."

In the next few days, we would find out just how great a weekend it was for Appalachian State University. The ratings for *College GameDay* were fantastic. An average of 2.2 million people watched for the entire three hours. In the final hour, it was 2.8 million. It was one of the top 30 all-time rated *College GameDay* shows. The social media mentions of App State over those three weeks were incredible. The school estimated that the exposure the university received from *College GameDay* was worth more than $500 million. There was a 25 percent increase in applications since the *College GameDay* appearance. Fall 2023 would see record enrollment for the university. Throughout the season, there would be references to what happened with the Mountaineers in September.

Daniel Jeremiah played quarterback for Appalachian from 1998-2000. He's made his mark as a draft analyst on the NFL Network. During the coverage of the NFL Draft on the network, there is always a reference to the Michigan upset between Jeremiah and NFL Draft Coverage host and Michigan grad Rich Eisen. Before the 2023 NFL Draft, Pat McAfee had Jeremiah on his radio show to talk about the draft. Before they started the interview McAfee brought up how much he loved doing *College GameDay* in Boone and they talked about Boone and App State for a couple of minutes. In a podcast, Rece Davis listed his top five favorite *College GameDay* sites and App State was number two behind only Clemson. The uniform reveals on social media continued to be among the most watched in the country.

So, what would the Mountaineers do for an encore for the Hail Mary? As I've mentioned earlier, I was very happy that James Madison joined the Sun Belt, and I was really looking forward to seeing them play. The Dukes were up next on the schedule. They would be coming to Boone for the first time since the classic 2007 first-round playoff game (See Chapter 7). Unfortunately, I was not able to make the game. I have a pet sitting business and that was the first weekend of fall break in the area I cover. We are always busy that week and I just couldn't make it to Boone. I watched the first half on TV and saw App State bust out to a 28-3 lead. The defense had forced two turnovers and quarterback Chase Brice was 9 of 11 for 129 yards and two touchdowns in the first half. JMU scored with about two minutes remaining to cut the deficit to 18, but the Mountaineers seemed to be in a commanding position in front of another raucous crowd at The Rock.

I had to go do some walks at halftime but listened on the radio to Adam Witten and Brandon Turner on the Appalachian Sports Network from Learfield. What I heard was very disturbing. The halftime adjustments the Dukes appeared to have made were working. They were pressuring Brice into incompletions and bottling up the run game. But the Mountaineer defense had held the Dukes without a first down on their first two drives. App State had the ball and faced a three and five at their 25. Brice was sacked. On the punt, the JMU returner called for a fair catch. Milan Tucker was bearing down on the returner and got blocked. There was contact and the returner fumbled the ball. The Mountaineers recovered the fumble, but there was a flag, Tucker was called for fair catch interference. Replays showed that the contact with the returner was from the JMU player blocking Tucker. But the play stood, and the Dukes took over at the App State 40. Seven plays later James Madison scored a touchdown.

Early in the fourth quarter, Madison pulled to within 3 with a touchdown and two-point conversion. On the first play of the next App State drive, Brice was intercepted, and the ball was returned to the App 9. It took the Dukes two plays to score and take the lead. After a three and out, JMU had a long drive but faced a fourth and one at the App 9. Trey Cobb, the senior leader at linebacker who had missed the Troy game because of an injury at A&M, showed his guts with a tackle for a loss. Once again, late in the fourth quarter, the Mountaineers would need a late touchdown to pull out a win. They picked up a couple of first downs but didn't get across the 50 as a fourth down pass was incomplete and the Dukes won 32-28.

"We just became lackadaisical," lamented senior tight end Henry Pearson. "We were up 28-3 and saying these guys need to go back to FCS and we got punched in the mouth. It was on the players and coaches. Players weren't communicating with coaches about what wasn't working, and the coaches didn't change things. We got embarrassed in the second half. There's no explanation for losing a game like that."

"You can second guess yourself all you want," said Clark. "We brought in a sports psychologist to talk to the team. Things were happening for us. Against James Madison, there were a couple of key plays. We had the ball on a two-minute drive to win and I was confident. It was four emotional weeks. We didn't handle it well as staff, and that starts with me. You have to play every single week, or you will lose."

"It seemed like we gave up after the fair catch interference," said Marcin. "It seemed like they had a hard time with motivation after that."

The following week and a 49-0 win over The Citadel made the JMU loss seem like an aberration. But the next week the Mountaineers fell behind early and lost at Texas State 36-24. App State had been 6-0 against the Bobcats. The son of the Aggie fan I met during the tailgate in College Station was correct. App beat A&M and lost to Texas State. I knew something was wrong. Kaiden Smith said the subject of what was wrong with Appalachian was a popular topic on his podcast.

"I think those early games were such national distractions it hid some of the flaws this team had." he said. "It was bad defense against UNC, and we played okay against A&M. Troy beat us and we stole the game at the end. That distracted from how poorly we played most of that game.

Those issues came to light. The creativity wasn't there. Some stuff behind the scenes of culture. Doubts about people stepping in. Who's next? Maybe there were some people who maybe didn't step up, like you had hoped they would."

"It seemed like it was more mental than anything else," said Marcin. "We had a few bad losses. We go to Texas State, and we were big favorites, and it made no sense to we lost that game. It seemed we had no motivation for that."

The team finally got some off time and rattled off home wins over Georgia State and FCS Robert Morris. The Robert Morris game was a late add to the schedule because the Marshall game was scheduled to be a non-conference game, but when they were admitted to the conference, it became a conference game. That gave the Mountaineers two FCS games. The problem with that is that you can only count one FCS game toward the six you need to gain bowl eligibility. That meant App would have to win seven games, something that was beginning to look questionable.

Road games at Coastal and Marshall brought two more losses. The Mountaineers were 5-5 and would have to win the remaining two games: at home against Old Dominion and at Georgia Southern to keep alive their bowl streak.

"People wanted better teams in our conference, and they got 'em," said Kirk Sherrill. "That's going to be no joke. There will be some great rivalries going forward."

"I don't think most students were disappointed about the season," said Mike Wolfe, Jackson's father and an Appalachian grad. "People who knew more about App, were a little more disappointed, but everyone just enjoyed going to the games."

The Senior Day crowd for Old Dominion was a sellout. There were 32,096 on hand to see a 5-5 team play a team they had no history with. That showed me a lot about the fans, and it was noticed by the players.

"People are sacrificing so many things to come and there are die-hard fans, and you can't express how appreciative you are about that," said Pearson. "Crowds are what makes college football special. Not something everyone has. For the town, fans, players, recruits. It brings everyone together and it's a beautiful thing."

All six games in Kidd Brewer Stadium in 2022 drew more than 30,000 fans, the listed capacity of "The Rock." The average for the season was 33,566 per game, a record for the school and the Sun Belt Conference. Sure, that number was buoyed by the UNC game, but for every game, on a cold Wednesday night against Georgia State or a late November game against ODU, the fans showed up.

"I think what that says, is the true fans are locked in and loyal and will support the team," said Sherrill. "I'm proud of the school. I take great pride in being a grad. I want to see that continue."

"Every year seems to build on itself," said Mike Wolfe. "Student attendance gets higher, seven straight seasons of bowl games. We have better competition coming to town. It's become an event that people want to be a part of."

The regular season closed with "Hate Week" against old rival Georgia Southern. The Eagles, who had won at Nebraska the same day App beat A&M, were 5-6 and needed a win to get a bowl bid. It was another crazy game between the schools, the Mountaineers would take a lead and the Eagles would come right back. A Southern touchdown with 4:22 remaining tied the game at 38. Brice would have a chance to redeem the season and gain bowl eligibility. But he could only manage one first down, and they had to punt the ball back to the Eagles. The App State defense forced Southern to punt it back, and Appalachian had the ball with 41 seconds left, but at their own 28. They did still have two time outs.

On first down, Brice was incomplete. Nate Noel took a handoff for 12 on the next play and Clark called time out. There were 28 seconds left; too early for the Hail Mary, but not too early for Brice to look for Christian Horn. He found him for a 45-yard gain down to the Southern 15. There was enough time for Noel to take a handoff and put the ball in the middle of the field at the 12. The Mountaineers called their final time out and sent kicker Michael Hughes in to try a 30-yard field goal for the win. He missed as time expired.

The teams exchanged touchdowns in the first overtime. In the second overtime, Hughes hit from 33 to give the Apps the lead. But Southern scored a touchdown and won the game. For the first time since they were eligible to earn a bowl bid as an FBS team, the Mountaineers didn't win enough games to secure the bid.

"I'm not a psychologist but I think it would be hard for anyone to go through what they did and not have a crash," said Witten. "Does that mean we finish 6-6? How JMU happened? It's hard to keep up that mental focus, going through everything they went through. I also believe there is such a fine line between winning and losing. In 2021, we won 10 games, and we won a lot of close games, Marshall, Coastal, fourth quarter comeback against Georgia Southern. Eventually that stuff balances out. When you are in a tough league, those games aren't going to always go your way."

No bowl meant one senior missed out on doing something that had become quite special for the players.

"Sad to say, I was holding out for bowl game," said Pearson about appearing in a uniform reveal. "I had an awesome idea. My first four years, I grew my hair out from July to December. My jersey idea was to go to the barber shop in Banner Elk where a lot of the players went and get the haircut in full pads. It was approved, but we didn't get to a bowl game."

If you were wondering how Troy handled the loss to the Mountaineers, they did okay. They rattled off nine straight wins to close out the regular season. They blew out Coastal 45-26 in the SBC Championship Game and beat number 22 UTSA in the Cure Bowl to close the season 12-2 and earn a number 19 ranking in the final AP Poll.

The Mountaineers didn't get any votes as one of the best teams in the nation, but they did get some notoriety as a team that played in some of the most exciting games. ESPN ranked the game against JMU as the 98th most exciting game of 2022. The same ranking listed the A&M game at number 11, the Troy game at number 10, and the UNC game was ranked as the ninth. No other school had more than two in the top 11. *The Athletic*'s ranking of the 50 top games for 2022 had the Mountaineers game against Georgia Southern at 49, A&M at 40, Troy at 31, and UNC at 26.

Injuries were more of a problem for App State in 2022 than they had been in a while. Positions that seemed the deepest on the team were the hardest hit. On offense, the running back position had two backs, Noel and Cam Peoples, who had each gained 1,000 yards in a previous season. The Mountaineers had a 1,000-yard rusher each of the past 10 years which was by far the longest streak in the nation, but with Peoples and Noel each missing three games that streak ended in 2022. Noel was the leading rusher with 604 yards in 2022. Daetrich Harrington, who had successfully come back from two knee surgeries was the only running back to carry the ball in all 12 games.

The linebacker position was expected to be the strength of the defense. Brendan Harrington went out for the season against UNC and the next week leader Trey Cobb had to leave the A&M game. Cobb returned to action but dealt with the injury all season. Of the nine players listed at linebacker on the depth chart for the UNC game, Andrew Parker and senior reserves Tyler Bird and Logan Doublin were the only ones to play in all 12 games.

Another stat that I think really shows the consistency of the program ended in 2022. App State had a streak of 37 straight seasons (eight Sun Belt, 29 Southern) with a conference record of .500 or better. Among current FBS programs, counting seasons before and after any transitions, it was the longest streak by 14 years. During 2022, Clemson, Oklahoma, and Boise State reached 24 in a row.

Clark isn't one to make excuses and went to work on things from his end. He fired defensive coordinator Dale Jones who had been with the football program for 26 years. He was replaced by Scot Sloan, who had been on the defensive staff from 2010-17. Offensive coordinator Kevin Barbay was hired by Mississippi State and Clark brought Frank Ponce in to run the offense. This is the third time Ponce has been an assistant in Boone. He spent 2022 with the University of Miami. Ponce was active in recruiting redshirt freshman Ryan Burger who was one of the candidates to replace Brice at quarterback for 2023. Clark also went back to hire a new strength coach. Ryan Greenhalgh had been the assistant from 2014-17 and was brought back to run things in December of 2022.

Something I think is an important reflection on how the players are feeling about the direction of the program is how many players leave in the transfer portal. Linebacker Jalen McLeod left for Auburn and that was a big loss, but many Group of Five schools had their rosters raided by Power 5 schools. Troy Everett had started the first six games at center, before being removed from the starting lineup. After spring practice, he apparently hadn't won his spot back and decided to leave. He was the focus of an article in *The Athletic* about Group of Five players transferring. He ended up at Oklahoma. Those were the main losses, and a few other players likely would have contributed in 2023 transferred out. Fourteen players were added to the roster through the portal, including two defensive linemen who transferred in from Rutgers and Michigan State.

The fans may have been grumbling among themselves and on internet fan boards, but once again showed their support for the program in record numbers. By early June season tickets for 2023 sold out. Some people thought the only reason season tickets had sold out in '22 was because of the demand for the UNC game. But even without a Power 5 school coming to Boone, more than 10,000 season tickets sold out even faster than the year before. The Yosef Club, the athletics department fund-raising group, had a record year of income.

As someone who had been there for the days when you could walk up to the ticket office on game day and get a good seat, this was truly amazing. It's hard to describe the pride I feel on those Saturday afternoons (or weeknight evenings) looking around and seeing the changes in the stadium. The premium seating, the packed Hill, the track being gone, and most importantly, all the people in the stadium. I am so proud of how the students have truly embraced their role in setting the atmosphere in The Rock. They arrive early and stay throughout the game, regardless of the score or the weather.

Obviously, I'm proud of what we've done, and the notoriety it's given the university. In the early '80s, when I was a student, most people outside of North Carolina had never heard of Appalachian State. Jay Bilas was a highly recruited high school basketball player from Los Angeles in the class of 1982. Duke was among the schools recruiting him. Bilas tells the story that in December of 1981 a coach from another school that was recruiting him called him one morning and asked if Bilas had ever heard of Appalachian State. Bilas said no. The coach proceeded to tell Bilas that Appalachian State had beaten Duke in basketball the previous night. Undaunted, Bilas went to Duke to play for Mike Krzyzewski. You aren't going to hear those kinds of stories very often now, especially with sports fans. The Michigan win and the aftermath gave App State a big splash. But they keep earning it again and again with performances like September of 2022 and consistent winning.

The student body has changed too. Many more students are coming to Appalachian from families who had a relative graduate from the school. It was unusual when I was a student to see another student who had grown up coming to Appalachian games. Now in our tailgate group of about a dozen families, there are four children who came to games with their parents who are or have been students there. In fact, four players on the 2022 team were sons of a former Appalachian player. So not only are there more legacy students enrolling, but it's also helping with recruiting. I've heard some of my contemporaries from App complain their child couldn't get in because the demand has created tougher admission standards. It's great seeing those families pass down the special experience of being a student at Appalachian State University.

As I stood there before the Hail Mary play against Troy feeling a little sorry for myself and my school because it looked like we were going to come up a little short again with the spotlight on us. But the fact is, even without the winning touchdown in that game, App State continues to put itself in situations to be in the national spotlight. There are even a lot of the so-called Power 5 schools that haven't had the bowl wins we've had, the wins over highly ranked teams or the memorable finishes. As athletic director Doug Gillin said, "It's always a great day to be a Mountaineer."

Former Chancellor Ken Peacock knew how football could unite a university and worked to ensure that alumni and fans could enjoy a beer while tailgating without getting an open container citation. He took those national championship trophies to alumni functions all over the Southeast so graduates could touch and pose for pictures with those trophies. He wanted us to have our fingerprints on those trophies because he understood that they belonged to everyone associated with Appalachian State. I have never gained a yard rushing or made a tackle, but I've given a lot of money. I get up at 6 a.m. on game days and drive five hours to Boone, enjoy several hours of tailgating, then go to the game, and drive home to Atlanta. (Thank goodness for satellite radio!) While I'm there, I'm screaming for the defense when the opponent has the ball, not just on third down. I'm trying to encourage the offense and applaud their success.

I stood in the rain for three and a half hours during the Wyoming game in 2015. I went to Troy in 2014 when we had a 1-5 record and were down 7-0 and had just lost our most experienced defender to a targeting penalty. I was there hollering when we tied the game on the next series and hollered all game as we kept scoring and went on a run that saw us win that game as well as the next five. We finished 7-5 and put the Sun Belt on notice there they had better look out for these new kids from the mountains. I like to think my yelling that day at Troy helped the team a little. There couldn't have been 5,000 people in the stadium, and I, and the other App fans with me, were making our voices known.

I sat there in frustration as Miami's Mark Walton broke that tackle and ran 75 yards in what was at that time the biggest game in Boone for App State. I sat there as we lost overtime games at Knoxville and State College. I celebrated on a golf course in Ann Arbor and on the field in Chattanooga after three national championships. In that same stadium, in 2010, I was there when we overcame two 21-point deficits in the final 17 minutes of the game to beat UT-Chattanooga. I showed up at work hoarse many fall Mondays. Win or lose, I enjoy the entertainment they give me, and I am going to give my all for Appalachian State from the stands to help them win.

I hosted a party at my house several years ago and I invited someone I hadn't known for very long, but I knew she would enjoy the theme of the party, and I wanted her there. At the party she heard that I went to Appalachian, and said, "I didn't know you went to App State." My good friend James Johnson overheard that comment and asked, "How long have you known McMackin? I haven't known him to talk to anyone for more than five minutes without bringing up App State!" I think he meant it as a little bit of a dig, but I took it as a compliment.

"I think that's the thing we overlook sometimes is it's a great experience to get there," said Witten. "Going to Boone in September or October, there's not a better environment in college football."

That experience could be important for the role App State may have in the future of college football. With all the realignment and name, image, and likeness (NIL) money, I'm not sure what the future holds for college football. Right now, Appalachian and the Sun Belt are in a great place. But will the biggest 40 or so schools break off and have their own super conferences? Could Appalachian join a conference with some of the Southern schools that may be left behind if the super conferences are formed? Will they find themselves back in another version of FCS? I hardly think the latter will happen, but who knows? I think because of the track record of the team as far as wins and losses, the support the team receives at home and on the road, plus our ability to handle big crowds, we would be attractive for a new prospective conference.

"Now we have new facilities," said Kaiden Smith, a defensive back from 2017-21. "We didn't have a nutritionist, now they do. We used to get a few T-shirts, now they get all the gear. It's about adaptability. For most G5 teams it's a small window of success. We have had a long window having a blue-collar culture. Can you still do what it takes to be successful? It's hard to measure wanting to keep that culture alive."

I don't care if App State puts the intramural flag football champions in Black and Gold and sends them out on the Kidd Brewer Stadium field, I will still love coming to Boone, tailgating with my friends, and cheering for the Mountaineers. I'm proud of all the kids who choose to come to Appalachian whether they play football or not. The kids who feel the special pull of the mountains and what it means to be a Mountaineer. It's truly a special place and it's not for everyone.

"I'm proud I played there," said App State Hall of Fame guard Ed Boyd, who played from 1981-84.

The guys in our tailgate group have been in these same spots for nearly 20 years now. It seems like each season we stand and look around with pride and talk about the changes in campus, how there are more people showing up to tailgate, how sophisticated some of the tailgates have become, and how the quality of the teams that come to The Rock has improved.

My journeys have taken me across the country to gridirons at Clemson, Texas A&M, Alabama, Auburn, Georgia, Tennessee, Penn State, and Michigan. Those crowds and environments are great. And they have been for years. One of the things that is so special for me to see is the changes and the growth in the program at App State. I have been there to witness it, nearly every step of the way. For all the changes in the stadium, the campus, and the town, one thing remains constant. I love making the journey to Boone to see the guys in Black and Gold give their all for Appalachian State on the gridiron.

Acknowledgements

When I was driving back home from Boone the Sunday after the Troy win, I was reflecting on a lot of the interesting college football games I'd seen. I was wondering if I should maybe write a book, but I had no idea of how to present it. Bob Inman was the news anchor at WBTV when I interned there, and we stayed in touch. He had published several novels and was by far the most accomplished writer that I knew. I told him what I was thinking about, and he told me, "Mike, it's all about the stories." That was like an epiphany for me. I thought, I can pick about a dozen games and do a story about each game.

That was how this book came to be. It has really been a lot of fun to research, re-live, and reconnect with friends about this project. There are so many people I am grateful to for the help and the motivation to get this to market. I wasn't sure if I should tell people I was working on it, or just start it, but I figured it would be helpful to have people asking me about it to make sure I followed through with it.

Obviously, Inman with his advice and support played a big part in making this book possible. He also told me to send him some chapters when I was halfway through it, and he would offer some feedback. My editor Betsy Rhame-Minor gave this beginning writer much needed guidance. My former colleague at The Weather Channel, Jill Cox-Cordova, was generous with her experience and gave me valuable advice on dealing with publishers. I love the cover Vanessa Lowry came up with incorporating all the tickets and press passes I had saved from all the games in this book.

Thanks is due to my trivia team, Roger Manis and Mike Stamus, for being a sounding board as well as helping me get in touch with some interview targets. So many people were so generous with their time to share their stories about college football. Ed Boyd, Tim Wooten, Brian Hoagland, Mack Brown, and Jeremy Sharpe of UNC Athletics helped arrange the interview with Coach Brown. My Sig Ep brother Mike McKay introduced me to John Phillips during the tailgate for the UNC game at App. Once I decided to do the book, I knew he would be a great resource for the Clemson-Georgia game. Pete Yanity has been a long-time friend and colleague.

When I was working at WBRC-TV in Birmingham, Paul Finebaum was a regular on several of the shows we produced, and we always had a nice relationship. I'm glad he has settled in so well in Charlotte. You can't write about Auburn athletics without talking to David Housel, who has such passion for his school and a wealth of knowledge of its history. Michelle Keesee offered insights of a teenager in Auburn that historic week in 1989 and helped arrange the interview with Stacy Danley.

Ray Melick and I spent nearly two hours reminiscing about things we had covered. It was good to see that Roger Shultz hadn't lost any of his personality in the 20-plus years since we had talked. Keith Rhodes shared his experiences as a student in New Orleans for the Sugar Bowl. Rob Rankin put me in touch with his fraternity brothers Murray Griffin, John Poteat, and Barry Owens, who had enough confidence in their team to see a rally for the win. It was fun experiencing the Esso Club for the first time with Mark Stackow, but I haven't forgiven him for trying to ruin the Michigan win for me with his play by play of Clay Bucholz's no-hitter against my Orioles.

I learned so much about weather from Dr. Jon Nese and the other Penn State grads who work at The Weather Channel (as well as all the meteorologists there!). I'm thankful for our long-time friendship and his hospitality when I visit State College. I'm so lucky he brought Mike "The Mailman" Herr into my life. Jen and Neil McGillis and I have shared wines along with football tales. Scott Stroupe has been a long-time friend, and his Penn State fandom came in handy for the book.

Mike Ladd has been a wonderful traveling partner as we have covered thousands of miles together to see our Mountaineers play. He won't need to read the book; he's heard all these stories a thousand times. Another frequent travel partner is Eric Race, who put me in touch with his friend from App State, Jake Stroot.

I can't say enough about all the guys in our wonderful tailgate crew: my brother Hunter, who introduced me to these guys; Andy Ebert; Jay Hellinger; Jim Macholz; Brian Metcalf; Mike Nauman and his daughter, Emily; Kirk Sherrill and his daughter, Paige; and Mike Wolfe and his son Jackson. We have shared many beers and many laughs. Many of the laughs have been at the expense of one another. What a great group of guys I'm proud to call friends. I can't believe anyone other than Ted Cabot has traveled from Europe see the Mountaineers play over the last few years. Kudos for dealing with international airline issues to make it from Italy to Boone to see the Apps host the Tar Heels.

Charlie Cobb was very generous with his time and experiences as AD at App State. Doug Gillin took over for Cobb and has continued to build the athletic department at App State. Mike Flynn spent several hours telling stories about the Armanti Edwards era, as well as the move up to FBS. His replacement, Joey Jones, was full of information about the Power 5 wins in 2019 as well as the crazy September of 2022. Alex Johnson and Charles Haynes show their passion for App State with their weekly podcast that I am happy to support and listen to. I met Dean Mills on the trip to Montana and it was nice to relive some memories. He put me in touch with his son Pat who really took me into the App State locker room. Paul Owens and I spent a great evening in Ann Arbor together.

It was great talking to Rece Davis, and I was grateful for his perspective on the Appalachian program and taking us behind the scenes of the roadshow known as *College GameDay*. Adam Witten has had a front row seat for some of the biggest wins the Mountaineers have had, and his radio calls will live forever for App State fans. Jeff Marcin was an internet sensation with one phrase calling the end of the Troy game for the Appalachian student radio station, WASU-FM, of which I am a proud alum.

Coach Shawn Clark took time from pre-season camp to share his experiences on the sidelines and what it was like during the COVID pandemic. Kindsey Green Reeder is a proud Mountaineer who has spent many years working for the university, and I appreciated her insight into the growth of fall Saturdays in the High Country. Two players who Gave Their All For Appalachian State, Kaiden Smith and Henry Pearson, were kind enough to share their experiences on the field. I met John

Myers at a road game and have run into him many times since. I enjoy his analysis of what is going on. Mike Smith has seen a lot of Appalachian football games, and I enjoyed sharing the end of the Troy game with him.

Good friends Tom Mattesky, Allison Gale, David Snepp, and Patrick Flynn provided a lot of support and some early feedback on my writing and the direction of the book.

I want to give a special shoutout to all the sports information directors around the country for all the great work you and your staff have done over the years and how valuable that was to me for this project. I've always enjoyed reading media guides and seeing the different things each school does that are a little different. My packrat mentality has me still possessing many old guides that came in handy for this project but thank goodness many are available online now as well.

And lastly, I'd like to thank all the students, parents, players, faculty members, administrators, and coaches who have made up the Appalachian Family all these years and have combined to create so many great moments for me to make a book out of! Thanks for reading and hopefully you will be entertained and learn something.

ABOUT THE AUTHOR

Mike McMackin is a graduate of Appalachian State University who spent 25 years working in various capacities in the TV industry. He is a winner of two regional Emmy awards and numerous state Associated Press awards. Email him at mcmackinwrites@gmail.com and follow him on X/Twitter at @mackthefan02